14.38

# How We Learn

# How We Learn

### A Christian Teacher's Guide
### to Educational Psychology

## Klaus Issler and
## Ronald Habermas

Baker Books
A Division of Baker Book House Co
Grand Rapids, Michigan 49516

Published by Baker Books
a division of Baker Book House Company
P.O. Box 6287, Grand Rapids, Michigan 49516-6287

Printed in the United States of America

**Library of Congress Cataloging-in-Publication Data**

Issler, Klaus Dieter
How we learn : a Christian teacher's guide to educational psychology / Klaus
Issler and Ronald Habermas.
    p.   cm.
Includes bibliographical references (p.   ) and index.
ISBN 0-8010-5039-1
1. Learning, Psychology of. 2. Educational psychology. 3. Christian education.
I. Habermas, Ronald T. II. Title.
LB1060.I87   1993
370.15pdc20                                                    94-6684

To our children, Daniel, Ruth, Elizabeth, Melissa,
and Susan, from whom we have learned much
about God and life
May you each learn from Jesus to take on his easy
yoke and find rest for your souls
(Matt. 11:28–30)

# Contents

# List of Tables and Figures

## Tables

## Figures

# Preface

Teachers must comprehend the basic features of instruction and learning. Whether the setting involves the school, church, or home classroom.[1] Christians must know *why* they do *what* they do in education that is Christian. Since we are commanded to follow and emulate the Master Teacher, as teachers we should first and foremost understand the dynamics of the teaching-learning process. While engaged in this task we will come to appreciate why Jesus was called "teacher" more than any other title in the Gospels.

The present book grew out of our desire to offer an evangelical perspective on educational psychology. The text naturally emerged from material initially presented in our *Teaching for Reconciliation: Foundations and Practice of Christian Educational Ministry (TFR)* (Baker, 1992) in which we attempted to articulate a new vision and framework for the educational ministry of the Church. Starting with chapters 5–8, we have rearranged and significantly expanded that text's concepts, resulting in the eleven chapters of *How We Learn*.[2]

No worthwhile project is without its lists of credits; this book is no exception. We're grateful to Don Ratcliff for reviewing the entire manuscript and offering a variety of insightful comments. Our heartfelt thanks extend to Jim Weaver, Baker's Editor of Academic and Reference Books, for recognizing the contribution of such a textbook. We've benefited from his consistent affirmation and helpful suggestions. Maria denBoer's extensive skills are evident throughout. As we valued her efforts in *TFR*, again we prize her labor of love and excellence in this volume.

Collegial encouragement has sustained us as well. Klaus appreciates the supportive affirmations of Talbot faculty members J. P. Moreland, Walt Russell, Scott Rae, and Bill Roth (who should be on the faculty). Ron expresses thanks to Bob Ferris at Columbia Biblical Seminary for his camaraderie and insights. Also, we acknowledge the conducive climate for writing nurtured by the administrators from our respective schools. Closer to home, the unconditional support of our families was ever-present. In the midst of numerous deadlines and rewrites, we still experienced a home context of love and learning together.

That we have been wonderfully made has been a recurring theme to us throughout this writing project. How we learn is a complex and delicate process. We present to you our considered reflections on this topic with the hope and prayer that they offer some insights for your teaching ministry as you help your students become mature followers of the Master Teacher themselves.

# Part 1

# *Perspectives about Learning*

# 1

# Why Worry about How We Learn?

Learning, like breathing, occurs every minute of the day. Because it is so natural, it is often unnoticed. Since learning is such a common experience, we overlook its complexity. These realities can foster misunderstandings about learning and teaching.

### Try It Out[1]

Asking "what if" questions can help us clarify our understanding of what we believe to be true. What if the following hypothetical principle of learning were true?

> "Students who run one lap around a track tend to learn better than those who don't."

How might this view affect the practice of education at school, home, or church? Perhaps the teacher would require each student to run a lap every morning, or even better, before each class! On further thinking, the teacher might raise the question, "What might two laps do?"

Can you come up with a few implications of your own from this hypothetical learning principle?

1.
2.

More specifically, how might this particular learning principle affect:
    (a) an elementary school class?
    (b) a Sunday school/Bible fellowship class?
    (c) preaching in the main worship service?
    (d) a home Bible study?
    (e) a college class?
Select one of these educational settings and suggest two implications of this unusual learning theory:
    1.
    2.

## The Purpose of This Book

Too often, an analysis of how we learn (i.e., matters of educational psychology) seems overly complicated. Little appears applicable to teaching practice. A helpful assessment of the problem comes from a Stanford University education professor:

> A finger of blame must be pointed at both the mystifiers [educational psychologists] and the mystified [teachers], at the former for spreading confusion and at the latter for tolerating it (Jackson 1986, pp. 37–38).

The purpose of this book is to "demystify" the subject—to outline a basic biblical theology and psychology of learning.[2] The goal is to make our teaching ministry more effective. This book is geared to the practitioner of teaching—it's not a technical manual. Only those ideas, analytical frameworks, and practices that are directly relevant to facilitating learning have been included. Other matters, particularly those of a more detailed nature, can be pursued through resources cited in the notes and references.

This book takes a distinctively *Christian* perspective on the subject matter. Whether or not they identify themselves as evangelical Christians, however, all teachers can benefit from this book. It offers an integrative synthesis of learning theories and practical suggestions. What is distinctive about the material is the inclusion of both the *natural* and *supernatural* realities directly related to the learning process. It is these latter elements that are typically missing from standard texts on educational psychology. Thus, a unique foundational (or additional) layer of insight, based on God's special revelation, is incorporated into the discussion.[3]

As a result of the readers' comprehension of the material, the development of three particular skills are anticipated.

1. *Selecting Teaching Methods:* Why does any particular teaching method "work"? How does it specifically contribute to learning? Under-

standing basic principles of learning can help us select the appropriate teaching method for our lesson aim and our students. For example, Jesus used parables in his public ministry. The parables he told required some thinking. Through this common method, he was able to accomplish two main goals: to reveal truth to those who were seeking God, and to conceal truth from those who had rejected God (Matt. 13:10–17). By understanding how methods contribute to learning, teachers can easily adapt any learning activity to intensify its learning effect.

2. *Diagnosing Learning Problems:* Why do some students easily learn the material while others struggle? A variety of factors contribute to our students' readiness or ability to learn. In the upper room, Jesus recognized that the disciples were having difficulty comprehending the material he had already given them. As a result, he didn't move on to newer material—material that the Holy Spirit would teach them after Jesus had returned to heaven (John 16:12–13). In some cases, simply identifying why a student is experiencing difficulty in learning is a major step toward solving the problem.

3. *Anticipating Teachable Moments:* We are all curious creatures, but our particular stages in life tend to develop in us differing interests. Paul acknowledged that single persons and married persons have different priorities (1 Cor. 7:32–35). Due to the similarity of human needs across the lifespan, however, we can have a fairly good idea when students might be most receptive to learning a particular subject matter. For example, toddlers are challenged by mastering skills such as fitting puzzle pieces together. Teens, on the other hand, are puzzled by self-esteem issues and how to fit in with their peers. We can build on these diverse interests and incorporate them into our teaching strategies.

## Perspectives about Learning

The thought experiment conducted at the beginning of this chapter reminds us that how we teach is significantly influenced by how we *think* about learning. With this in mind, let's look more closely at a few of our assumptions about the learning process. For each principle identified, employ the same "what if" thinking you used earlier. What if teachers held this particular "theory" about learning? What would the instructional component of the class look like? What would teachers have students do? What anticipated results could be stated?

If this approach were taken, what would teachers be required to do? First, teachers would not worry much about lesson preparation. Why should they, if only God is involved? Second, teachers would not need to have any training at all. Since it wouldn't matter what the teacher did, training (or lack of training) is irrelevant. Third, there would be no need

## Proposition #1

# What if learning among believers resulted *solely* from the work of God?

for human teachers. If God is the *sole* teacher in the lives of students, as this first principle states, then he is all we need. All human effort is unnecessary!

But we know—both biblically and experientially—that there *is* a human role in education that is Christian. God has bestowed a variety of gifts upon believers for ministry. One of these gifts is teaching (Rom. 12:7; 1 Cor. 12:28; Eph. 4:11). Human effort in Christian education, therefore, cannot be discounted.[4] To the contrary, such gifts imply responsibility and accountability. But how much responsibility? Consider a second, contrasting view about learning.

## Proposition #2

# What if learning among believers resulted *solely* from human effort?

If this principle were true, then learning for Christians would not be unique. It would not be any different for Christians than it is for non-Christians. Moreover, we could cancel the word "Christian" from "Christian education."[5] Only knowing matters of educational psychology and empirical research of the learning process would be necessary. Also, there would be no need to pray for our students' personal growth.

Among other problems, this faulty view obviously gives the Christian teacher *too* much responsibility. God is presumptuously cast out of the picture. It's clear that these two extreme theories of learning are faulty. Neither divine nor human teachers can be ignored. We must realize that the Divine Teacher works both within and alongside the human teacher. In fact, one name for the Spirit—the Paraclete—means "One who counsels alongside us."

Identifying exactly how the Divine Teacher works alongside the human teacher and within the student is difficult to unravel, but Scripture does give us some general guidelines. Notice the interplay of divine and human effort in the following verses:

> But by the grace of God I am what I am, and his grace to me was not without effect. No, I worked harder than all of them—yet not I, but the grace of God that was with me (1 Cor. 15:10).

> Therefore, my dear friends . . . continue to work out your salvation with fear and trembling, for it is God who works in you to will and to act according to his good purpose (Phil. 2:12–13).

> May the God of peace . . . equip you with everything good for doing his will, and may he work in us what is pleasing to him, through Jesus Christ, to whom be glory for ever and ever. Amen (Heb. 13:20–21).

God's grace supplies the resources we need to accomplish his will, but students must continue to make an effort to contribute to their learning and growth.

In some cases, God directly (i.e., immediately) intervenes to accomplish his purposes. For example, when Peter confronted Ananias and Sapphira for lying, they died instantly by the stroke of God's hand (Acts 5:1–6). But in most cases, God works through the natural laws within his creation, and particularly through human beings (i.e., mediately). For example, God used the Corinthian church to administer discipline. As a result, the sinning believer repented of his sin. Paul then urged the church to restore him to fellowship (2 Cor. 2:6–8). The norm for us as human teachers, then, is to teach to the best of our abilities, as God enables both teacher and student.

The Holy Spirit's ministry of illumination is one divine means of participation in the learning process that is specifically outlined in Scripture. According to 1 Corinthians 2:12–14, the fullest learning is only possible for Christians who are receptive to the teaching ministry of the Spirit.

> We have not received the spirit of the world but the Spirit who is from God, that we may understand what God has freely given us. This is what we speak, not in words taught by human wisdom but in words taught by the Spirit, expressing spiritual truths in spiritual words. The man without the Spirit does not accept the things that come from the Spirit of God, for they are foolishness to him, and he cannot understand them, because they are spiritually discerned.

Paul is not saying that non-Christians cannot read the Bible or understand the basic message of the gospel.[6] If he were, our ministry of evangelism and apologetics with non-Christians would be a waste of time—

there would be no common ground of communication. The point is that the Spirit aids the believer in "accepting" or "welcoming" the significance of God's truth for full application in his or her lifewalk. And it is this welcoming of God's truth into the lives of our students for which we pray.[7]

Consider a third principle of learning.

---

**Proposition #3**

# What if Christian students *fully understood* whatever they heard?

---

What implications does this principle have for teaching? Some examples might include these practices: schools would only require large lecture halls. Teachers would present just the facts. They would never need to review material. Instructors wouldn't have to answer any student questions since none would be asked. Student-teacher dialogue would disappear. In fact, students could listen to an audio cassette or view a video cassette in their homes and never set foot in a school building. Best of all, pop quizzes and final exams would be unnecessary!

To uncover the difficulties with this particular principle, let's take a look at three implicit fallacies that create formidable barriers to learning. They can be summarized as follows:

---

# To Teach Is to Tell

# To Tell Is to Know

# To Know Is to Do

---

### To Teach Is to Tell

This misconception equates teaching with verbalizing facts. Instruction occurs, the myth states, when information is given to students. But at least two related errors appear. First, subject mastery is falsely viewed as the teacher's *primary* (if not sole) responsibility. Second, it involves a reductionistic fallacy: it assumes that *one* of the parts of teaching (in this case, the exclusive activity of verbalizing facts) can be substituted for the *whole* concept.

This erroneous concept may provide the impetus for an exclusive dependence on the lecture method for information distribution. We can understand its prominent use *before* the invention of the printing press—a time when lecture was the primary means for transmitting knowledge in an expeditious manner. But, with the availability of the printing press, information could be disseminated in various written forms: books, pamphlets, and newspapers. Today, in an age of high technology, we have advanced audio media (records, cassette tapes, compact discs) and visual media (overhead projectors, films, video tapes) that aid us in knowledge transmission. Coupled with photocopying and computer technology, we can communicate information in a more efficient and permanent manner than we could using the lecture method.

Does this mean that we should avoid the lecture method? Does lecturing have no value at all for teaching and learning? Quite the contrary. These technological inventions have removed the burden of information transfer as the *primary* purpose of lecturing. Now the lecture method can focus on other benefits. For example, students are able to witness a live and passionate presentation of reasoning and convictions that are enthusiastically endorsed by the lecturer. Thus, lecture can serve as an *affective* and *motivational* tool to arouse student interest in the subject matter. Some professors become the historical character whose writings are being studied—adorned with costume and wig. Others use effective rhetorical devices to engage the students' minds and hearts. Students are not tape recorders. We must use all available resources and methods to encourage learning.[8] The "teaching = telling" misconception, therefore, reduces to a very simplistic notion. At best, we are left with a superficial formula for teaching.

### To Tell Is to Know

This second misconception assumes that a student will correctly and fully comprehend everything the teacher says. This misleading view of learning is humorously described by a veteran teacher:

> The Sunday School teacher had told her class of kindergartners about God's decision to destroy Sodom and Gomorrah. As the teacher explained, "God wanted to spare Lot, so He told him to take his wife and flee." With that, the teacher sat back and watched the silence of comprehension take over the faces of each class member. Finally, one little guy ventured a question. "What happened to the flea?" (Schimmels 1989, pp. 19–20).

Sometimes, even carefully planned instruction goes awry. Good intentions don't guarantee success. Using a class demonstration for an object lesson, one sixth-grade teacher wished to communicate the dangers of alcohol to her students:

> She filled one beaker with water and another with alcohol. She dropped a worm into the beaker filled with water; and the worm frolicked around in an obvious joy. She then fished the lively worm out and dropped him into the beaker filled with alcohol. Immediately, the worm sank to the bottom, dead.
>
> "Now," the teacher asked in her finest teacher voice, "what have you just learned from this lesson?"
>
> The silence which followed suggested that the students were working on an answer. Finally, one young man proposed a possibility. "I think I know," he said seriously. "People who drink don't have worms" (Schimmels 1989, p. 226).

In both examples what was intended and what was actually learned were worlds apart. This discrepancy is recognized partly because each teacher provided an opportunity for student feedback. But think about what happens when such feedback is not available. How many other cases of *mis*education could be cited?

### *To Know Is to Do*

The third and final misconception assumes that students automatically change their conduct once they acquire new information. Such a "student-proof" view of teaching falls decisively short of the mark. Among other points, it neglects the "inner factors" of students noted by LeBar (1958/1989): sin tendencies, motivation, response to the Holy Spirit, and the complexities of making and persevering in choices. Information and understanding are necessary components of growth. But when it comes to change within the student's life, several other factors deserve consideration. A discussion of barriers to learning is included later in the chapter.

---
### Try It Out
---

Reflect on your own experiences of learning.
1. For each of the two sentence fragments, provide at least three responses:
    a. "I learn best when . . ."
    b. "It bores me when a teacher . . ."
2. Study your responses.
    a. What do you discover about your own way of learning?
    b. Do any of your responses relate to the different principles or misconceptions of learning? Explain why. If not, what other learning

misconceptions could be found in your reflections? Create your own list of myths.

## Elements of Learning

Learning is largely a mystery. No one fully understands how it actually works. And, for Christians, because of God's active involvement in the learning process, explaining precisely what happens when we learn is even more problematic. Although we may not have 100 percent knowledge of the subject, we can identify broad principles that have been and continue to be effectively used to facilitate learning in students.

### Table 1.1
### Five Elements of Learning

**L**evels of learning—What can we learn?

**E**xtent of learning—How well can we learn?

**A**venues of learning—In what ways can we learn?

**R**eadiness for learning—Are we prepared to learn?

**N**ature of learning—What is the essence of learning?

For ease of analysis and use in teaching, a proper understanding of the learning process minimally includes five basic factors (Table 1.1). Figure 1.1 provides a conceptual overview of how the rest of the chapters of this book relate to each of these five elements.[9] And, to help the reader move beyond a survey of the material presented, each chapter ends with an application section. The purpose is to explore one implication for the practice of teaching in light of what was introduced in the chapter. For those wishing to pursue further study, resources in the notes and references may be consulted.

A basic definition of learning is provided at the outset and, in the rest of the book, the various concepts will be unpacked chapter by chapter.

> **Learning for Christians is change that is facilitated through deliberate or incidental experience, under the supervision of the Holy Spirit, in which they acquire and regularly integrate developmentally appropriate knowledge, attitudes, values, emotions, skills, habits, and dispositions into an increasingly Christ-like life.**

**Figure 1.1**
# Conceptual Outline of *How We Learn*

| Chapter 2 | **Levels** of Learning |
|---|---|
| Chapter 2 | **Extent** of Learning |
| Chapter 3–5 | **Avenues** of Learning |

| Chapter 3 | • Information-Processing Learning Family |
|---|---|
| Chapter 4 | • Conditioning Learning Family |
| Chapter 5 | • Social Learning Family |

| Chapters 6–9 | **Readiness** for Learning |
|---|---|

| Chapter 6 | • Willing: Student Motivation |
|---|---|
| Chapters 7–9 | • Able |
| Chapter 7 | Physical Growth and Ability |
| Chapter 8 | Cognitive Growth and Ability |
| Chapter 9 | Personality Growth and Ability |

| Chapters 10–11 | **Nature** of Learning |
|---|---|

| Chapter 10 | • Goal of Learning: Christian Maturity |
|---|---|
| Chapter 11 | • Learning Is Lifelong |

## Barriers to Learning

Although learning is a natural process for human beings, it is beset by some limitations and stumbling blocks. Before we embark on our study, we should first remind ourselves of these hindrances to learning. Our worldview as Christians gives us insight into the battle that is being waged against God and his people. Four broad categories summarize the main factors that can hinder students from fully learning all that God has for them—factors related to students, stumbling blocks and relationships, worldview perspectives and cultural values, and Satan and demonic activity. Our discussion will not be exhaustive but illustrative of the kinds of forces that move *against* our students in the learning process.

**Table 1.2**
## Students: Factors Within That Hinder Learning

**1. Physical Body.**
   a. Body organs (e.g., brain) have limited and decaying capacities as a result

of the curse (Gen. 2:17; 3:19). Some students have specific disabilities that affect learning (e.g., visual impairment; see Table 7.1 in Chapter 7).

b. Some students may be experiencing sleep deprivation, nutritional deficiency, or a more severe chemical imbalance in their bodies that prevents them from concentrating on learning. A comprehensive physical examination may identify the appropriate problem.

2. **Psychological Distress.**

a. Stress—Most learners will experience some degree of stress, frustration, or disappointment in their lives—stress that can temporarily distract their attention to learning (e.g., a favored possession is stolen; their team loses an important game; rejection by a friend; moving to another state or country; financial, job, or marital difficulties).

b. Trauma—Some students may have experienced more severe cases of stress due to life crises or previous instances of abuse. Thus, aspects of their mental faculties may be dysfunctional. They cannot look outward because the inner pain is so intense. Therapy with a qualified Christian counselor may provide the necessary support to address the problems in order to move on to maturity.

3. **Forgetfulness.** Students' memory retention rates vary. (More comments will be made about this factor in Chapter 2.)

4. **Avoidance of Change.** Many adult students gravitate toward the status quo—what some have called the "hardening of the categories." They prefer their comfortable routines and lifestyles. Learning involves change and change is disruptive, unsettling, and often painful. Our general antisuffering bias also hinders us from welcoming trials as means to growth (James 1:2).

5. **Laziness and Wrong Priorities.** Growth in godliness takes effort and discipline (1 Tim. 4:7–8), but some students may be unwilling to pay the price. Some students tend to take the path of least resistance, and expect learning and growth to come to them. Being entertained to soothe bodily appetites is more important than activities that minister to the deeper needs of one's soul.

6. **Specific Sins.** By persisting in self-destructive habits or thought patterns (e.g., bitterness, Heb. 11:15) some students close themselves off to the working of God's grace, which moves them ahead toward maturity. One specific debilitating sin is that of pride. Learning requires a posture of humility—an admission of ignorance—and a willingness to be guided and corrected. In Proverbs, humility is associated with wisdom (11:2), and pride is a characteristic of the fool (12:15; compare the receptivity to learning of Apollos, Acts 18:24–28, with that of the Pharisees, John 9:24–34).

7. **Past Sin Tendencies.** If students are not in an active process of presenting their bodily members to serve God in righteousness, then they can easily revert back to old sinful patterns of former days—for adult students those patterns were ingrained through years of habit (cf. Rom. 6:15–22).

8. **Weakness of Will.** "The spirit is willing, but the body is weak" (Matt. 26:41). Students are susceptible to temptation, and may not do what they ought to do.

9. **General Apathy to Grow.** We cannot assume that all of our students actually have the Spirit of God dwelling in them. It may be that some students have never entered into a personal relationship with Jesus Christ. Without the Spirit working in them it is no wonder they have little interest for spiritual things (cf. 2 Cor. 13:5).

### Students

We need look no farther than the students themselves to find formidable barriers to learning. Table 1.2 lists a variety of factors that can affect their receptivity to learning. As teachers we must be sensitive to these. In some cases, students may have no conscious awareness of their particular problem. Persistent prayer and unrelenting sensitivity on our part are necessary tools for fighting this kind of spiritual battle. We must encourage our students to "keep in step with the Spirit" (Gal. 5:25) through diligent meditation on the word of the Spirit (Eph. 6:17).

### Stumbling Blocks and Relationships

"Bad company corrupts good character" (1 Cor. 15:33). Peer pressure may prevent some students from doing their best to please God (Rom. 14:13). The Book of Proverbs contains a number of warnings about the kinds of persons who can drag us down. Students need like-minded friends and support groups who desire to grow in God's grace (2 Tim. 2:22). The American spirit of independence and individualism pulls us away from a healthy interdependence with other believers. For example, adult students may lack the close friendships that provide support and accountability for continuing growth. The ministry of admonishment—receiving constructive criticism from trusted others—is a key ingredient for learning (Rom. 15:14; Col. 3:16).[10]

### Worldview Perspectives and Cultural Values

We may be in a post-Christian era in which the dominant values and ideas of our culture are opposed to developing Christian virtues, but the "earthly" wisdom has *always* been contrasted with the "wisdom that comes down from heaven" (James 3:13–18). Continual exposure to such "earthly" perspectives can slowly turn our students' thinking away from a Christian worldview (Rom. 12:2). As a result they may become less receptive to—even skeptical of—accepting biblical truths with any degree of validity. Our task as teachers is to help our students fully develop a Christian worldview and, in the process, to critique this "earthly" wisdom.

In contemporary circles, especially in the sciences, an empiricist theory of knowledge pervades our American culture. In this view, all that exists is only what can be observed by the senses or measured with instruments. Thus, any "unscientific" beliefs, particularly religious ones, have no basis of credibility. But does that theory of knowledge best explain all that exists? Actually this materialistic notion of reality is inconsistent and self-refuting. Scientific theories themselves are not material objects—they are theoretical propositions. And think about "numbers." We use numbers for purposes of scientific quantification. We can read the symbols that represent each numerical concept (e.g., "3"), but no one has or ever will actually see a number! It's a theoretical concept. We can have much more confidence in the Christian worldview since, by recognizing both *material* and *immaterial* substances, it best explains the reality that we know.[11]

### Satan and Demonic Powers

Satan seeks to hinder our Christian students from becoming fully mature believers.[12] We must help our students strategize both defensively and offensively regarding this supernatural foe (Eph. 6:10–13). Over the years of human history Satan has successfully tempted God's people to disobey. But we have a greater power on our side (1 John 4:4). As teachers, we must view our instruction within the larger picture of this often unseen spiritual warfare—a battle that will, in the end, be decisively won. In the interim period, we must be on our guard (1 Pet. 5:8–9) not giving any foothold to Satan (Eph. 4:27). Above all, helping our students pursue a close and growing relationship with God is the best way to maintain their readiness for learning and to keep them on the path toward growth in maturity.

## Theory and Practice

Earlier in this chapter we examined certain beliefs about the learning process. Whether our views are accurate or not, our understanding of the learning process will directly affect our practice of teaching. If we hold to faulty learning principles, we may actually hinder our students from learning. To further explain the relationship between theory and practice, we'll take a look from another angle—from the pages of medical history.

Bloodletting was one of the more peculiar techniques utilized by doctors. The early Greeks practiced it. In America, the general practice continued until the nineteenth century.[13] The word means just what it says: letting blood drain out of the body. But it had nothing to do with a Red Cross blood drive! When we give blood for the Red Cross today, the blood is stored for later use. But in that day, the blood was discarded after the patient was bled. What was worse, many doctors of that time actually used *leeches* as a convenient method of bloodletting![14]

Doctors perpetuated this practice because of medical *theory*. Before modern science, it was assumed that the body contained four basic fluids, called "humors": (1) blood, the chief fluid; (2) phlegm; (3) choler, or yellow bile; and (4) melancholy, or black bile.[15] A healthy body, it was believed, possessed a balance of these humors. Thus, all disease stemmed from imbalance. Diagnosis of disease was simple. Accurate diagnosis determined the imbalance among the humors. Bloodletting was the most direct way to normalize the blood humors, since all four were interconnected. Drawing off one area would drain off the other, and a healthy ratio would be reestablished.

What's the point of this history lesson? Simply this: what we *do* is *always* based on what we *think*. To rephrase it: *theory drives practice.* The practice of medicine is based on assumptions or theories about how the body functions. Moreover, faulty assumptions about physical processes lead to faulty medical *practice.* In like manner, we teachers have our own theories about how students learn best. And sometimes our instructional methods in the classroom contain "faulty theories" comparable to "humoral theory."

As the physician works within God's design of the human body to facilitate healing, so the teacher works within God's design of the mind and heart to facilitate learning. Effective physicians and instructors master their respective disciplines in harmony with God's purposes. An older definition of Christian education affirms one conceptual basis for this book:

> **Christian education is a reverent attempt to discover the divinely ordained process by which individuals grow in Christlikeness, and to work with that process (Harner 1939, p. 20).**

## Key Concepts and Issues

barriers to learning

Christian education

definition of learning

diagnosing learning problems

dissemination of information

educational psychology/learning theory

elements of learning:

    Levels of learning

    Extent of learning

    Avenues of learning

    Readiness for learning

    Nature of learning

lecture method

myths of learning process

relation of theory and practice in learning

role in student learning: divine and human teacher

selecting teaching methods

teachable moments

**L** evels
**E** xtent
**A** venues
**R** eadiness
**N** ature

*2*

# What Can We Learn?

**Cognitive Level: Knowledge and Intellectual Skills**
**Behavioral Level: Physical Skills and Habits**
**Affective Level: Emotions and Attitudes**
**Dispositional Level: Values and Tendencies to Act**
**Application: Evaluating and Measuring Learning**

## Try It Out

Imagine that you are teaching a series of lessons to teens on compassion in the Christian life. Listed below are indications that your students are learning compassion. At what point are you satisfied that your students have become more compassionate? Look at the following items and check the one that comes closest to this standard.

_____ 1. Each student can recite Ephesians 4:32.
_____ 2. Each student can explain the concept of compassion in his or her own words.
_____ 3. Each student can identify an example of compassion when seeing one.
_____ 4. Each student can share an experience from this past week when he or she was compassionate to someone else.
_____ 5. Each student can provide a testimony from an adult who saw the student being compassionate to someone else.

None of these listed indications of learning compassion are unimportant to our students. Each one gives evidence that some learning has taken place. Furthermore, each succeeding option offers signs of more substantial learning. These items show that learning can involve a variety of outcomes with various degrees of mastery.

The purpose of this chapter is to explain what *kinds* and *degrees* of learning are possible. Technically, these are called "Levels" and "Extent" of learning, respectively. Any approaches to teaching and learning that we use must reflect the way God has made us. The following four-part "ABCD" framework complements God's design of people. Teachers can use this model both in planning lessons and in evaluating student learning.

1. **A**ffective Level (emotions and attitudes)
2. **B**ehavioral Level (physical skills and habits)
3. **C**ognitive Level (knowledge and intellectual skills)
4. **D**ispositional Level (values and tendencies to act)

Educators are familiar with the first three categories, usually labeled as the affective, psychomotor (what we term "Behavioral Levels") and cognitive domains. Certain published curricula refer to these three Levels (for their instructional aims) by using such terms as, "to feel" (affective), "to do" (behavioral), and "to know" (cognitive). But a word of explanation is needed regarding the fourth category.

Wolterstorff (1980) suggests that another category replace the affective domain, that of dispositional or tendency learning.

> A program of Christian education will take that further step of cultivating the appropriate tendencies in the child. It will have tendency learning as one of its fundamental goals. . . . It is also necessary that the students' tendencies, ranging all the way from their unreflective habits to highly self-conscious commitments, be those of acting in accord with the normative laws for right action. Education, accordingly, must have among its goals to secure—always in morally defensible ways—*the formation of right tendencies* (pp. 14–15, emphasis added).

These tendencies are so distinctive, especially for Christian education, that they merit a separate category. This volitional or "conative"[1] dimension in learning has received little attention in the educational literature, largely because contemporary conceptions of human nature do not take into consideration an immaterial soul, or the function of a will. But to eliminate the other more passive or transitory aspects of affect, as Wolterstorff suggests, seems to be unwise.

As it currently is conceived in the educational literature, the affective domain is overly cumbersome. It seems to be a catchall collection of whatever does not fit in the more defined cognitive and psychomotor domains. It includes such diverse elements as feelings, emotions, moods, aesthetic appreciations, attitudes, values, and motivation.[2] Consequently, in this book, two distinct categories are identified: the *Affective Level* of learning, which will include emotions and attitudes in general, and the *Dispositional Level,* which will be comprised of values and tendencies to act. Also, student motivation and attitudes toward subject matter—overlapping both categories—receive a chapter-length discussion later in this book. Although it seems more helpful to divide these various factors into two such groupings, we must realize that our affective life is much more holistic than any academic classification system can describe.[3]

Besides the question of what *kinds* (or Levels) of learning are possible a complementary issue is how *well* students have learned. Is learning relatively simple or more sophisticated? Reflect on the "Try It Out" task earlier. Certainly we are pleased that our students can recite Ephesians 4:32, but we also want them to learn much more about compassion and being compassionate.

In the following section each of the four *Levels* of learning is described. *Extent* of learning is also featured, in that various degrees of mastery for each Level are suggested. (Although it is necessary, in practice, to separate these domains for the purposes of analysis and description, we must remember that learning is much more holistic and interrelated.) Since the Cognitive domain is the most familiar to us in our teaching, it will be described first, followed by the Behavioral, Affective, and Dispositional Levels.

## Cognitive Level: Knowledge and Intellectual Skills

The most popular understanding of learning views it as the acquisition of new information. We typically associate this category with the primary purpose of formal education. Acquisition of facts, however, also includes the cultivation of a more sophisticated thinking skill—the ability to process facts.[4] For example, teachers often help students learn how to determine God's will for their lives, interpret a Bible passage, or understand a foreign language for a missions project.

New information can be comprehended with differing degrees of mastery. The standard taxonomy of educational objectives within the cognitive domain of learning was developed by Bloom and his colleagues (1956). This taxonomy identifies six degrees of cognitive functioning. Ford (1978) grouped five of these categories under the heading "understanding," to distinguish them from the elemental category of "awareness." Christians would add "wisdom" as a final degree of cognitive mastery, indicating the ultimate need to consistently apply knowledge to life (See Table 2.1).

Thus, we have, in order of complexity, (1) *awareness* (being conscious of some concept); (2) *understanding* (having a better perception of a concept's meaning and significance); and (3) *wisdom* (consistently using this information to make an important decision).[5] By way of illustration, we could know that the earth is a round globe (awareness). We could then deduce that, since it is a globe, someone could travel around the world and eventually return to the starting point (understanding). Furthermore, we could decide whether it would be good judgment to actually take a trip around the world (wisdom).

**Table 2.1**

# Cognitive Level of Learning

| | |
|---|---|
| • Awareness: | basic recognition of a concept |
| • Understanding: | more in-depth perception of the meaning and significance of a concept |
| • Wisdom: | using the concept in an appropriate manner in making decisions according to a Christian worldview |

### Awareness and Understanding

*Awareness* and the five categories of *understanding* can be best described using a bicycle as an illustration.[6]

#### Awareness[7]

Imagine that someone explains the concept of "bicycle" to you for the first time. After this brief instruction, you can recognize a bicycle. You are able to select a picture of a bike from several pictures that include a car, a shopping cart, and a skateboard. "Awareness," or such recognition, signifies that a mental conception is associated with the appropriate object.

#### Comprehension

Comprehension means that you can demonstrate basic knowledge by drawing a picture of a bicycle. Your picture shows the essential features of a bike. It portrays the proper relationships of each part to other parts (although probably not to scale). This task requires you to outwardly express the concept based on your personal understanding. In contrast to "awareness," the picture that is drawn originates from *inside* you, rather than from an external source.

#### Application

Assume that you don't know what a unicycle or a tricycle is, but that you do understand what a bicycle is. You are presented with pictures of all three objects. Again, you recognize only one. Reasoning from the two-wheeled vehicle, you ask yourself, "If we call this a 'bicycle,' what should these other two be called?" You may not use the exact term, but you could use your understanding of "bi" and "cycle" to name the remaining objects. That is, you apply or transfer known principles to a new situation involving some unknown factors.[8]

*Analysis*

Analysis requires the learner to know the operational or functional parts of a subject as well as the relationships of the parts to each other. To test for mastery of this category, you might be presented with a broken bicycle that needs repairs. Or, you might be given a box of bicycle parts to assemble. In order to complete either of these tasks you need to know the intricacies of each component and what contribution each one makes. Analysis allows you to perform such problem-solving tasks.

*Synthesis*

Could you gather all known parts of a bicycle and rearrange them into a new form? That's the challenge of synthesis. It's the challenge of creativity. For instance, using the basic parts (e.g., seat, handlebars, wheels, pedals), could you design a different sort of "pedaled," nonmotorized mode of transportation for use on land? Options might include a reclining bicycle or a tandem (two-seater) bicycle.

*Evaluation*

Evaluation requires the learner to make a judgment about an object based on a set of criteria.

---

### Try It Out

---

Of the following modes of transportation, which one do you think is best?

    a. 10-speed touring bicycle
    b. 18-speed mountain bicycle
    c. tricycle
    d. tandem bicycle
    e. unicycle

---

Your answer to the "Try It Out" question depends, of course, on the standards of assessment you use. For what purpose and in what situation will this vehicle be used? Who will use it? Does the rider possess the necessary skills?

*Remembering and Forgetting*

One other relevant topic for learning awareness and understanding is short- and long-term retention. Having ready access to what we have learned is critical to the learning process. We might picture our memory as a filing cabinet full of files. Not being able to locate the specific file that is needed at the moment would be very frustrating. Circumstances that require this retrieval ability include adding the prices of grocery items, fixing a flat tire, or answering a question about the resurrection of Jesus. In one sense, it may be true that no one ever really forgets—almost everything that is experienced is retained, either in conscious or unconscious memory storage. Yet if we could consciously remember everything, our minds would be cluttered with information. It's a blessing that we have some form of memory decay.

But in the educational setting, forgetting is a real problem. Current research on how we forget offers two main reasons for our inability to retrieve information that has been learned. "What you don't use, you lose" *(inactivity)* points to the first reason for memory loss. Using the filing cabinet analogy, we all possess many "inactive" files. The frustrating response, "I know it's here somewhere!" does little good unless we actually reclaim what we are trying to locate.

The second reason for memory loss involves *interference*. In this case old learning prevents new learning. For example, it's often difficult to write the new year on personal checks. Again, using the filing cabinet il-

## Table 2.2
# Understanding—Categories of Critical Thinking

| Category/Meaning | Relevant Verbs | Relevant Activities/Questions |
|---|---|---|
| **Comprehension** | | |
| To integrate new data with existing information | Interpret Paraphrase Translate Illustrate | In your own words, summarize Moses' thoughts and anxieties during the burning bush experience (Exod. 3). |
| **Application or Transfer of Learning** | | |
| To use information in new situations | Construct Demonstrate Implement | Conduct an "interview" with one of the servants who saw Moses' confrontation with Pharaoh during the plagues. |
| **Analysis or Problem-solving** | | |
| To distinguish facts in their relationships | Categorize Diagram Outline | How was Moses' burning bush experience similar to and different than Paul's Damascus road experience? |
| **Synthesis or Creating** | | |
| To reorganize or integrate facts into a new whole | Design Develop Plan | Create a script for a 2-minute radio spot newscast, using the sea crossing event in Exod. 14. |
| **Evaluation** | | |
| To judge facts, using a specified standard | Appraise Rank Rate | Read Exod. 15:1–21. Now read vv. 22–24. Assess your feelings as if you had experienced this situation as Moses did. What if you had been Miriam? |

*Source:* Unknown; categories from Bloom, et al. (1956).

lustration, it's like trying to relocate a file of past sermons that were cat-alogued *topically*, but are now filed according to the *Scripture texts*. To employ a sports analogy, a good racquetball player may have difficulty becoming a good tennis player since the swing of the racquet is very different in each game. Another kind of interference involves the reverse problem: new learning "erases" or blocks out what was previously learned. For example, studies show that when a list of grocery items is given, unless some special memory device is used, the items near the end of the list tend to be remembered more than the first few items.[9]

"Forgetting" about the Creator and his mighty acts is a prominent sin of God's people (Deut. 4:9; 6:12; 8:11). In the New Testament, believers are commanded to remember the personal work of Christ—the Lord's Supper is one regular reminder to be used for this purpose (1 Cor. 11:23–30). Various strategies encourage better retrieval of learned information: overlearning, deeper understanding of concepts (versus rote learning), and emphasis on meaningful learning and memory devices.[10]

In summary, we have looked at two of three major degrees of learning: awareness and understanding. Within these two categories, we have identified six factors that provide one effective way to assess many of the diverse cognitive tasks we require of our students. For instance, are we challenging them to analyze or synthesize concepts? Or are we interested only in comprehension or awareness? Table 2.2 provides a summary of five of the factors of understanding, along with sample discussion questions. Table 2.3 presents an alternative taxonomy for the cognitive domain. This typology was developed to provide more guidance for higher-order test item construction.

### Table 2.3
## LOGIQ: Logical Operations for Generating Intended Questions

**REITERATION** is a task that requires an individual to recognize or produce information in essentially the same form as that in which it was originally received. Examples of reiteration are recalling names, facts, and principles; locating places and things on previously seen maps and models; reproducing maps, diagrams, and formulae; restating material verbatim. Reiteration can be employed with all three types of content, as the following sample items show:

- **Facts.** State the sum of 4 + 6. (The student has already learned this problem.)

- **Concepts.** Give four defining attributes of mammals. (Again, the student has learned these attributes.)

- **Principles.** State a principle that governs the prediction of rain. (The student has been taught "When dew is on the grass, rain will not come to pass.")

**SUMMARIZATION** requires an individual to report the substance of a message accurately as opposed to recalling the message verbatim. In summarizing, information irrelevant to a current goal or situation may be omitted while especially relevant information is highlighted. All three types of content can be summarized:

- **Facts.** Summarize the events leading up to the Boston Tea Party.
- **Concepts.** Describe in your own words the distinguishing characteristics of infants with phenylketonuria.
- **Principles.** Describe in your own words the effects of a continuous schedule of reinforcement on learning rate (acquisition) and on resistance to extinction.

**ILLUSTRATION** requires the student to demonstrate understanding by recognizing or providing previously unseen or unused examples of a concept or principle. Only two types of content can be used in illustration:

- **Concepts.** State which of the following are examples of romantic poetry. (The student is given several lines from each of a number of previously unencountered works.)
- **Principles.** (*a*) Name the principle used by the defensive coach in the following play. (The student is given a description of an athletic contest in which a change in offensive strategy by one coach is countered by a change in defensive strategy by the other.) (*b*) Name one principle of foreign policy on which the following action could be based. (The student is given a description of an international event and the official action of the U.S. government.)

**PREDICTION** Confronts an individual with a previously unencountered situation and asks him or her to employ a rule to predict (*a*) changes in the situation at a later time, or (*b*) changes in related situations. Like illustration, prediction can be based only on concepts and principles.

- **Concepts.** Given the following account of the findings of history and physical examinations, describe the findings you would expect in concurrent x-ray investigations and laboratory studies. (The account the student is provided describes a classic cardiovascular problem.)
- **Principles.** (*a*) Given the following long-term environmental changes, forecast the relative chances of survival for the two species named. (The student is given specified changes and the names of two species that differ in genetic endowment). (*b*) Describe how consumer behavior will be altered by the following changes in Federal Reserve Banking policies. (Specified actions of the Bank are described.)

**EVALUATION** involves the use of criteria in making a decision or selection. It consists of careful analysis of a problem or situation to determine factors to be considered in making the decision and the careful weighting of each factor.

Evaluation is based on the use of principles, as it normally involves anticipating the consequences of an act and then judging the acceptability of those consequences on the basis of appropriate standards. This process holds even when historical precedent is the apparent basis for a decision because such precedent is normally based on the anticipated consequences of an act.

Evaluation items may require the test-taker to complete an entire process of evaluation or any of the following component parts: (*a*) selection of criteria, (*b*) operationalizing of criteria, (*c*) using given criteria to make a judgment, or (*d*) determining what criteria were used in making a judgment. One example of an evaluation item follows:

- **Principles.** What factors should be considered in deciding the degree of emphasis to be placed on nuclear generation of energy for the next ten years? (The question asks for discussion of appropriate criteria to be used in making the decision.)

**APPLICATION** is the reverse of prediction. Here the individual is given a desired outcome and a description of the initial state or situation and is asked to arrange the conditions necessary to achieve the desired outcome. Application involves using other types of behavior (summarization, prediction, etc.) in sequences and includes those activities commonly referred to as problem solving and creative thinking. Application is normally based on use of principles. One major characteristic that differentiates application (and evaluation) from illustration and prediction is the requirement that the examinee *formulate* possible courses of action rather than just choose among options provided.

- **Principles.** Given the following description (of environmental conditions such as degree days, amount of direct and indirect radiation, latitude, etc.), develop plans for a fuel-efficient home.

For example, the principle, "A stitch in time saves nine" can be used in various ways. It may be recited verbatim (reiteration). It may be restated in different words (summarization). Individuals may be asked to provide or identify examples of the rule in use (illustration). The rule or principle may be used to anticipate the consequences of certain acts, for example, one may observe that failing to sew up small rips in clothing leads to larger tears (prediction). Or a principle or procedure may be employed to make a judgment, for example, one may decide to sew the rip up now rather than wait (evaluation). The rule or principle may also be used in arranging conditions and initiating procedures to produce a desired outcome (application).

*Source:* Williams and Haladyne (1982, pp. 165–66).

### Wisdom

Wisdom is the ultimate goal of all cognitive learning. How should we distinguish among the three major categories of awareness, understanding, and wisdom? Lee (1985) offers two guidelines. "[U]nderstanding and wisdom, unlike [awareness], can be gained only through firsthand experience" (p. 178). Second, "As understanding judges [awareness] and subsequently corrects and illumines [it] as a result of this judgment, so too does wisdom judge understanding and subsequently corrects and illumines it" (p. 193, n. 138). Throughout the Book of Proverbs, wisdom and the person with righteous judgment are placed in stark contrast to the foolish, wicked person. The former person is recognized as one who lives by truth, who is shaped by and embodies truth.

No doubt God is concerned about the believer's awareness, understanding, and wisdom (2 Cor. 10:5; Phil. 4:8); but there is much more to learning for Christians. We turn our attention now to the three other Levels.

## Behavioral Level: Physical Skills and Habits

This Level of learning primarily relates to bodily actions. Whether it's serving a ball in tennis, operating a printing press, sewing clothes, or driving a car, we have all mastered numerous skills. Even activities like praying or evangelizing include learned competencies. Learning good habits and persevering in the routines of our lifestyle contribute to the development of Christian character.

Although no standard taxonomy of educational objectives has emerged as the dominant summary of the behavioral (or psychomotor) domain, a few have been developed.[11] Ford's study (1978) provides a brief introduction to the psychomotor domain, using Simpson's (1966) categories. This seven-part framework may be organized into three kinds of instructional phases (see Table 2.4).

**Table 2.4**

# Simpson's Taxonomy for the Behavioral Level

**Phase 1: Preparation**

- Perception—becoming aware of objects and their qualities through one or more of the human senses.

- Set—possessing the readiness to perform a particular action.

**Phase 2: Supervised Practice**[12]

- Guided response—performing under the guidance of a skilled trainer.

**Phase 3: Increasing Excellence in Performance**

- Mechanism—performing a task consistently with some degree of confidence and proficiency.

- Complex overt response—performing a task with a high degree of confidence and proficiency.

- Adaptation—performing new but related tasks based on previously learned motor skills.

- Origination—using understanding, abilities, and skills developed in the psychomotor area, the student creates new performances.

*Source:* Modified from Simpson (1966).

Within the human body, God has designed great potential for action, as indicated in the following story.

When he heard a woman scream, "My baby, my baby!" at a neighbor's swimming pool, James Patridge knew he had to act. The Vietnam veteran, who lost both legs in a 1966 land-mine explosion, raced his wheelchair 180 feet as the mother ran into her home near West Chicago, Ill., on June 4 [1986] to telephone authorities for help—only to get a recorded message.

Blocked by thick trees and brush, Patridge, 38, left his wheelchair and crawled 60 feet to reach 1-year-old Jennifer Kroll, who had been pulled from the pool by her mother. "The baby wasn't breathing, and her face was blue," Patridge says. He began the cardiopulmonary resuscitation (CPR) he had learned in a hospital course. The baby came back to life with a cry. The father, Michael Kroll, who had never met Patridge, now thanks him daily. Patridge insists, "God saved that child—not me."[13]

In developing skill mastery and habits, our bodies seem to develop a "memory" of their own. A good illustration is the complex task of driving a car. When most of us were first learning to drive, we were overwhelmed by all that we had to keep in mind. But, after years of experience, we now drive to and from work for miles in "autopilot" fashion; we hardly give any thought to what our body is doing. This "body memory" is the key to success for Olympic athletes. They couldn't progress toward excellence without it.

## Affective Level: Emotions and Attitudes

The Christian life necessitates love for others: being compassionate, kind, humble, and gentle (Col. 3:12–14). God desires "willing hearts" who serve him (Exod. 35:5; 36:5–6). These virtues take time to mature since they are more often "caught than taught." Analogous to gardening, convictions require patient cultivation. Motivation, emotions, and attitudes are also learned.

---

### Try It Out

---

Listed below are a number of feelings and attitudes. Fit as many as you can in the blank spaces available.

feel/was obligated
rejoice(d)
am/be bored
desire
moan
be glad
hate

"I _____ to do your will, O my God; your law is within my heart" (Ps. 40:8).
"But may all who seek you _____ and _____ in you" (Ps. 40:16).
"I _____ with those who said to me, 'Let us go to the house of the Lord.'" (Ps. 122:1).

---

Some of the combinations probably sound very familiar, but others come across as absurd or hilarious (e.g., "I feel obligated or hate to do your will, O my God."). The psalmist highlights the fact that our attitudes and feelings are an important part of the Christian life. And they don't come fully developed at birth—we learn them.

The affective domain includes a wide variety of learning outcomes. Some people like math, some dislike economics; some look forward to Bible study, some avoid ministries to preschoolers. In every educational situation, students develop personal, affective responses to the teacher, the subject matter, and the classroom. Certain motivations need to be checked as potentially sinful attitudes (e.g., constant neglect of and dislike for witnessing about Christ). When it comes right down to it, it should be no surprise that all such attitudes (positive and negative) affect future learning.

### Table 2.5
# Krathwohl's Taxonomy for the Affective Level

- Receiving—A person is willing to receive (or attend to) a particular viewpoint. For example, a student might show an openness to listen to the claims of the Gospel.

- Responding—A person shows sustained consideration to do something with that particular viewpoint. Here, a student might decide to "stay after class" to discuss the Gospel even more.

- Valuing—A person expresses a preference for or a commitment to that particular viewpoint. The student actually makes a personal decision for Christ, at this point, by valuing a biblical worldview over other perspectives.

- Organization—A person internalizes and rearranges his or her life according to this particular viewpoint. The student's priorities change. Now, for example, she attends a home Bible study and becomes involved in an outreach project within her neighborhood.

- Characterization by a particular value or set of values—A person develops a way of life that is built around this particular viewpoint and its value system. Over time, the student's reputation reflects godly living.

*Source:* Modified from Krathwohl et al. (1964).

A taxonomy of learning objectives developed by Krathwohl et al. (1964) provides one way of seeing progression in affective development (see Table 2.5). Included with each of the five factors is an illustration of someone who sequentially evidences a growing commitment to the Good News about Jesus Christ. A global outline like this one may not be that helpful on a day-to-day basis. Krathwohl's taxonomy appears to give more attention to attitudes and values, and less to the emotional life. Attempting to relate together such factors as emotions, attitudes, values, and motivation into *one* useful framework may be an impossible task.

Though it is more difficult to measure, the affective domain is critical to learning—more so than we usually acknowledge. Chapter 6 is devoted to practical classroom matters involving student motivation, attitudes, and feelings.

## Dispositional Level: Values and Tendencies to Act

It's common in Christian circles to speak of personality as being made up of intellect, will, and emotions; but we never seem to get around to talking about the *will*. In this final Level of learning, the purpose is to discipline the will to choose and act in accord with the indwelling Spirit of God. Wolterstorff (1980) suggests that a major focus in Christian learning ought to be on such "tendency" learning. "Tendencies are grounded in desires, wishes, commitments, values, and the like" (p. 4).

For the Behavioral Level, treated earlier in this chapter, established habits and "body memory" were regarded as significant factors. But this "body memory" also can work to our disadvantage in the spiritual realm. Although we Christians are alive to God and not under bondage to sin, in most cases we still retain the particular desires and habits that characterized our lives before salvation. With the Spirit's indwelling, we have power to freely choose to do good and not to sin. But we carry with us old baggage—our bodies, in particular, retain those unrighteous dispositions we learned in the past. Willard (1988) explains:

> After conversion our will and conscious intent are for God. . . . But the layer upon layer of life experience that is embedded in our bodies, as living organisms born and bred in a world set against or without God, doesn't directly and immediately follow the shift of our conscious will. It largely retains the tendencies in which it has so long lived (p. 86).

Thus, we are not working with a level playing field regarding our desires and habits—initially we are at a disadvantage. But this status does not need to remain unchanged.

As we systematically strive to form new and godly habits, we anticipate a time when each habit will become a natural part of our lives. Like experienced drivers who no longer need to mechanically contemplate every separate and precise aspect of driving we will live the Christian life naturally. Willard (1988, p. 117) elaborates: "We consciously direct our bodies in a manner that will ensure that it eventually will come 'automatically' to serve righteousness as it previously served sin automatically" (cf. Rom. 6:12–13). To illustrate it another way, "Habits are like railroad tracks. You lay them down with a lot of effort so that later you can get where you want to be, smoothly and easily" (Mininnger and Dugan 1988, p. 129).

Figure 2.1 pictures the process by which we develop dispositions as related to habit formation. Before cultivating a new habit, the particular behavior and desire are largely uncontrolled (Phase 1). Then, through systematic human efforts within the boundaries of godly living—efforts exerted by ourselves and those to whom we hold ourselves accountable—and by God's grace, we gain control—step by step—over this area (Phase 2). Concurrently, a positive disposition is also being formed *along with* this new habit. If these practices are continued the behavior and disposition can become routine (see Phase 3A). At this point, we often call this accomplishment a "second nature" habit. Yet, in areas for which we are

**Figure 2.1**
# Phases in Formation of Habits and Dispositions

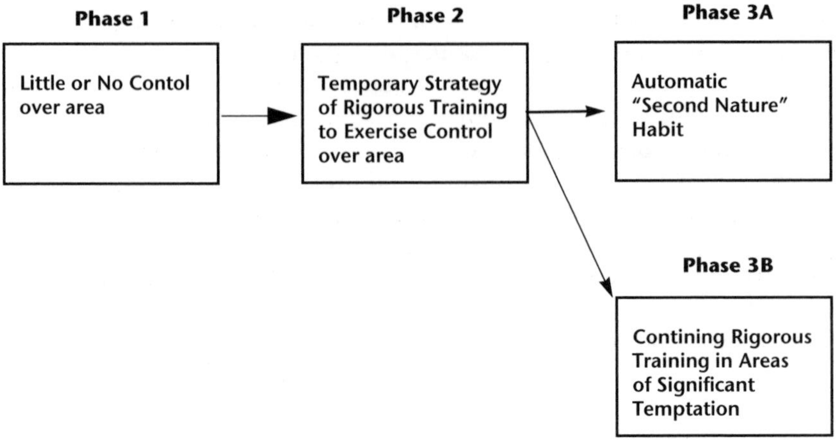

| Phase 1 | Phase 2 | Phase 3A |
|---------|---------|----------|
| Little or No Contol over area | Temporary Strategy of Rigorous Training to Exercise Control over area | Automatic "Second Nature" Habit |

**Phase 3B**

| |
|---|
| Contining Rigorous Training in Areas of Significant Temptation |

*Source*: adapted from Watson and Tharp, 1989 p. 97

very susceptible to temptation, we must guard ourselves from falling by continuing in this systematic training program for godliness (Phase 3B; cf. 2 Tim. 4:7–8).

If we *don't* move ahead in developing dispositions toward godliness, we endanger our relationship with God. Due to the habits and inclinations of our former life apart from God, at any time we can revert back to our old "self." This is the same part of ourselves that Paul tells us to put off, in order to "put on the new self, created to be like God in true righteousness and holiness" (Eph. 4:22–24). "Virtue is the habit of a heart firmly inclined toward right values, hungry and thirsty for them" (Holmes 1991, p. 64).[14]

## Application: Evaluating and Measuring Learning

One important teacher responsibility includes providing helpful feedback to students regarding their progress. In order to assess our students' learning, we must know *what* they learn (i.e., Level of learning). We also need to have some idea of the progressive learning phases they go through (e.g., Extent of learning).

During his earthly ministry, Jesus regularly evaluated the disciples' faith, or rather their lack of faith (Matt. 8:26; 14:31; 16:8; 17:20; Luke 17:6). Yet, following the Day of Pentecost, we see no wavering as they boldly walk in faith. Paul praises the Thessalonian church for their significant growth and ministry (1 Thess. 1:2–10), and yet he urges them to keep growing (1 Thess. 4:1). Evaluation offers us progress reports about our learning.

Students are accustomed to one form of evaluation: tests. God also tests his children. God evaluates every thought, word, and deed (Matt. 12:36; Rom. 2:16; 1 Cor. 3:13; 1 Thess. 2:4). We're familiar with how God tested Abraham to see whether he loved God more than his only son (Gen. 22:1). To learn of their love and obedience, God repeatedly tested the nation of Israel in the wilderness (Deut. 8:2–3). We have specific records about how God allowed Job (Job 1–2) and Peter (Luke 22:31–32) to be tested by Satan himself. And God allows us to undergo trials and tests so that we may be approved in our faith. "Blessed is the man who perseveres under trial, because when he has stood the test, he will receive the crown of life that God has promised to those who love him" (James 1:12). An ultimate form of divine approval comes from the parable of the talents: "Well done, good and faithful servant! You have been faithful with a few things; I will put you in charge of many things. Come and share your master's happiness!" (Matt. 25:21).

### Tools for Evaluation

For each of the four domains (Affective, Behavioral, Cognitive, and Dispositional Levels) we have described conceptual frameworks that value the comprehensive nature of learning. These analytical tools can guide our evaluation efforts. Such specialized outlines focus on greater detail, whereas more holistic charts provide "at-a-glance" perspectives. For example, Richards' (1970) five-part integrative outline is presented in Figure 2.2. Although any analytical framework has its limits, the various guidelines described in this chapter get us on the right track.

### Guidelines for Evaluation

The following general principles are useful to keep in mind when evaluating students:

1. *Many Samplings:* Make many assessments. Don't base your judgment on just one or two evaluations.

2. *Variety in Method:* Use different kinds of evaluative strategies: oral, written, structured experiences, or simple observation of student activities (see Table 2.6).[15]

3. *Short- and Long-Term Learning:* Pursue observations over a longer period of time. More complex learning takes a while to manifest itself. The Christian life is not a one-hundred-yard dash; it's a marathon.[16]

4. *Different Circumstances:* Make evaluations within diverse settings. Signs of growth in the classroom do not guarantee maturity outside of class. What we ultimately desire, for example, is that our students can effectively teach the Bible, resist personal temptation, and demonstrate faithfulness to their commitments.

5. *Many Evaluators:* Several mature leaders should be involved in the assessment process. Scripture refers to the importance of having two or

## Figure 2.2
# Richards' Phases of Learning

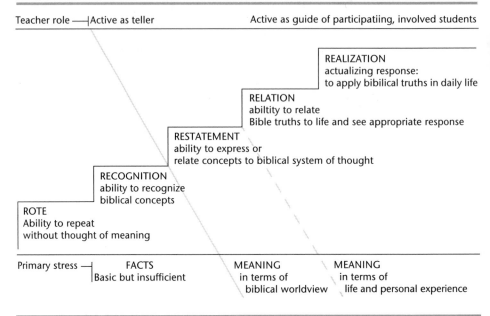

Source: Richards (1970), p. 75.

three witnesses verify an interpersonal judgment (Deut. 19:15; Matt. 18:16).

## Table 2.6
# Diverse Kinds of Methods for Evaluating Learning

*(Examples relate to a local church ministry.)*

1. Testing (e.g., using a Bible knowledge inventory test)
2. Attitude Measurement (e.g., various published attitude scales could be used)
3. Survey Questionnaires (e.g., survey members' past involvement in various ministries of the church)
4. Interviews (e.g., interview mothers regarding requirements of a nursery)
5. Observation Methods (e.g., shadow a pastoral staff member for one day, collect information from a typical morning worship service)
6. On-site Evaluation Methods (e.g., visit several members' homes or go camping or a week together)
7. Unobtrusive Methods (e.g., count children's Sunday School papers, etc., left in the hallway of the church building on Sunday)
8. Delphi Technique (develop consensus through series of mailed questions instead of face-to-face meetings—when you want to avoid possible emotional entanglement among participants/experts)
9. Q-Sort (when a number of set statements need to be ranked/prioritized; it is easier to manipulate cards than just ranking items printed on a sheet of paper)

10. Content Analysis (e.g., look at the last five years of deacon board minutes)
11. Experimental & Quasi-Experimental Design Methods (e.g., compare the effects of two visitation/evangelism programs)
12. Investigative Journalism Methods (e.g., try to determine why the church has a long-standing pattern of not giving very much to world missions)

*Source*: Worthern and Sanders (1987, pp. 298–327).

The chapter began with a "Try It Out" exercise that asked when you might be satisfied with your students' learning of compassion. Looking back on that exercise, we teachers must realize another important factor: students vary according to how quickly they learn something. Also, our expectations about student accomplishment and progress both help and hinder their learning.[17]

How do these basic guidelines translate into teaching in various areas? For example, when teens are just trying out the new mental abilities of adult reasoning (explained in chapter 8), do we expect them to recite our church's doctrinal statement word perfect? Or can we allow them freedom to try out their thinking—which may initially yield some heresy? Remembering how long our own pilgrimage has taken may help us be more sensitive and flexible in giving our students freedom to grow. Such a "developmental" perspective in teaching guards our expectations from being too rigid or unrealistic.

Another caution: what can be learned in the classroom may not fully represent the more holistic learning indicated in Scripture. In this light, "capability" and "performance" are two concepts we should remember. Capability refers to what we ask students to do in class, indicating their learning. That's an important step. But we are also interested in their lifestyle changes. That's what performance represents; what students *normally* do in life, right or wrong. Figure 2.3 provides one way to look at the

## Figure 2.3
## Capability and Performance

| Level | Capability | Performance |
|-------|------------|-------------|
| Affective | ? [Certain Attitudes, Motivation] | Christian Attitudes and Feelings |
| Behavioral | Skills and Exercises | Skill Mastery and Christian Lifestyle Habits |
| Cognitive | Awareness and Understanding | Christian Wisdom and Thought Life |
| Dispositional | ?[Certain Values, Tendencies] | Christian Dispositions with Lifestyle Habits |

More easily measurable during class

various Levels of learning based on these two concepts. We may not easily measure performance-types of learning in class, but we must keep this broad concept of performance in our overall teaching perspective. For anything we do to cultivate the right convictions, lifestyle habits, godly wisdom, and dispositions—ultimate learning goals—will be well worth our time and effort.

## Key Concepts and Issues

Bloom's Taxonomy of the Cognitive Domain
    Awareness, Comprehension, Application, Analysis, Synthesis, Evaluation
body memory
capability and performance
Extent of learning
    Cognitive Level: awareness, understanding, wisdom
evaluating and measuring learning
habit formation
Krathwohl's Taxonomy of the Affective Domain
Levels of Learning
    affective, behavioral, cognitive, and dispositional
remembering and forgetting: inactivity and interference
Simpson's Taxonomy of the Behavioral or Psychomotor Domain

# Part 2

# Process of Learning

# Learning by Processing Information

**Identification Avenue**
**Inquiry Avenue**
**Age-Appropriate Learning**
**Application: Facilitating Discussion among Adults**

Imagine that you are a newly trained health worker in a Third World rural community. You want to help impoverished parents keep their babies from getting diarrhea. Diarrhea among infants is widespread in Third World nations due largely to the use of unclean baby bottles. This habit contributes to the high infant mortality rate. You plan to teach mothers to choose the more hygienic practice of breast feeding. But such education sounds easier than it really is. You become frustrated when your instructional sessions do not bring about the desired change. Eventually you are clued in to local perspectives. The reason why these parents are not easily persuaded by your logic is because they believe that the actual cause of diarrhea is the "evil eye." They think that any person's glance at a healthy infant brings ill effects. In order to prevent evil eye, mothers tie various charms around their babys' necks or wrists. Of course, they hide their precious infants from public view to avert such lethal glances. Compliments about healthy babies are not very welcome (Rogers 1983, p. 102).

Our ideas and beliefs directly affect our actions. In short, both *what* and *how we think* are critical. This holds true whether we live in a rural village in a Third World country or in a metropolitan city in America. It also holds true whether our ideas are right or wrong. And our ideas about how people learn will directly affect our practice of teaching. In chapter 1 we addressed various misconceptions about the educational process: "to teach is to tell," "to tell is to know," and "to know is to do." Our practice of learning and teaching will improve in proportion to our altered perceptions, which must be aligned with truth.[1]

In what ways do we actually learn? Every teacher makes assumptions and judgments about specific learning processes. We regularly employ teaching methods that we think best help students learn: presentations to introduce new subjects, small group discussions to encourage interaction and decision-making, and projects to facilitate deeper understanding and personal application. Each method, whether we realize it or not, is undergirded by particular learning principles.

In the next three chapters we will focus on the specific *ways* that we learn. These are summarized in six principles, or *Avenues,* of learning. They represent the substance of each of the three learning "families" outlined by Dykstra (1990): cognitive, or Information-Processing Learning theory; associational, or Conditioning Learning theory; and observational, or Social Learning theory.[2] Each learning family contains a pair of contrasting Avenues. These half-dozen categories are *not* mutually exclusive; each shares characteristics with other Avenues. Figure 3.1 presents the six Avenues of learning in relation to the three major learning families.[3]

## Figure 3.1
## Learning Families and Related Avenues of Learning

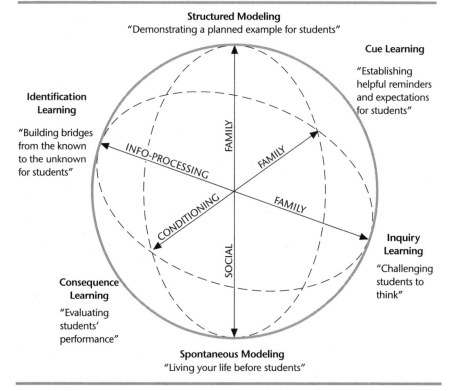

**Structured Modeling**
"Demonstrating a planned example for students"

**Cue Learning**
"Establishing helpful reminders and expectations for students"

**Identification Learning**
"Building bridges from the known to the unknown for students"

**Consequence Learning**
"Evaluating students' performance"

**Inquiry Learning**
"Challenging students to think"

**Spontaneous Modeling**
"Living your life before students"

Information-Processing theories,[4] which will be discussed in this chapter, assume an active role for the learner's intellect. Specifically, the learner calculates, classifies, coordinates, contemplates, and criticizes information. The "Identification Avenue" and "Inquiry Avenue" feature the two major cognitive means of learning. To illustrate each Avenue with Scripture, we focus on the miraculous feeding of the five thousand—one of the few miracles of Jesus recorded in all four Gospel accounts.[5]

## Identification Avenue

At the outset of the feeding of the five thousand, the twelve disciples were anxious about the crowd's needs. The multitude had followed Jesus all day. They were exhausted and famished. No food was available in the immediate vicinity (Luke 9:12). Jesus empathetically responded to these needs. But he did so in an unexpected way. The crowd's physical needs were met in concert with their spiritual needs.

The next day following the miracle, in a discourse with the same crowd, Jesus referred to himself as the "bread of life" (John 6:35). This metaphorical imagery provided a specific reference to the miraculous feeding (John 6:26). It also recalled God's provision of manna for the Israelites in the wilderness (John 6:31).

The Identification Avenue that Christ employed here attempts to locate some meaningful connection with the student's life situation and experience. It uses the student's relevant background as the means to teach new information. The term "identification" is used in the sense that teachers attempt to *identify with* their students' current level of understanding—to see life from the students' point of view and level of experience. This "life-to-lesson" approach moves from the *known* to the *unknown*. It builds bridges from the students' present understanding to new concepts.[6] In the passage above, Jesus consciously connected the crowds' experience of the miracle with the fact that he alone could provide eternal sustenance as the bread of life.

Consider a few more examples. To explain how the human conscience functions, a teacher may suggest several real-life comparisons: a fire bell clanging at a fire station; a flashing red warning light on a car dashboard, indicating engine trouble; a smoke alarm sounding to awaken a sleeping family. We often use familiar objects to introduce students to new ideas. But we must be cautious because such word pictures are very culture-specific; they assume a common experience base between teacher and student.

A more elaborately structured analogy uses a "picture within a picture." For instance, one simple metaphor explains prayer as a phone conversation with God. Wanting to stress that God is always attentive to our supplications, a mother told her third-grader, "No, you don't have to wait for a dial tone to talk to God. There are no busy signals. And no need for a call-waiting service."

The foremost biblical example of the Identification Avenue is the incarnation. "The Word became flesh and made his dwelling among us" (John 1:14). In addition to his becoming "one of us," Christ's teachings overflow with relevant life illustrations. Recall his references to culturally appropriate analogies, such as shepherds (Matt 18:12) and vineyards (Matt. 21:28). Other New Testament metaphors explain Christ's relationship to the church: the head and the body (1 Cor. 12; Eph. 1), the cornerstone and the stones of a building (Eph. 2; 1 Pet. 2), and the bridegroom and his bride (Rev. 19:7). The Christian life is pictured as a military battle (Eph. 6), a foot race (1 Cor. 9; Heb. 12), a boxing match (1 Cor. 9; 1 Tim. 6), and the sowing and harvesting of a field (2 Cor. 9).[7]

In John's Gospel, Jesus conveys to Nicodemus the reality of the Spirit's work in regeneration. He cites a simple word picture from nature: "The wind blows wherever it pleases. You hear its sound, but you cannot tell where it comes from or where it is going. So it is with everyone born of the Spirit" (John 3:8). Not only does Jesus proceed from the known to the unknown, but he includes an excellent tool for memory retention. He constructs a play on words. The Greek word *pneuma* is translated as both "spirit" and "wind." Since spiritual realities are typically unseen, Christ shows us that such realities must be comprehended in terms that are more familiar to the hearer. The fact, again, represents the essence of the Identification Avenue.

Another popular approach to the first Avenue is a strategy known as the advance organizer.[8] Prior to the introduction of new material (i.e., in "advance"), the teacher first presents a theoretical framework, indicating how the new concept fits within the larger body of knowledge already familiar to the student (i.e., "organizer"). For example, when teaching an Old Testament lesson, the instructor helps students organize Old Testament history by using a simple chart of three basic time periods (see Table 3.1). Each period revolves around the one well-known period of history: the period of the kings.

**Table 3.1**

## Advance Organizer for Old Testament History

| Pre-Kingdom Period | | Kingdom Period | | Post Kingdom Period | |
|---|---|---|---|---|---|
| Patriarchs Moses Joshua | Judges | United Kingdom | Divided Kingdom | Exile | Return |
| | | Saul David Solomon | Israel Judah | | |

# Inquiry Avenue

Just before Jesus performs his miracle of feeding five thousand people, he intentionally poses the "problem" of feeding the hungry crowd to the Twelve (John 6:5–6). Philip claims the task is impossible (John 6:7). But Andrew, with a little more faith, attempts to deal with the problem by presenting a boy's small lunch (John 6:8–9).

In this manner, our Lord affirms the place of Inquiry learning. The Inquiry Avenue is utilized when difficult situations are faced, when perplexing questions are raised. In such cases, learners are encouraged to seek solutions for themselves. Contemplate a contemporary example. Someone who doesn't feel confident about buying a car may seek advice from others, read a pertinent magazine, or engage in a comparative study of potential vehicles. This learning situation transforms into a teachable moment. It is based on the features of the Inquiry Avenue.

---

### Try It Out

God intended Israel's routine ceremonies and family habits to encourage children to ask questions—to actually create teachable moments. This afforded adults the opportunity to transmit their faith legacy to the next generation. We read about such intentional learning strategies as they pertain to the Passover meal (Exod. 12:23–27), the sacrifice of the first animal offspring (Exod. 13:11–16), and the memorial stones of the Jordan River (Josh. 4:5–7).

List at least two more biblical examples of Inquiry learning that you recall—educational moments that made the learners think.

1.
2.

---

God tests the Christian's faith through the trials of life (James 1:2; 1 Pet. 4:12–19). Trials provide opportunities to think about, clarify, and integrate our theology and lifestyle. It's often a time to ask, "What are you trying to teach me, Lord?" Learning gained through such deep wrestling in the crucible of life is not easily forgotten.

In the classroom, we teachers incorporate the Inquiry Avenue when we use critical questions, provocative statements, debates, case studies, puzzling events, and integrative homework assignments. Encouraging students to reflect on personal experiences stimulates lifelong critical thinking skills.[9] In contrast to the Identification Avenue (which builds on the student's previous knowledge base), the Inquiry Avenue focuses on solving newly encountered problems. To put it another way, the former highlights issues that *make sense* and the latter matters that *don't make sense*.

Table 3.2 suggests a few appropriate teaching methods for both Identification and Inquiry Avenues.

**Table 3.2**

# Teaching Methods for Identification and Inquiry Avenues

| Identification Avenue: | Inquiry Avenue: |
| --- | --- |
| *"Building bridges from the known to the unknown for students"* | *"Challenging students to think for themselves"* |
| 1. Graphic imagery: metaphors, analogies, parables | 1. Discussion questions, troublesome statements |
| 2. Advance organizers; organizational frameworks | 2. Case studies, moral dilemmas |
| | 3. Exploration of "live" puzzling events |

---

**Try It Out**

Consider your own learning experiences through these two Avenues of the Information-Processing family. Select one experience for each particular Avenue. Or, pick a concept you would like to teach others. Think of one way you could utilize each Avenue. To help you get started, here are a couple of examples.

a. **Identification Avenue:**
   In one sermon on forgiveness, a pastor used the analogy that forgiveness was like the lubricating oil of relationships.[10] At the close of the sermon, the members of the congregation were challenged to check their oil levels!

b. **Inquiry Avenue:**
   One summer day, a man needed to sharpen the blades on his lawn mower. The twin blades were so tight, a dilemma arose. To loosen them, should he unscrew the bolts in the normal pattern (i.e., rotate counter-clockwise) or in the reverse pattern? If he chose the wrong way he might overtighten the bolts and possibly strip the threads. A call to the local shop helped solve the problem: normal threads. With more confidence and effort, the bolts easily came off.

Now it's your turn. Again, provide either a personal learning experience *or* an anticipated teaching illustration. Give one example for each avenue.

   1. Identification Avenue:
   2. Inquiry Avenue:

## Age-Appropriate Learning

Effective teaching is accomplished *through*—not *despite*—the needs and characteristics of our students; it requires the skill of knowing how students learn the material best. Mark 4:33 offers relevant insight into the Master Teacher's balanced strategy: "With many similar parables Jesus *spoke the word* to them, *as much as they could understand.*" All Christians value the first part of the Lord's example (i.e., teaching "the word"). Yet many of us forget the value of or lack skills for the second half: the need to know our students so well that we, like Christ, know their limits. Like him, we must adapt our teaching to their ability to comprehend truth. Our instruction must be balanced by the student's ability to receive instruction.

As a general rule of thumb, all three learning families and related Avenues pertain to each age group: adults, teens, and children. As we scrutinize teaching strategies that are age-appropriate, however, a more discriminating look is necessary. In light of particular human needs, each age division *has been matched* with *one* particular learning family. Again, although the remaining two categories are permissible to use, one learning family best correlates with each age group. These pairings are based on comparative consideration of developmental theories. Figure 3.2 portrays these recommended combinations.

### Figure 3.2
## Age Groups and Learning Families Emphases

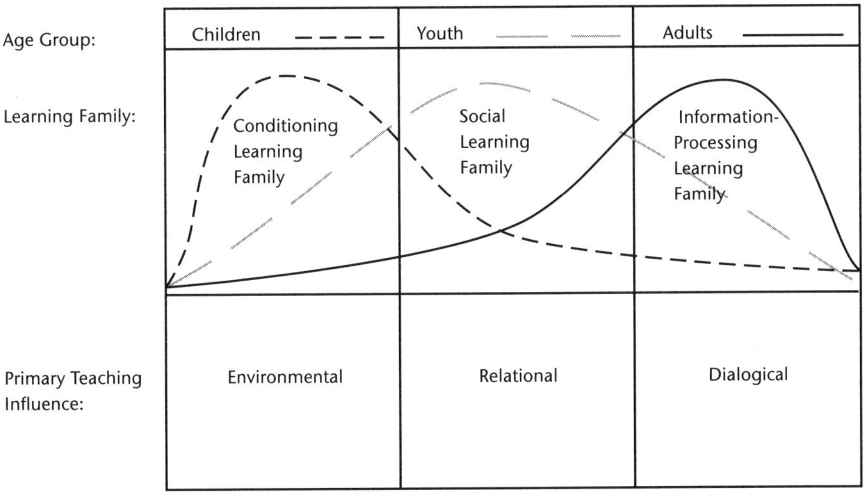

*Source:* Adapted from Kohlberg (1981, 1984) and Ward (1989, p. 94).

These matched sets primarily derive from implications of moral reasoning theory, as developed by Kohlberg (1981, 1984) and adapted by

Ward (1989, p. 94). For example, children are basically motivated by reward and punishment (Kohlberg's Level I). These positive and negative reinforcements are represented in the Conditioning Learning family. Mature youth (Level II) are morally persuaded by societal rules and role models. Social Learning theory exhibits a parallel perspective. Finally, mature adults (Level III) are motivated by dialogue and interpersonal transactions. Information-Processing Learning theory fits here, since growth is seen to be generated by sophisticated thought and interpersonal interaction.

Remember: these pairings between age groups and learning families only indicate *heightened tendencies, not exclusive associations,* as depicted in Figure 3.2. In this chapter and the next two, for each learning family some practical guidelines are offered for use with the respective age group. Now let's look at implications for teaching adults based on the Information-Processing family.

## Application: Facilitating Discussion among Adults

Class discussion is a highly valued learning method since it can foster critical thinking in students. In practice, however, good discussions are few and far between. Teachers may plan to have a class discussion, but they often do not develop the questions ahead of time. Consequently, students must work with questions off the top of the teacher's head. Following the typical silence, the teacher may then rephrase the question, or call on a reluctant student, who responds with, "Could you repeat the question?"

Framing good discussion questions takes time and plenty of thought—they should be prepared before class. The phrasing and rephrasing of questions should take place on paper, not in front of students. But even preparing questions before class may not guarantee a good class discussion. In the following section, three key principles are offered to help students talk more in class. These ideas are largely based on *Questioning and Teaching: A Manual of Practice* (Teachers College, Columbia University, 1988), a book by J. T. Dillon, an excellent teacher at the University of California, Riverside.

### Use the Right Kind of Question

First, let's clarify the role of classroom questions. Educative questions either *review* material students already know, or encourage students to *discuss* and inquire further about an issue. Our major problem may be that we use the wrong type of question. Here's a typical example of one classroom discussion.

> **Teacher:** What does Scripture tell us about the concept of forgiveness? (hand is raised) Bob?

> **Bob:** That we're supposed to do it! (laughter)
>
> **Teacher:** Okay. You have a knack for the obvious, Bob. (hand raised) Carol?
>
> **Carol:** The first verse that came to mind was Ephesians 4:32, a verse I memorized as a child. We are to forgive others as God has forgiven us.
>
> **Teacher:** Good point. (writes item on board) Anyone else? (hand raised) Gary?

In this classroom discussion, the teacher actually uses a review question that assumes that students have a basic knowledge of the issue. The assumption is that *both* student and teacher know the answer. And it follows that the teacher's purpose is to provide affirmative or corrective feedback for students.[11]

In contrast, a discussion question makes no assumptions about student knowledge of the matter. The purpose of a guided discussion is to encourage student inquiry into new options and implications related to the main issue—to let them think out loud. In this situation, the teacher has an understanding of the matter and guides student thinking to greater depths of comprehension. The key element of a discussion question is that it stimulates students' desire to know more. For example, the teacher may pose a problem (e.g., from the Bible or a contemporary scenario) for the class to solve.

> In Matthew 18:22, Jesus commanded us to always forgive other believers as often as they ask us. Yet in Titus 3:10 we are commanded to reject divisive persons after warning them twice. How do you resolve these two passages of Scripture? What is God teaching us about forgiveness?

Review questions are usually matched with one correct answer. Convergent thinking is encouraged. Discussion questions permit divergent thinking and exploration, usually with a range of helpful responses. Of course, class discussions to clarify the meaning of Scripture are unique in that there is only one interpretation—though many possible applications. But in most other kinds of discussions, a variety of solutions are possible.

Griffin (1982) suggests that we use vivid imagery in forming our questions. People tend to think in pictures. It's easier to focus on issues that are placed in a concrete context. For example, instead of asking, "What do you think God is like?" Griffin posed this scenario:

> Christmas is only a few weeks off. Suppose you came down Christmas morning and discovered a big package under the tree. They say that good things come in small packages, but you've always been partial to the big presents. You eagerly tear off the shiny red paper and discover a genuine

do-it-yourself Make-a-God kit. It's not the artificial plastic model, but the authentic original. You read the instructions and discover that you can make any kind of God you want. The only requirement is that once you've made him, you have to live with him. I know this is ridiculous. There is no such thing as a Make-a-God kit. But what if there were? Suppose it were possible to create a god to match our desires. What kind of god would you make? (p. 98).

With this kind of question any response is correct, because it has a viewpoint in mind. And timely probes help students understand their inconsistencies. "If someone asserts that she'd make a God powerful enough to stop all wars, I point out that he'd have enough clout to force his will on them as well" (p. 98). And from student responses, discerning teachers can gauge comprehension of the various attributes of God.

---

### Try It Out

1. Think of one of your past lessons or one you plan to teach. Identify one or two issues that would lend themselves to discussion. Design one discussion question.

2. Edit your discussion question at least five times. As you edit, ask yourself if this is exactly what you want the students to discuss.

3. Reflect on any insights you gained from doing items #1 and #2 in this exercise.

---

### *Step into the Background*

Even great questions can bomb because of a more difficult barrier. The traditional pattern of classroom interaction requires the teacher to talk at every turn. Reread the brief classroom excerpt on pages 56–57. It becomes obvious that the hidden curriculum of class etiquette is that the teacher *always* has the floor. Students first seek permission to speak and, after being acknowledged, make their comments. No free-flow discussion is possible. All comments are directed toward one place—the teacher—and then, typically, the teacher responds to each comment.

As teachers, the secret of facilitating good discussion involves removing ourselves from that focal point of playing the gatekeeper for every student comment. It is a hard habit to break—even for very experienced teachers—because we have been so conditioned to speak at every turn. If we are serious about developing a new habit, we'll first need some way to measure our progress. Because we tend to be preoccupied with getting the discussion going, we can easily fall into old habits of speaking at every turn. We need some form of empirical assessment to keep us in line with our intentions. The easiest indicators are the number of times we talked compared to how many times students talked, and how long we talked compared to the length of student comments. Good discussions are characterized by many lengthy student comments, with the teacher participating about as much as the majority of students. We can try to keep track of the frequency of comments ourselves (just doing the tabulating itself may get us out of the spotlight). But we may want to validate our results by asking a trusted friend or student to do the counting. Then we have some data on which to make judgments about our progress.

Two simple ideas can provide a lot of help. First, we need to attend to the physical arrangement of the classroom. How the seats are placed can help or hinder dialogue. It's best when no one sits behind another person. Some kind of circular format works well. Teachers should make sure they are not in a highly visible location; they should be just as visible as the students. Teachers should try to avoid continual eye contact with students who are speaking, especially at the beginning stages of the discussion. Without eye contact, teachers don't have to respond after every comment. Looking down when taking notes of the discussion (or counting comments) is a useful distraction for the teacher. Students will tend to look at other students. See Table 3.3 for ideas on how to keep students talking by the kind of responses we make.

### Table 3.3
## Alternate Responses to Student Comments during Discussion

- Statements
  (e.g., repeat comment, state what is on your [teacher's] mind, make reference to a related thought from another student)
- Student Questions
  (e.g., let student state the comment in the form of a question; allow other students to pose their own questions)
- Signal
  (e.g., an affirmative uh-huh; indicate to a student to make their comment)
- Silence
  (e.g., deliberative silence until speaker continues)

*Source:* Dillon (1988, pp. 132–167).

Habits change slowly, so we can't expect a free-flowing discussion immediately. It may take several sessions for students (and teachers) to get comfortable with this new arrangement. Once students get used to good discussions, they usually enjoy talking so much that it becomes harder to rein in conversation about tangential issues, or even to close the discussion. But these kinds of problems are much better than *not* having students talking and learning.

### Foster Perplexity in Students

The final guideline for good discussions relates more to the general procedural expectations of teaching than to the discussion per se. The main problem is that classroom norms are not that supportive of student questions. What hinders students from asking? In general—strange as it may seem—it's inappropriate for students to show ignorance in class, as evidenced by some teachers' responses or the groans of other students. In addition, in order to ask a question, students must be recognized to gain the floor. And, if recognized, only questions about the subject at hand are permitted—even though changing the direction of the thought may raise an important implication of the issue. Teachers may respond with, "We'll get to that later," or "We just covered that. Weren't you listening?" Other teachers tend to view student questions as interruptions. Consequently, students have a number of good reasons *not* to ask questions in class.

Dillon highlights the fact that an experience of perplexity is "the *precondition* of questioning" (1988, p. 18). The desire to inquire is prompted by such states of educative bewilderment. Student questions represent pronounced teachable moments—they provide windows into students' current states of knowing and wondering. God intended that Jewish parents would pass on their faith at times when their children wondered about the meaning of the Passover meal (Exod. 12:26–27) or the memorial stones on the bank of the Jordan River (Josh. 4:21–24). We, too, need to regard our students' questions as opportunities for learning. Cultivating a climate of inquiry and perplexity permits students to ask the questions that burn in their minds.

In studies about the Master Teacher, most analyses focus on the questions that Jesus asked. Just as important for our instruction are the questions that the disciples asked (see Table 3.4). These inquiries offered opportunities for significant teaching. If we make room for and welcome questions in our teaching, we can affirm our students' natural curiosity. Such inquisitiveness will often provide the momentum needed to sustain good class discussions.

### Table 3.4
# Questions for Jesus Posed by the 12 Disciples

(in chronological order)

"Rabbi, where are you staying?" (Andrew and another disciple; John 1:38).

"Why then do the teachers of the law say that Elijah must come first?" (Peter, James, and John; Matt. 17:10; Mark 9:11).

"Why couldn't we drive it [the demon] out?" (Matt. 17:19; Mark 9:28).

"Who is the greatest in the kingdom of heaven?" (Matt. 18:1).

"Lord, how many times shall I forgive my brother when he sins against me? Up to seven times?" (Peter; Matt. 18:21).

"Lord, do you want us to call fire down from heaven to destroy them?" (James and John; Luke 9:54).

"Rabbi, who sinned, this man or his parents, that he was born blind?" (John 9:2).

"Where, Lord?" (Luke 17:37).

"Who then can be saved?" (Matt. 19:25; Mark 10:26; Luke 18:26).

"We have left everything to follow you! What then will there be for us?" (Peter; Matt. 19:27).

"Why wasn't this perfume sold and the money given to the poor? It was worth a year's wages." (Judas, John 12:2–8; cf. disciples, Matt. 26:8; Mark 14:4–5).

"Where do you want us to make preparations for you to eat the Passover?" (Matt. 26:17; Mark 14:12; Luke 22:9).

"Lord, are you going to wash my feet?" (Peter; John 13:6).

"Lord, who is it?" (John; John 13:25).

"Lord, where are you going?" (Peter; John 13:36).

"Lord, why can't I follow you now?" (Peter; John 13:37).

"Surely not I, Lord?" (Matt. 26:22; Mark 14:19).

"Lord, we don't know where you are going, so how can we know the way?" (Thomas; John 14:5).

"But, Lord, why do you intend to show yourself to us and not to the world?" (Judas [not Iscariot]; John 14:22).

"Lord, what about him [John]?" (Peter; John 21:21).

"Lord, are you at this time going to restore the kingdom to Israel?" (Acts 1:6).

## Key Concepts and Issues

advance organizer

alternate teacher responses to student discussion comments

Conditioning Learning Family

discussion questions

fostering perplexity

guided Discussion

Identification Avenue

Information-Processing Learning Family

Inquiry Avenue

learning families matched with age groups

review questions

Social Learning Family

# Learning by Association

**Consequence Avenue**
**Cue Avenue**
**Application: Guiding Children's Learning**

Placed near a highway off-ramp, a provocative traffic sign simply read, "Keep Moving." The location had been the scene of much traffic congestion and several accidents. It made sense that something had to be done consequently. What was actually done, however, was most intriguing.

The message of the new traffic sign was encouraging drivers to respond differently at this particular site—to develop *new driving habits*. The unusual directive was just the *opposite* of the road signs we are used to—like "Slow Down," "Proceed with Caution," and "Stop." It will take many months to see whether this new approach will alleviate earlier traffic problems. One thing, however, is certain. The city officials who requested the new sign realized that current driving habits had to change at that particular intersection. The sign serves as a visible reminder to drivers as to what they should do.

A basic feature of learning is making an association between two items—just like the traffic sign and the requisite driving behavior. Some of the connections we make help us remember facts. For example, the acrostic "HOMES" can help us name the five Great Lakes. Other associations we have learned influence us to change our thinking, attitudes, or actions. For example, we've learned that a good day's work earns a good day's pay. Imagine that you suddenly stopped receiving a paycheck at work. If your financial need was great, how long would it take before you started looking for another job? Or if someone keeps making disparaging remarks to you, you eventually avoid that person to prevent hearing these personal insults.

Some of our experiences have been etched deeply in our memories. At the very moment we attend to certain cues—a phrase, a sound, even a smell—the projectors of our mind are activated so that we relive the whole experience again, even down to smallest details. For example, many of us can remember the specific time and place where we were when we heard that President John F. Kennedy had been assassinated. It was such a tragic and unexpected event in American history that it stands out in our memory. Or we may remember when we learned of the space shuttle *Challenger* disaster (those in school may have even viewed it on television). And we have all learned that certain kinds of green paper that are six inches long and two and a half inches wide (with numbers, pictures of a president, and "Federal Reserve Note" printed on them) can be exchanged for such items as food, clothes, books, and music tapes.

All learners can be influenced, or "conditioned," by people (e.g., parents who praise, teachers who give constructive criticism), objects (e.g., road signs), and activities (e.g., free donuts at break every Friday). This truism expresses the primary contribution of the Conditioning Learning family.[1] Though the concepts underlying such conditioning appear to be very simple, this particular family of theories represents a very powerful form of learning. Two major subcategories include the "Consequence Avenue" and "Cue Avenue."

## Consequence Avenue

In chapter 3 we saw how Christ's miraculous feeding offered illustrations of the Information-Processing family. Again, this miracle will be analyzed for evidence of the Conditioning Learning family. The miraculous feeding of the five thousand led to certain consequences. Despite the apostles' insistence that only a minimal supply of food was available (Mark 6:37–38), the crowd eventually had plenty to eat. In fact, the disciples collected twelve baskets of leftovers (John 6:12–13)! What an embarrassing—and enlightening—homework assignment! We can imagine how the disciples might have been convicted about their lack of faith in Jesus.

We, too, experience learning consequences regularly. Largely based on such feedback, we either repeat or discontinue specific thoughts, feelings, words, or actions. Some consequences we judge as good; we feel encouraged to perform the action again. Others we determine to be bad. We feel discouraged. Chances are we will curtail any related behavior.

Virtually every activity carries a consequence. For instance, in simple conversation, a nod indicates agreement or approval, while a frown suggests the opposite. Take a more complex example. What happens when a key does not easily move into the tumblers of a door lock? Based on previous experience (i.e., previous consequences), we make quick judgments. The problem, we tell ourselves, may be with the key or with the lock. Perhaps the key is upside down; it could even be the wrong key. The lock may be broken or "frozen." Consider a third example. When term papers are returned, students expectantly read the teacher's comments to find out how well they did. Technically, these are consequences in written form. Most students feel cheated if a significant number of remarks are not made. Such feedback reinforces what was done well.

Encouragement is one appropriate way to offer a constructive "consequence" for believers. Paul modeled this educational strategy through his encouragement to the Thessalonians (1 Thess. 1:2–10). Since our self-concept is largely determined by feedback we *receive* from others, the kind of feedback we *give* to others should be carefully chosen (Eph. 4:29–32). Admonishment can at times provide believers with needed feedback. Correction helps those veering away from God's principles (see Matt. 18:15–20; 1 Thess. 5:14; James 5:19–20). In Proverbs 15, we're taught that significant learning comes from listening to correction (vv. 31–32); we play the part of fools to resent it (vv. 10, 12). Likewise, our errors also provide signals that improvement is needed. Listen to one student's reflections about the value of mistakes in her life:

> In my own life, my mistakes stick out more in general than do my achievements. I can still remember what answers I got wrong on some of my tests and quizzes through the years, whereas the right ones have vanished from memory. I think that negative consequences tend to cause deeper learning than positive consequences in some cases. Pain is always easily recalled and I believe the Lord uses this aspect of our mind to His advantage.
>
> Where I am going with this is to suggest that I think the Lord does not stop us from making some mistakes so that we will experience the negative consequences and therefore learn better what kind of behavior and action we want to avoid.[2]

The consequence system of feedback represents, among others, one intentional plan for learning that God built into our nature.[3] He designed this pattern of learning for us so we can grow in our relationship with him and with each other.[4]

## Cue Avenue

For the Consequence Avenue, the focal point is on feedback or what *follows*. But for the Cue Avenue, the key factor is what comes *first*, that is, the "cue." Here, a symbol or object (most often involving one or more of the five senses) is linked with a distinctive mental, affective, or behavioral response on our part. If the connection between the symbol and response becomes well established, then whenever that particular symbol is encountered, it evokes the linked response. For example, hearing eerie music (sound cue) may prompt someone to experience anxiety or fear (an *affective* response). Whenever drivers see a red traffic light (visual cue), they have learned automatically to step on the brake (a *behavioral* response). A written comment (visual cue) in a daily planner can help us remember (*cognitive* response) that we have a lunch appointment tomorrow.

Jesus observed that the religious leaders correctly interpreted the signs (or "cues") of the weather, but failed to read the more significant signs concerning the Messiah (Matt. 16:1–4; Luke 11:29–32). In his Gospel, Luke portrays the feeding of the five thousand as the last event that confirmed Jesus as the Messiah (Luke 9:10–20).[5] This miracle offered the final sign or "cue" for the Twelve to arrive at this understanding.

A major benefit of the Cue Avenue is that, for the most part, we do not need to relearn such links—they can become very permanent parts of our lifestyle. God has given each of us programmable memory storage for various kinds of learned sequences—mental, affective, and behavioral. For well-established linkages, little thought is necessary for our response. The Cue Avenue helps explain the development of our memory, emotional reactions, skills, and habits of life. These learning processes are quite commonplace, yet they are often unconscious for both teacher and student.

Since both the Cue Avenue and the Identification Avenue involve some kind of a linkage, how do they differ? In the Cue Avenue, the teacher presents or uses a *symbol* (related to one of the five senses) in order to prompt student response—*behavioral* (a spoken response is expected when the student's name is called), *cognitive* (a correct definition is recalled and given for a particular term used in class), or *affective* (the student feels good when the teacher nods approval of the correct definition).

Both the Cue Avenue and the Identification Avenue make associations, but they are different. Notice, first, that these Avenues come from different learning families. For the Identification Avenue, the teacher attempts to use the student's *previously existing base of knowledge or experience* in order to explain or clarify a new concept (moving from the known to the unknown). The Identification Avenue primarily links two *conceptual* pieces of information, and thus is primarily limited to the cognitive domain, as part of the Information-Processing Learning family. The Cue Avenue, within the Conditioning Learning family, makes associations between a symbol and a conditioned response to that symbol. It *may* involve linkages in the cognitive domain, but it *also* includes affective, behavioral, and dispositional associations.[6]

---

### Try It Out

---

Certain cues can really set the mood for us.

1. Think of music that soothes and relaxes you, or the type of music that lifts you up. Why do you think it has that kind of effect on you? Do you remember any particularly memorable occasions when listening to such sounds?

2. Odors, fragrances, scents—God designed us with noses to appreciate a variety of aromas. What specific smells do you really enjoy? How do they make you feel? Can you think of any particularly memorable occasions when special scents were very meaningful to you?

3. Many of our experiences have become associated with certain sounds and scents that are now cues for memory retrieval.

### Cues as Reminders

Cues—and the links we make—help us remember facts. Have you ever tied a string around your finger? The visual cue or object and its associated message are like pairs—when you see one, the other comes to mind. Through repeated experiences, the first one becomes the cue for the second.

Familiar links include these categories: personal names that evoke memorable characteristics (e.g., Babe Ruth, Adolf Hitler), important passages in Scripture (e.g., Ps. 23; John 3:16), and physical or geographical locations with distinctive reputations (e.g., the White House, Las Vegas, Wall Street). Throughout America, various places are designated as significant historical sites (e.g., Abraham Lincoln's birthplace) or have commemorative significance (e.g., Vietnam Memorial). Religious ceremonies and habits practiced by the Israelites were reminders of their special relationship with God. Recall the altar on the banks of the Jordan River. These stones were intended as a "witness," an object lesson for the eastern tribes (Josh. 22:21–28). The Lord's Supper reminds Christians of the Lord's earthly pilgrimage and suffering sacrifice. Furthermore, the ordinance also serves as a cue that he will return someday (Matt. 26:29).

Diplomas, plaques, and trophies are contemporary reminders that we display to acknowledge major milestones and accomplishments in our pilgrimage. "Modern Western societies are poor in symbolism. One of the results is that on a personal level, we fail to incorporate symbols into our lives and give them the emphasis which they need. Christian adults need concrete material ways of summarizing the learning and growth they have experienced in some epoch of their lives."[7] Just as the nation of Israel used the stones on the Jordan River bank as a witness to their faithfulness, we should devise and use contemporary memorials testifying to our own walk of faith—whether as individuals, families, friends, or churches.

Table 4.1
# Categories of Memory Devices

A. Organizational: Relating Unrelated Units
  1. Peg
     a. *Loci*—associate words or concepts with a specific physical location
        (e.g., for theology exam on the Holy Spirit: verse cards on "illumina-
        tion" are located by the *window*, verse cards on "filling" are placed by
        the bathroom *sink*;  or main points of a sermon associated with rooms
        of your home)
     b. *Pegword*
        (1) Acrostics—(e.g., "HOMES" for 5 Great Lakes; notes on the treble
            clef, EGBDF: "Every Good Boy Deserves Fudge")
        (2) Peg System—"1-bun, 2-shoe, 3-tree, 4-door, 5-hive, 6-sticks, 7-
            heaven, 8-gate, 9-line, 10-hen" and associate unusual imagery;
            (e.g., cf. Table 4.2)
  2. Link
     a. *Verbal*—
        (1) Storyline or common phrases: "A *piece* of *pie*."
            Substitute words: Greek: "My *gramma* wrote me a *letter*."
        (2) Rhyme: days of month—"30 days hath September . . ."
     b. *Visual*—One item: country of Italy looks like a boot
        Series—For each concept, imagine a ridiculous image and then link
        images together: e.g., airplane and tree: a gigantic tree is flying, or an
        airplane is growing
        In developing ridiculous images, use four rules:
        (1) substitution,
        (2) out of proportion,
        (3) exaggeration,
        (4) action
     c. *Musical*—(e.g., putting Scripture verses to music: "Seek ye first . . .";
        spelling "sovereignty" with the old "Mickey Mouse" tune)
     d. *Kinesthetic*—(e.g., Walk Thru the Bible Seminars: certain hand move-
        ments associated with key words—Creation, Fall, Flood, Nations)
B. Encoding or Transforming the Concept
  1. Concrete Reference (e.g., for "mountain" think of a specific mountain like
     Mt. Everest)
  2. Abstract Reference
     a. *Semantic or Conceptual* (e.g., for "origin" think of image of egg)
     b. *Phonetic Pun*—Substitution: (e.g., for "Minnesota" think of "mini soda";
        "Minneapolis" think of "many apples")
        In memorizing the states in alphabetical order: Maryland & Massa-
        chusetts: "*Mary land*ing among a *mass* of people who *chew* and *sit*."
        Portuguese word for "father": "A gigantic *pie* is your *father*."
  3. Number—use a coding scheme with digits as consonants,
     1 (t,d), 2 (n), 3 (m), 4 (r), 5 (l), 6 (j,sh,ch,g),
     7 (k,c), 8 (f,v,ph) 9 (p,b), 0 (z,s,c)
     (e.g., "*no time*" in Los Angeles for the area code [213])

*Source*: Adapted from Bellezza (1981) and Lorayne and Lucas (1974).

The Cue Avenue is employed in various instructional systems. Table 4.1 provides an overview and categorization of various memory devices that can be used. Famous orators used comparable devices to recall the outline of a speech (Lorayne and Lucas 1974). These proven techniques have relevance today for retrieving an array of facts. Lists of Bible characters, telephone numbers, persons' names, and personal identification numbers (PIN) for automated bank tellers are but a few ways we utilize the Cue Avenue. Table 4.2 offers one way to remember the seven miracles recorded in the Book of John. Memory devices can help us retrieve information until it becomes part of our working memory through continual usage. We can use them like training wheels on a bicycle, and discard them when no longer necessary. As another example, the acrostic "LEARN," can be used to help us remember the five major aspects of the concept of learning. In addition, each of the learning families and their respective Avenues begin with the same letter of the alphabet, for ease of memorization.

### Table 4.2
# Remembering the Seven Miracles in the Gospel of John

1. Changing water to wine (John 2)
   *Memory peg and imagery* "One—Bun": think of a large wedding cake made from a large bun (the miracle took place at a wedding); on top of this cake, instead of having miniature bride and groom figures, substitute two wine glasses (the number two indicates the chapter in John)
2. Healing the royal official's son (John 4)
   *Memory peg and imagery* "Two—Shoe": think of the royal official wearing shoes made of gold, golden shoes; he walked to Jesus wearing those shoes and he walked home wearing those golden shoes; at home he found his son healed; his son also wore golden shoes—making four golden shoes (the number four indicates the chapter in John)
3. Healing the man by the pool (John 5)
   *Memory peg and imagery* "Three—Tree": think of a large *palm* tree located near an oasis—in this case, a *pool* of water; this pool had five *porches* (John 5:2) (the number five indicates the chapter in John)
4. Feeding the 5000 (John 6)
   *Memory peg and imagery* "Four—Door": think of a very large door that is being carried horizontally by the disciples at waist-height; many loaves of bread have been loaded on the door—so many that loaves are falling off; the door is so large and the burden so heavy that it takes six disciples to hold the door—one at each of the four corners and two at the middle of the door (the number six indicates the chapter in John)
5. Jesus walking on the water (John 6)
   *Memory peg and imagery* "Five—Hive": think of a large bee hive; out of that hive flows water, not honey; so much water is gushing out that it covers the ground; though not mentioned in John's Gospel, the parallel accounts in the Synoptic Gospels record that Peter also walked on the water; if Jesus had not rescued him, he could have drowned—one idiom for death is "being buried six feet under" or being "deep sixed" (the number six indicates the chapter in John)

6. Healing the blind man (John 9)
   *Memory peg and imagery* "Six—Sticks": think of a blind man with a white cane or stick, tapping along a sidewalk; he was blind and now he can see, in other words, his world was turned upside down—turn the "6" upside down and you get a "9" (the number nine indicates the chapter in John)
7. Raising Lazarus from the dead (John 11)
   *Memory peg and imagery* "Seven—Heaven": Lazarus should have gone to heaven, but he didn't, he came back to earth; after being in the tomb for four days Lazarus is thirsty, so he buys a large soft drink at a "7–11" convenience mart (the number eleven indicates the chapter in John)

### *Attitudes in Learning*

As significant as the recollection of facts is, certain cues also remind us of important feelings, emotions, and values. Note that attitudinal responses are initially developed through the Consequence Avenue. For example, a student is bored with a particular class session. If this feeling persists in subsequent class sessions, the course itself becomes a cue for boredom whenever the student enters the classroom. Just thinking about the course can evoke feelings of apathy.

Certain feelings and values—even expectations—emerge with particular cues. For instance, the sounds of favorite hymns may stir earlier, poignant moments of worship. Smelling favorite foods, reliving pictures from a family photo album, and learning the high-pitched sound of the dentist's drill signal memorable cues for us. They elicit earlier attitudes and experiences. Skilled teachers enable students to acquire (and then to associate) positive attitudes with their teaching (cf. Mager 1984).

Contemplate one summative example of the Cue Avenue. Through each of our senses, complementary cues confirm a nearby fire. We *see* bright flames; we *smell* pungent smoke; we *touch* scorching heat; we *hear* crackling flames; and we *taste* hot ash filtering through the air. In addition, accompanying fears grip us. Parallel behaviors become automatic, like getting some water or running to safety. Each cue is learned at some point; such knowledge is not innate.[8]

Both Avenues of the Conditioning Learning family work together, although in contrasting ways. The Cue Avenue focuses on that which *precedes* the activity; we see the red light (cue), so we step on the brake to stop the car (activity). In contrast, the Consequence Avenue centers on what *follows* our activity; we step on the brake to stop for the red light (activity) in order to avoid having an accident or receiving a traffic ticket (consequence). Table 4.3 offers teaching suggestions for the entire Conditioning Learning family.

The Conditioning learning family is especially useful for developing new affective, behavioral, and dispositional learning outcomes (Levels of learning were treated in chapter 2). These particular learning outcomes relate to the formation of Christian character—a complex process involving both divine and human initiatives. And habits become the building

### Table 4.3
# Teaching Methods for Consequence and Cue Avenues

| Consequence Avenue: | Cue Avenue: |
|---|---|
| "Evaluating students' performance" | "Establishing helpful reminders and expectations for students" |
| 1. Verbal (spoken/written) (e.g., "good", "you can do better") | 1. Use of the arts: music (singing, recorded); visual (posters) |
| 2. Nonverbal (e.g., smile, nod) | 2. Classroom routines, "habits" |
| 3. Rewarding achievements | 3. Drill and practice in class |
|    a. concrete reward: (e.g., candy, free time) | 4. Memory devices |
|    b. symbolic rewards: (e.g., points, grades) | |

blocks of our character. The thoughts, feelings, and actions we participate in today form the kind of persons we will be tomorrow. As Ralph Winter has said, "Nothing that does not occur on a daily basis will ever dominate your life." Diligent and thoughtful use of both the Cue Avenue (see Table 4.4) and the Consequence Avenue (see Table 4.5) can help us change undesirable habits we have acquired and develop new ones. As stated in chapter 2, these strategies are temporary; they are needed only until the new habit becomes automatic or "second nature" (See Figure 2.1 in chapter 2).

### Table 4.4
# Changing Habits: Using Cue Avenue Factors

Modifying Old Cues to Avoid or Lessen Undesirable Habits

1. *Avoid Preceding Cues:* Identify and avoid the Cues that immediately precede the undesired habit, particularly noting the time and place for the recurring habit (e.g., for overeating: one man didn't accept dinner invitations until he had lost twenty pounds) (cf. 2 Tim. 2:22a).
2. *Refocus (and Distract) Thought Patterns:* Do this particularly for those Cues that cannot be avoided or narrowed (e.g., rather than thinking about the temporary pleasure of eating dessert or smoking a cigarette, think about the long-term benefits of having a healthy body—the temple of the Holy Spirit—by not doing the habit). Focus on the "cool" or abstract qualities rather than the "hot" or pleasurable features (e.g., think about the components of the dessert—artificial additives or coloring—rather than focusing on the taste, or think about a completely different subject to take your mind off the cake; view your date as a brother or sister rather than as a sex object (cf. 1 Tim. 5:1–2).
3. *Take a Break* in the midst of the thought or action for well-established, "automatic" undesirable habits. During the pause ask questions about the habit or keep a record about the habit and gradually increase the length of the pauses (e.g., have a two-minute pause in the middle of each meal; count to ten be-

fore reacting when feeling angry; as you feel a temptation come on, pause and rate the strength of the temptation on a 3 by 5 card you carry).

4. *Rearrange the Chain of Events* that typically lead to the undesired habit in order to interrupt the "automatic" nature of the problem. First, identify the chain of events by carefully observing yourself (thoughts and actions) and tracing the chain of cues back to its logical beginning. Then analyze what change or interruption can be made (e.g., don't keep chocolate or cigarettes around the house; rather than watching TV after dinner, walk around the block or play a game with the family; or place the TV in a closet—when you want to watch it you have to get it out and set it up, providing sufficient time to think whether or not it's something you really should be doing). Substitute alternate or incompatible thoughts and actions for the undesirable habit (e.g., pray for and do good to your enemies [Matt. 5:44]; chew some gum instead of smoking a cigarette; read a book or magazine instead of watching TV; instead of talking too much, learn to actively listen).

5. *Develop a Graduated Plan and Narrow the Range of Cues* that prompt the habit or narrow the undesired habit to occur in a certain situation in order to gain some self-control over the habit (e.g., start controlling a sulking temper tantrum habit by only doing it when in the basement away from others, then only when seated on a particular "sulking stool"; some businesses and hospitals only allow employees to smoke on their break outside the facility). Continue to narrow the range of cues until the undesirable habit is completely within your control (sometimes this approach is called "paradoxical therapy" since the person is encouraged to continue the habit, but within limited parameters).

Arranging New Cues to Develop New Habits

6. *Think Truthfully, Mediate on Scripture, Talk with God, and Initiate Healthy Self-instructions* (by the power of the Spirit, put off old ways of thinking and put on new ones, cf. Eph. 4:17–24, and don't believe the lies and deception of Satan, cf. 2 Cor. 11:3, Eph. 4:14, Rev. 12:9; spend time alone and be honest with God, cf. Luke 5:16, Phil. 4:4–7; e.g., recite Scripture verses, remind yourself of scriptural principles, or state the positive steps of action in your mind or out loud as you begin a new action). Substitute good thought habits for negative thinking patterns (cf. Phil. 4:8; see Backus and Chapin 1980). Just as gymnasts rehearse their routines in their minds before a meet, rehearse the new actions over and over in your mind, especially when facing difficult situations.

7. *Face Temptations with a Plan* (e.g., to deal with sexual temptations when away from family on speaking trips, one pastor reminded himself of his goals by reading a list of consequences that would befall him if he yielded to temptation; invite friends and family to remind us of our goals [e.g., another pastor has a close friend ask him probing questions after he returns from a trip]).

8. *Set Up New Cues* to encourage habit formation (similar to #5 above, this provides opportunities for early success; use a special location (e.g., only use a certain desk or table for a devotional time or for studying); use the buddy system (e.g., regularly meet with someone for the express purpose of a devotional time or for studying, cf. 2 Tim. 2:22b).

9. *Stretch Your Comfort Zone* and perform the habit in similar situations (e.g., speak in front of three friends at first, then speak in front of a larger group that includes your three friends—your friends help bridge your speaking to a larger group).

---

*Source:* Adapted from Watson and Tharp (1989, chap. 5).

## Table 4.5

# Changing Habits: Using Consequence Avenue Factors

In developing a habit, every new thought or action usually requires some positive Consequence. If the thought or action itself does not have this effect, then additional positive Consequences may be necessary. A Consequence is anything that will *increase* repeated occurrences of the thought or behavior that it follows. It can be related to *people* (e.g., praise, approval, a date, doing something together with friends) *objects* (e.g., new dress, a dessert, new compact-disc player), or *activities* (e.g., playing a game, going out to dinner, any special occasion, loafing with friends).

1. *Provide Positive Consequences Immediately,* when possible. When developing a new habit, the sooner the positive Consequence occurs following the habit, the more effective is its role in encouraging the habit to be repeated. Especially in the case of changing strong habits, it is important to provide yourself the positive Consequence as immediately as possible.

2. *Use Tokens* when you cannot arrange to have the positive Consequence follow immediately after the habit. Tokens provide a means to bridge the delay between the new habit and when the positive Consequence can be given (e.g., use a point system or gold stars to keep track of improvement and redeem these at the end of a week).

3. *Develop a Graduated Plan for Developing a New Habit* and reward each new level of improvement with a positive Consequence. Most undesirable habits were developed over years, so it may take some time to change the habit (e.g., for the first two weeks of a diet, limit intake to 2000 calories per day and reward appropriately; for the next two weeks, limit to 1800 calories per day). If you find yourself "cheating" more than 10 percent of the time (i.e., enjoying the positive Consequence without meeting the goal) then rework the graduated plan to make it more realistic. This is especially important in the early stages of developing a new habit. Any small step of improvement is better than no step at all.

4. *Monitor Thought Patterns* following an occurrence of the new habit (e.g., did you criticize yourself for not doing more, or commend yourself for making progress toward your goals?).

5. *Use the Premack Principle:* Follow a new habit with an activity you enjoy doing (e.g., eat the dessert after eating vegetables; watch TV after completing your homework or jogging around the block).

6. *Identify the Particular Positive Consequences* that support undesirable habits and use such positive consequences to work for you (e.g., only talk with friends in the library *after* you have completed a certain amount of homework).

7. *Use Close Friends and Family to Help Award Positive Consequences:* (e.g., allow spouse to help with weight loss program—to model good eating, to assist in record-keeping and to encourage and reward habit change; a friend might be given $40, to be returned in $10 weekly increments if you keep to your study schedule for a week; otherwise the friend would donate the money to a political candidate that you do not agree with; support groups serve as positive consequences). The effectiveness of such help depends on how consistent the person is carrying out the agreement.

8. *Use the Cooperation of Others and Share Your Positive Consequences with Them:* Cooperation is necessary for this approach, since both would miss out on the activity if the goal is not met (e.g., one woman selected going to a movie with a boyfriend as a positive consequence: if she met her goals, they would see a movie; if she didn't meet her goals, they would not).

9. *"Self-Punishment" Alone Is Usually Not Enough* because it does not teach new habits; it only focuses on old habits. Positive Consequences for the new habit are also necessary. Also, some may not be consistent in punishing themselves, which weakens the whole plan. If self-punishment is one component in your strategy to develop a new habit, it usually is better to give up a positive consequence than to use a painful consequence as a punisher (e.g., if a goal has not been reached during the week, then you can't rent a video to watch during the weekend, rather than making yourself do twenty push-ups).

*Source:* Adapted from Watson and Tharp (1989, chap. 7).

## Try It Out

1. Think of some foods that you like and dislike. Explain what attracts or repels you about these foods. Consider the five senses (sight, taste, smell, touch, sound) as a guide to your analysis. Can you remember how you initially came to like or dislike each selected food? Some people dislike the "fishy" taste of seafood because of regular doses of cod liver oil administered during childhood. Some can't stand drinking orange juice because their juice was laced with cod liver oil. What is the source of any of your likes or dislikes?

2. We tend to like and dislike certain subjects of study (e.g., theology, physical education, math, physics). What subjects do you like and dislike? Identify possible reasons for your feelings about these subjects.

3. As Christians, we are attracted to or avoid certain Christian activities and spiritual disciplines (e.g., class socials, personal Bible study, witnessing, singing, prayer, fasting). Select a few Christian activities that you tend to practice and others that you tend *not* to practice.

a. Using the Cue Avenue theory, identify factors that *preceded* any participation in these activities that may have influenced your continuing involvement in the Christian activity or your avoidance of it.

b. Using the Consequence Avenue theory, identify factors that *followed* any participation in these activities that may have influenced your continuing involvement in the Christian activity or your avoidance of it.

## Application: Guiding Children's Learning

Children enter life helpless. Other people make choices for them. They cannot look after themselves; they must receive constant care. Though they are helpless, children possess an innate, God-given capacity to learn. During these early years, we teachers guide their growth by various means. For instance, as adult caregivers, we are role models for our children (Social Learning family; see chapter 5). Furthermore, we stimulate their cognitive abilities (Information-Processing family; see chapter 3). But our primary responsibility is shaping Christ-like attitudes and habits.

Such nurturing strategies express the essence of the Conditioning Learning family.

In Chapter 3, we suggested that there is greater potential to encourage learning in children when using the paired Avenues of the Conditioning Learning family (see Figure 3.2 in Chapter 3). Some people may react negatively to this match of children and Conditioning theory, in part, because of their limited understanding of this learning family. To be fair to its fullest meaning, Conditioning Learning is much more than a system of rewards and punishments. It shouldn't be associated with the narrow view of behavior*ism*.[9] Conditioning Learning affects our thinking, attitudes, values, and skills. Such learning often occurs through what is known as "socialization."

Patterns of childrearing outlined in the Old Testament consistently point to this informal mode of education. In the Jewish home of that day, all the experiences of the young child's life—both the common and the special, the unplanned and the routine—became potential learning opportunities (Deut. 6:5–9). Children experienced multiple activities of family and cultural life (e.g., Sabbaths, Passover, and other annual feasts). Initially, they were simply expected to participate in these customary practices. Again, the basic features of Conditioning Learning and Social Learning are quite evident. Later, interpretation and meaning were imparted (Exod. 12:24–27), primarily through Information-Processing Learning.

Since life patterns for children largely developed without significant mediation of language and thought, even the attitudes of small children were purposefully shaped. These formative years provided a critical opportunity to lay the foundation for godly dispositions and virtues. "Aristotle is the classic point of reference in this regard. The moral training of children, he pointed out, requires the inculcation of habits, and habit formation in early years is the responsibility of parents and teachers" (Holmes 1991, p. 62). Although not writing from a distinctively Christian perspective, Levin (1990) affirms much of this educational strategy:

> Moral behavior is the product of training, not reflection. As Aristotle stressed thousands of years ago you get a good adult by habituating a good child to doing the right thing. Praise for truth-telling and sanctions for fibbing will, in time, make him 'naturally' honest.
>
> Abstract knowledge of right and wrong no more contributes to character than knowledge of physics contributes to bicycling. Bicyclists don't have to think about which way to lean, and honest people don't have to think how to answer under oath (pp. 113–114).

We help cultivate our children's acquisition of Christian values through the Consequence Avenue (e.g., an adult saying "good girl" for a child's appropriate action) and through the Cue Avenue (e.g., bedtime habits of prayer and singing). Self-image in children results exclusively from environmental feedback. How others respond to children fashions the opinions they initially hold about themselves. As teachers and parents, we should soberly assess this image-shaping influence on children. We must monitor both explicit and implicit communication with youngsters so that God-honoring self-perceptions emerge.[10]

How, then, can adult caregivers implement basic principles from the Conditioning Learning family? Effective work with children involves balancing four "R's": *relationship, responsibility, recognition,* and *remediation.* The last three "R's" illustrate the use of both the Consequence and Cue Avenues.

### Relationship

Children need to be unconditionally accepted—to feel loved. This is fundamentally communicated in classroom demeanor by kind, affirming words and personal interest in their lives. Yet a deeper level of relationship requires nurturing out-of-class involvement as well. Doug Lay, a sixth-grade Sunday school teacher in Portland, became convinced of this out-of-class potential. He discovered the positive difference in the classroom behavior of Jim, a rambunctious child of a church family. Doug invited Jim and another Sunday school classmate to play golf with him one Saturday. The special time together opened up new opportunities for trust and communication. As teachers and parents, we embody God to our students. Our loving demeanor and interest in their lives help pave the way for their response to a loving God who cares for them.

### Responsibility

What expectations do we have of our children? We usually underestimate their capabilities. Rocco Morabito, age five, of Port Chester, New York, is one young boy who demonstrated his well-developed coordination skills. He was able to drive the family station wagon through rush hour traffic—obeying all the traffic rules—two and a half miles from home! The only reason he was pulled over was because the police officer thought "it looked like the Invisible Man was driving that car. . . . I observed that the car was being driven pretty well, but all I could see was a small girl [Rocco's 2 year-old sister] standing in the back seat." The police officer used the lights and siren to try to stop the car "and the car pulls over to the curb, in perfect accordance with the laws of New York state."[11] Rocco, who stood about three feet tall, had moved the automatic seat as far forward as possible and could just touch the accelerator. Children can learn much more than we expect them!

A century earlier, in the *Little House on the Prairie* series, Laura Ingalls Wilder writes about Almonzo Wilder (her future husband) who trained his own oxen team at age ten and then, during the winter, used his team to haul timber. With the passing of our agrarian lifestyle, many of the family responsibilities that children performed have disappeared. Yet opportunities still exist for children to make similar, notable contributions. One first-grade teacher assigned classroom responsibilities to each child, on a weekly rotating basis. These assignments were not just busywork, but involved important aspects of school life, like delivering and picking up lunch boxes, changing the date on the board, opening and closing doors when the class left for recess and lunch, and taking messages to the principal. The children lived up to the expectations of their teacher.

How can we apply this principle to local church education? How can we challenge children, yet respect their various levels of responsibility? One example, for Sunday school, would encourage children's involvement in a self-chosen Bible learning activity when they arrive in the classroom. These diverse activities might relate to art, drama, music, oral communication, creative writing, service projects, Bible games, or research. Adults could team-teach this segment by having each one coordinate one or two of these activity centers in the classroom. Some children prefer to write new words to an old tune. Others want to play the role of a news reporter, interviewing a Bible character. Still others enjoy making billboard posters or bumper stickers. Children need "hands-on" experiences while studying God's Word. Much of class time can be devoted to these diverse activities, because for children, guided play *is* learning.[12]

But participating in learning activities is only part of instruction. During the latter part of the session, children must be given an opportunity to present their findings and projects in a time of group sharing, application to life, and singing. Early in their development we need to let children be responsible participants with us in our mutual growth in Christ. As was stated so poignantly in *Stand and Deliver,* the movie about high school math teacher Jaime Escalante, "Students will rise to the level of expectation."

### Recognition

We fail our children when we do not honor the times they act appropriately ("Thank you for paying attention, Marla. That means a lot to me," or "I appreciate the way you are working hard at your project, Desi"). Instead, we tend to emphasize their negative behaviors ("Sit down, Jason!"). Viewing one of our long-term teaching goals, we want children to become self-disciplined, mature adults. Therefore, attention to positive character traits is a necessity. In keeping with the Consequence Avenue's heightened emphasis for children, it is prudent to select various modes of recognition—some more tangible honors (e.g., earning points for meaningful prizes) and more intangible rewards (e.g., compliments, hugs). This feedback encourages children's interest and effort to learn.

We should not be too critical of their egocentric desires. By nature, children come into this world with a very narrow perspective on life: *they* are all that exists. As they grow, their mental faculties develop so they can broaden their view if they so chose. One aspect of maturity is recognizing that we are not the center of the universe. Having an exclusive focus on self is a natural characteristic of young children. In time, with appropriate maturation and learning, they can become more decentered. Second, we should be more sensitive to the kinds of motivation toward which they will give effort to the learning task—whether that motivation is based on tangible or intangible rewards. A "reward" is truly a reward if it encourages children to persist in the task. We need to learn what interests them and, without being manipulative, we should utilize this interest to motivate them for learning.

Just a quick note must be added to suggest the difference between "rewards" and "bribery." A *bribe* manipulates a child to act in a way that is primarily for *our* benefit (e.g., to keep the child quiet so the teacher can teach the lesson). A *reward* encourages a child to primarily respond for the child's own benefit—that is, it facilitates actions that help the child mature. Teachers using rewards must insure that *both* the reward itself (e.g., points toward a pizza party) and the *means* to that goal (e.g., memorizing a Bible verse as a part of a contest) are ethical. Without some sort of consistent and explicit indicators of progress (i.e., rewards), young children will be ignorant of the Christian virtues they are being asked to acquire.

### Remediation

Dealing with inappropriate behavior represents a "catch-22" dilemma of discipline: nobody likes to do it; but if nothing happens, behavior usually gets worse. Surprisingly, a good number of children's classroom "behavior problems" stem from teacher error: lack of good lesson planning, poor pacing of the lesson ("dead time" between activities), or use of irrelevant activities.

Furthermore, our discipline strategy at this juncture assumes an "all or nothing" posture. Just as a car needs all four tires to operate successfully, so must our four "R" guidelines work in harmony. If we have not given attention to close *relationships,* failed to identify meaningful *responsibilities,* or infrequently *recognized* growth, then we have not earned the right to correct our students' behavior. Effective classroom management strategies utilize recognition (reward) *and* remediation (punishment) efforts in two directions: at *individual* levels (e.g., extra points; a "time out" corner) and *group* levels (e.g., earning or losing class privileges such as playing a favorite group game).[13] In the end, these summative concepts depict the essence of the Conditioning Learning family.

## Key Concepts and Issues

attitudes in learning

changing habits

Conditioning Learning Family

Consequence Avenue

Cue Avenue

children and the Conditioning Learning Family:

　　relationship, responsibility, recognition, and remediation

memory devices

**L** evels
**E** xtent
**A** venues
**R** eadiness
**N** ature

5

# Learning by Example

**Structured Modeling**
**Spontaneous Modeling**
**Application: Guiding Teens to the Right Models**
**Six Avenues Converge for Productive Learning**

Chris Bencze, a ten-year-old from Auburn, Washington, saved his eight-year-old brother's life. Chris and Alex were home alone one Friday evening when Alex began to choke on an orange. Chris got behind his brother and squeezed his chest—using the Heimlich maneuver—until the fruit came out. Where did Chris learn the technique? From watching a recent episode of the cartoon show, "The Simpsons." The publicist for Fox Television, producer of the show, had heard of one other instance in which a choking victim had been helped, based on learning the maneuver from that episode.[1]

We can learn a lot by watching others, whether live or on television. The phrase "like father, like son" points out the impact of observational or vicarious learning in the home. Yet this principle of social influence applies to virtually all other environments, too. Social Learning theory—an integration of the Information-Processing Learning family (see chapter 3) and the Conditioning Learning family (see chapter 4)—combines reflection with imitation. We observe what others say and do and evaluate the particular consequences that result. We analyze what we see and make value judgments to either follow or to avoid these observed practices. If the former course of action is selected, we adapt the observed practice to our own setting, as indicated in the opening story.

Each sphere of life has its heroes. In the business world, they are called "mentors." Sports enthusiasts have their superstars. Media buffs treasure television and movie idols. And we all admire those who show courage in the face of death. Annually, the Carnegie Hero Fund Commission identifies a number of individuals who try to save the lives of others while risking their own. At last year's ceremony, fifteen people were honored for their bravery—four of them had died in their rescue attempts.[2]

The concept of role model, or "being an example to others," receives significant attention in the New Testament. In the epistles, three Greek word groups are used in most occurrences of the concept:

> a. *mimementes* ("imitator"; used eleven times; e.g., 1 Cor. 4:16).
>
> b. *tupos* ("example"; used nine times with this meaning, the word group is used a total of seventeen times; e.g., 1 Tim. 4:12).
>
> c. *hupodeigma* ("example"; used six times with this meaning, the word group is used a total of fifteen times; e.g., James 5:10).

On two occasions Paul combines the use of the first two word groups in exhorting his readers:

> Join with others in following my example [*summimementes*], brothers, and take note of those who live according to the pattern [*tupos*] we gave you (Phil. 3:17).
>
> For you yourselves know how you ought to follow our example [*mimeomai*]. . . . We did this [earning our own financial support], not because we do not have the right to such help, but in order to make ourselves a model [*tupos*] for you to follow [*mimeomai*] (2 Thess. 3:7, 9).

Paul acknowledges that Israel's failures are examples to avoid (1 Cor. 10:11). John exhorts us to be cautious regarding which models we emulate (3 John 11). Believers are encouraged to imitate the faith of their leaders (Heb. 13:7) and other believers (Heb. 6:12). Luke records that a student "who is fully trained will be like his teacher" (6:40). No wonder James warned teachers about their stricter judgment (3:1)!

The continuing effect of the example of a Christian community can be seen when the Judean churches and Paul's missionary team proved to be models for the Thessalonian church (1 Thess. 1:6, 2:14; 2 Thess. 3:7–9). The Thessalonian church, in turn, became a model for the believers in Macedonia and Achaia (1 Thess. 1:7–8).

Bandura (1977, 1986) identifies three primary modes of modeling, or what has been called Social Learning theory. *Direct modeling* involves first-hand experience. Watching a parent hug a child, having someone greet you with a warm smile, or viewing two antagonists engaged in heated argument depict direct modeling. Who hasn't looked to the host or hostess at a formal dinner to determine proper dining etiquette? In addition, even the results of an action are pertinent to modeling. Noticing what kind of clothes a person wears, the type of car a person drives, how the seating in a classroom has been arranged, or even the attractive appearance of a term paper portrays direct modeling.

*Verbal modeling* involves either written or spoken "how-to" explanations. Have you been compelled by a moving biography of a great Christian leader,[3] or the public testimony of a new Christian? Then you've experienced verbal modeling. As expected, direct and verbal modeling can be combined to increase learning potential. When a teacher sits at the terminal and demonstrates how to use a computer (direct) while also explaining how to use the computer (verbal), we see a combined application.

In training the Twelve, Jesus emphasized direct modeling (at least as recorded in the Gospels). In his first call to Simon and Andrew he said, "Come, follow me . . . and I will make you fishers of men" (Mark 1:17). Regarding the appointment of all of the apostles, the Gospel writer notes, "He appointed twelve . . . that they might be with Him" (Mark 3:14). In the Upper Room, Jesus challenged the disciples: "My command is this: Love each other as I have loved you" (John 15:12). In giving the written Word to the church, God has provided a form of verbal modeling, although this Word is to be studied within the context of a practicing community of faith (direct modeling).

The visual mass media, like television, movies, video tapes, magazines, and newspapers, represents the third mode of modeling. Bandura labels it *symbolic modeling*. It can also be harnessed for beneficial educational use. For example, in the field of human resource management, training videos help managers and salespersons perform their jobs more efficiently. Correspondingly, the past decade has produced scores of useful Christian education instructional programs—from simple children and family videos to elaborate mediated teacher-training programs. In the discussion that follows, the two avenues of the Social Learning family— "Structured Modeling" and "Spontaneous Modeling"—are delineated.

## Structured Modeling

The explicit purpose of Structured Modeling is to provide a regular standard for emulation. Structured Modeling involves "planning your work, then working your plan." For the teacher, this means carefully prepared classroom activities, such as lecturing, staging a dramatic scene, showing a full-length movie, or reading poetry. Each of these forms suggests preparation, editing, and even rehearsal before the final "performance."[4]

Films, television programs, and magazines also represent a variety of Structured Modeling possibilities. In its fullest expression, symbolic modeling is a twentieth-century phenomenon within the modeling repertoire. Bandura notes the power of the mass media for the dissemination of ideas and values over large geographic areas:

Whereas previously modeling influences were largely confined to the behavior exhibited in one's immediate community, nowadays diverse styles
of conduct are brought to people within the comfort of their homes through
the vehicle of television. Both children and adults acquire attitudes,
thought patterns, emotional bents, and new styles of conduct through symbolic modeling. In view of the efficacy of, and extensive public exposure to,
televised modeling, the mass media play an influential role in shaping human thought and action (1986, p. 70).[5]

---

### Try It Out

---

Television and movies are basic features of our lives. Recall a particular
television program or movie that has significantly affected you in either
a positive or negative way. What specific influence did it have on your
life? How do you think the show or movie prompted this influence? What
specific factors were involved?

---

In the two previous chapters, the biblical miracle of the feeding of the
five thousand highlighted both the Information Processing family and
the Conditioning Learning family. Jesus challenged his followers to reflect
about the crowd's need and the experience of feeding them. This miracle
also demonstrates yet another approach to teaching and learning.

During his earthly pilgrimage, Jesus was personally involved in ministry. His compassionate healing became a normal feature of his disciples'
daily observation. Just prior to the feeding of the five thousand, the disciples once again saw our Lord's compassion. Although Jesus was tired, he
healed the sick (Matt. 14:14). He taught the people about the kingdom of
God (Luke 9:11), a familiar theme of his messages. Following the miraculous feeding, the Master Teacher's structured modeling continued. Jesus
sought solitude for a time of prayer (Matt. 14:23), a prominent and
planned discipline during his earthly pilgrimage (Luke 5:16). In these
ways, Jesus' intentional example focused the disciples' attention on how
to live in the kingdom of God.

## Spontaneous Modeling

The miraculous feeding of the five thousand was prompted by a mo-
mentary need. In light of all the miracles Jesus had performed previously
(e.g., healing the sick, the blind, the lame, and lepers; raising the dead),
never had the Twelve asked Jesus to feed the masses. So special was this
miracle for the disciples, that it confirmed for them that Jesus was the
Messiah. So overwhelming was the miracle for the crowds that they
wanted to make him king (John 6:15). Yet Jesus dismissed them and sent
the disciples away (Matt. 14:22). It was not time for him to establish his
kingdom. This example of Spontaneous Modeling must have perplexed

the disciples.[6] "Did not the Messiah come to reestablish his reign on earth?" "Did he miss a golden opportunity to get the crowds behind him?" Some of them must have asked themselves these questions.

Spontaneous Modeling is not planned—it just happens. It is characterized by how we live our lives before others, how we respond to various circumstances of life. What do we say and how do we react to a flat tire, spilled coffee, or a "C" on a final exam? Deuteronomy 6:6-9 catches the spirit of this pervasive learning Avenue. "These commandments that I give you today are to be upon your hearts. Impress them on your children. Talk about them when you sit at home and when you walk along the road, when you lie down and when you get up. Tie them as symbols on your hands and bind them on your foreheads. Write them on the door frames of your houses and on your gates."

Certainly an intentional feature of Christian education exists in this command, akin to Structured Modeling. But because of the dynamic nature of life much of our instruction is necessarily unplanned. For teachers, preparing to use Spontaneous Modeling well is not easy—it literally takes a lifetime. The bottom line is that Spontaneous Modeling reveals our true character—what we really are like in last-minute conversations prior to class, in unscheduled counseling sessions, in moments of unexpected confrontation, and in how we talk about and treat others of the opposite sex.

The contribution of Spontaneous Modeling to learning is that we can observe positive expressions of faith in the lives of others. We represent living "commentaries" of the truth. We answer the question: "What does God's truth look like in day-to-day living?" In essence, this principle is the foundation for discipleship—as expressed by Paul to his spiritual son, Timothy: "And the things you have heard me say in the presence of many witnesses entrust to reliable men who will also be qualified to teach others" (2 Tim. 2:2). We demonstrate the validity of what it means to be "Christian" through our intimate relationships with God and others. "By this all men will know that you are my disciples, if you love one another" (John 13:35). Spontaneous Modeling demands that we attend to the development of consistent Christian character, since modeling necessarily requires that our private lives become public domain to those around us.

It's contradictory to say we can teach students and instructors to plan for "Spontaneous Modeling." But consider impromptu moments of questions and answers. As teachers, what is exhibited about our character at such times? Do we become defensive when students ask questions? Do we use our status as teachers to intimidate? When appropriate, do we honestly admit that we don't have an answer to a particular question? Is our nonverbal communication consistent with our verbal feedback, and are these both harmonious with the John 13:35 litmus test? Question and an-

swer times are not interruptions in the lesson. They provide a distinct opportunity, in class, for the public to view us transparently. In many ways
such sessions are more real-to-life than fully planned presentations. They
offer opportunities for revealing the more sophisticated expressions of
Christian community.[7]

The decision for us Christians is not *whether* to learn from the example
of others, but *which* behavior we decide is most appropriate to emulate.
Furthermore, it is not a question of *whether* we'll be models, but rather,
what *kind* of models we will be. How can we utilize the two learning Avenues of the Social Learning family in our teaching? Table 5.1 suggests a
few teaching methods for Structured and Spontaneous Modeling.

### Table 5.1
### Teaching Methods for Structured
### and Spontaneous Modeling

| Structured Modeling: | Spontaneous Modeling: |
|---|---|
| "Demonstrating a planned example for students" | "Living your life before students" |
| 1. Live demonstrations | 1. Open question and answer sessions; class discussions |
| 2. Reading excerpts of biographies | 2. Classroom "town hall" meetings |
| 3. Viewing training video tapes | 3. Field trips |

## Application: Guiding Teens to the Right Models

In chapter 3, we suggested that youth are highly influenced through
the Avenues of the Social Learning family: Structured and Spontaneous
Modeling (see Figure 3.2). In this section, we focus on two important
uses of these Avenues in the ministry to teens: role models[8] and the
mass media.

### Role Models for Teens

One beneficial summary of effective modeling principles was compiled
by Richards (1975, pp. 84–85). Richards' study affirms theological direc-
tives while being informed by social science theory. This subject primarily
attends to Spontaneous Modeling influences. A modification of his seven
points sets us on track to provide youth with the kind of learning experiences they require (see Table 5.2). Kagan (1972) reminds us of the importance of peers to youth: "The earliest adolescent wants many friends, for
he needs peers to help him sculpt his new attitudes against an alien set
to evaluate their hardiness, and obtain support for his new set of fragile
assumptions" (p. 103).

## Table 5.2
# Principles of Effective Modeling

1. Youth need to have frequent, long-term contact with models.
2. Youth must experience a warm, loving relationship with models.
3. Youth should be exposed to the inner values and emotions of models.
4. Models for youth need to be observed in a variety of life settings and situations.
5. Models need to exhibit consistency and clarity in behavior and values.
6. There must be compatibility between the behavior of the models and the beliefs and standards of the models' larger community.
7. There should be explanations of the models' lifestyle, along with accompanying life demonstrations.

*Source:* Adapted from Richards (1975, pp. 84–85).

Keyes (1976, p. 183) refers to the "especially impressionable stage" of adolescence. He reverses the traditional view that teens are strongly influenced by adult values. Keyes instead claims that "adult values grow directly out of high school" (p. 182). Yaconelli and Burns (1986) report on the impact of peer pressure and social groupings. Curriculum materials consistently attest to the significance of social ties for teens.[9]

In the end, it comes down to modeling. It's not a question of *whether* youth will emulate others; it's a question of *whom*. Who will be their heroes and heroines? The church has the responsibility to provide alternatives to worldly leaders through two sources: godly peers and godly adults. Technically, the first category of group influence is called "peer ministry." Yaconelli and Burns (1986, p. 107) offer their rationale for such an emphasis:

> Today's youth worker has no excuse for not using his best programming resource—the kids in the youth group. Kids can participate in almost any aspect of the program, often more effectively than an adult. *They aren't always* more effective. The kids may do worse or they may botch a program, but then, failure is one of the best ways to learn. And youth groups always seem to be able to accept the failure of their peers. High-school students are much less critical of other high-school students than they are of adults. Peer ministry is credible exactly because it is not profession.

The following constructive suggestions for healthy peer ministry are proposed by Yaconelli and Burns (1986, p. 107).[10]

1. Adolescents should not just *go* to youth group; they should be allowed to *do* the youth group. They should have the opportunity to use their gifts in the youth ministry program, not just occupy a seat and watch.

2. Provide lots of small group activities in which adolescents (without adults or with silent adults) discuss the lesson and come up with their own conclusions. Small group activities are the primary source of peer

ministry opportunities. Too many youth groups either don't have small groups, or, when they do, use them to accomplish some activity rather than to share with each other.

3. Keeping a journal and letter writing provide great opportunities for peer ministry.

4. Service projects are another great environment for peer ministry.

When it comes to the complementary need for *godly adults,* a team is also required. Christie (1987) cautions against the Lone Ranger mentality. This counterproductive attitude prevails not only in megachurch youth ministries but in small teen groups as well. Christie advises youth pastors to recognize the value of an adult team and to foster a variety of adult models. He details a helpful rationale.

> Maybe you're wondering, *Why do I need other adults working beside me? I can handle these few kids on my own.* Even if I had only a handful of kids in my group, I would still recruit other adults to work with me—not because of *my* needs, but because of the kids' needs. Kids need a variety of adult models.
>
> Any adult who will interact with kids regularly becomes a model to them. In recruiting a team of adults, look for a variety of role models: married couples, singles, young adults, older folks. Youth will respond differently to different people. Kids need to see the quiet adults, the thinkers, the huggers, the zanies, the serious, the jocks, and the nerds. They need to see the deeply religious and experienced as well as the recently committed Christian (1987, pp. 17–18).

In addition, Christie suggests two overarching purposes for an adult group of youth workers. One is to model, among themselves, many of the relationships (such as marriage, friendship, older Christian with younger Christian, and so on) in which youth will eventually find themselves. The second goal is to have at least one advisor on staff with whom each adolescent can identify. Grandmothers and grandfathers make great youth workers, but an entire team of senior saints is not advisable. The same is true of college students, who tend to be energetic and lively, but often lack stability, experience, and maturity. We need an *intergenerational adult* team for youth ministry. We need people who are fully committed to the basic principles of the Social Learning family—those who will be godly models.

Finally, Stevens (1985, pp. 127–28) provides very practical means by which adult team members can get to know their young people. Remember: intentionality and incarnational ministry lie at the heart of effective youth work. Table 5.3 expresses a modified version of Stevens' ideas.

**Table 5.3**

# Practical Ways to Strengthen
# Relationships with Teens

*Get to know your teens as you:*
   Go to a school athletic event.
   Take a teen along on one of your errands (driving time in a car facilitates conversation).
   Play miniature golf.
   Go to a worthwhile movie.
   Go to the beach or lake.
   Go out for ice cream.
   Work on or fix something.
   Loan a teen a good Christian book or CD and discuss it later.
   Make a casual telephone call.
   Attend a school play or musical.
   Drive a teen home after school.
   Watch a television show together.
   Arrange to meet a teen during the lunch hour.
   Drive a teen home after a youth-group event.
   Meet for breakfast before school.
   Have a girls' slumber party or a guys' overnight (based on the leader's gender).
   Help a teen with homework.
   Write a letter, note, or card.
   Following an activity, go out to eat on the way home, to talk.
   Play games like ping-pong, basketball, or chess.
   Take a walk or go hiking.
   Drop by with one of their friends.

*Begin this relationship-building process as you:*
   Develop a roster of the youth group.
   Make a note to yourself of teens to see and call.
   Call them up.
   Make an appointment at the youth group meeting.
   Volunteer to pick them up.
   Ask their good friends to bring them.
   Call to confirm just ahead of time.

*Source:* Adapted from Stevens (1985, pp. 127-28).

## Evaluating Media

A second important objective of youth ministry includes the proper assessment of music videos, soaps, commercials, and sitcoms. This approach primarily confronts Structured Modeling influences. The explosive potential of youth is exacerbated by the media in general and by television in particular. Postman (1985) offers an exceptional and concise critique of this latter point. He claims that television replaces facts with emotions and opinions; that commercials portray all problems as easily solvable; that television implies "being sold solutions is better than being confronted with questions about problems" (p. 131); and that present-centeredness is valued above historic contributions or the call to prepare for the future. In brief, television teaches adolescents that theirs is a quick-fix world. Postman states that the media, which advances such life perspectives, affects us all—but it particularly influences teens.

> One can hardly overestimate the damage that such juxtapositions do to our sense of the world as a serious place. *The damage is especially massive to youthful viewers who depend so much on television for their clues as to how to respond to the world. In watching television news, they, more than any other segment of the audience,* are drawn into an epistemology based on the assumption that all reports of cruelty and death are greatly exaggerated and, in any case, not to be taken seriously or responded to sanely.
>
> I should go so far as to say that embedded in the surrealistic frame of a television news show is a *theory of anticommunication,* featuring a type of discourse that abandons logic, reason, sequence and rules of contradiction. In aesthetics, I believe the name given to this theory is Dadaism; in philosophy, nihilism; in psychiatry, schizophrenia. In the parlance of the theater, it is known as vaudeville (p. 105).

One youth study guide that deals with contemporary music is *Hot Topics: Youth Electives* (Elgin, Ill.: David C. Cook, 1989). Among other emphases, this curriculum helps youth analyze lyrics, discuss absolute standards, and evaluate related ideas like album cover graphics and artists' lifestyles. Student interaction sheets include such items as the effect that music has on us through commercials, as well as through clothes, hairstyles, habits, and thought life. Another music-based resource is David C. Cook's *Spectrum* series. In this curriculum, youth take a look at such issues as self-image, hard questions, friendship, and the Bible. Each study contains a cassette with six contemporary Christian tunes, lyrics, discussion questions, a half-dozen Bible studies and meeting plan outlines, and thirty related activity ideas. Table 5.4 offers basic guidelines for media critiques.

## Table 5.4
## Guidelines for a Biblical Critique of Media

1. To encourage a silent member in discussion:
   "Teresa, from your perspective as a senior, how do you interpret this biblical imperative, as it pertains to the sitcom you observed?"
2. To support expression of feelings and Christian values:
   "How does this Scripture passage challenge one typical way our culture views this moral controversy?"
3. To call attention to issues that have not been raised:
   "Is something missing here? If you take an alternative perspective to what has already been stated, what do you come up with?"
4. To foster reflective skills and statements of personal experience:
   "In two minutes, I will ask for each of your responses to this topic. So, jot down one or two relevant examples you can share about this question: 'How does this video exaggerate—even lie—about what you know to be true?'"

5. To maintain the focus of the discussion topic:
   "That's interesting, Sid. Now, how do we bring these comments to bear on our subject?"
6. To utilize conflict constructively:
   "Since we can't seem to come to a conclusion on this theme, can we move on to the next point? Perhaps further information will clarify the issues at stake."
7. To suggest that additional information is needed to continue productive discussion:
   "Look carefully at the context of this passage. Notice what the author says just before and after our Scripture. Does this new information shed any light on what's been said?"
8. To cite the source of information: "Okay, that's a good caution to remember, Ted! Can someone other than Ted tell us where in the Bible this warning is found?"
9. To check the degree of acceptance for a particular viewpoint:
   "Some of the commentators agree with that perspective; some don't. By raising your hands, how many here agree?"
10. To concentrate on the subject rather than on distracting personalities or groups that might be connected:
    "Are we placing too much attention and emotion on secondary topics here? Perhaps we're overreacting or being uncritical of heroes and heroines we have."
11. To prevent a few monopolizers from dominating the conversation:
    "Excuse me, Yvonne. Before you continue, may we hear from someone who hasn't expressed an opinion?"
12. To raise the need to make a procedural decision:
    "Now, we've spent about ten minutes on this particular subject. Earlier we planned to discuss two more, related themes. Do you want to continue with our present topic or discuss the other two?"
13. To state the need to close the discussion:
    "May we have two or three more final remarks as we close tonight?"
14. To address the matter of follow-up:
    "In review, what have we all decided to do in preparation for our next Bible study session?"

*Source:* Adapted from Potter and Andersen (1976, pp. 51–52).

## Six Avenues Converge for Productive Learning

Now that we've completed our survey of the six Avenues of learning, let's take a summative look at them. We've observed that the feeding of the five thousand was an important learning opportunity for the Twelve. All six Avenues were evident in their training (see Table 5.5). The Master Teacher knew that when several complementary approaches to learning are involved, a greater potential for growth exists.

### Table 5.5

## Avenues of Learning and the Feeding of the Five Thousand

**INFORMATION-PROCESSING LEARNING FAMILY**
Identification Learning: The disciples were naturally concerned for the hungry crowd. Jesus responded to their concern and dealt with the crowd's hunger. What

Christ did "made sense." The miracle *identified* with their concerns. In a subsequent discourse, Jesus called himself the bread of life. Thus, he moved from the known to the unknown. His reference incorporated both the previous miracle and the manna given to the Israelites in the wilderness.

Inquiry Learning: When Jesus performed the miracle, he did so in an unexpected way. Our Lord asked the disciples to participate in the miracle. He asked them to solve the food problem. By discussing the crowd's limited food resources with the Twelve, what Christ did initially "did not make sense." It encouraged mental reflection and probing.

### CONDITIONING LEARNING FAMILY

Consequence Learning: The disciples also participated by collecting twelve baskets of leftover food—more than they had started with. Simple arithmetic may have prompted convicting thoughts about their lack of faith in God.

Cue Learning: This miracle ignited subsequent insight for the disciples. It provided a significant, additional memory link to confirm Jesus was the Messiah.

### SOCIAL LEARNING FAMILY

Structured Modeling: Jesus was compassionate. He routinely and faithfully taught the crowds and healed their sick. In this case, he fed them. Often, he would leave the disciples to pray to the Father.

Spontaneous Modeling: Although Jesus had certain planned (i.e., structured) approaches to ministry, he also responded to impromptu needs. Following the miracle, in response to the public acclaim of the crowd to make him king, rather than yielding to it, Jesus dismissed the crowd and sent the disciples away.

---

The pairings between age groups and learning families only indicate *heightened tendencies, not exclusive associations,* as depicted in Figure 3.2. Given this reminder, consider some practical implications of such pairings via the six Avenues (see Table 5.6). Also, we have noted that, although each Avenue is operative in almost every learning situation, some Avenues tend to be more effective in achieving specific learning Levels. The arrangement (Table 5.7) between learning the three Levels and six Avenues suggests distinctive contributions for various instructional approaches. Our learning goals help us select appropriate Avenues. These Avenues, in turn, allow us to choose related teaching methods and learning activities.

### Table 5.6
# Age-Related Learning Families and Sample Methods

| Age Group | Learning Family and Avenues | Strategies |
| --- | --- | --- |
| ADULTS **Information-Processing Family** | Identification | • Study subjects based on needs and interests (e.g., finances) |
| | Inquiry | • Organize learning according to thought-provoking ends (e.g., case studies, dilemmas) |

| YOUTH **Social Learning Family** | Structured Modeling | • Select good media (music, magazines, TV, movies/videos, books)<br>• Evaluate heroes/heroines |
|---|---|---|
| | Spontaneous Modeling | • Provide superb role models (i.e., friends, youth leaders, adult sponsors)<br>• Extend opportunities for varied experiences and examples (e.g., cross-cultural trips) |
| CHILDREN **Conditioning Learning Family** | Consequence and Cue | • Develop godly attitudes (e.g., love, joy, peace, patience)<br>• Foster godly habits/lifestyle (e.g., daily Bible reading, prayer, conflict resolution) |

**Table 5.7**

## Levels and Avenues of Learning

| Level | Prominent Avenues |
|---|---|
| Affective Level (Attitudes, Motivation, Feelings) | Cue and Consequence, Spontaneous Modeling |
| Behavioral Level (Skills) | Structured Modeling, Consequence and Cue |
| Cognitive Level (Knowledge) | Inquiry, Identification, Consequence |
| Dispositional Level (Tendencies/Values) | Cue and Consequence, Spontaneous and Structured Modeling |

**Table 5.8**

## Educational Settings and the Avenues of Learning

| Good Sermon or Sunday school Lecture | Significant Use:<br>• Identification: illustrations, familiar words, stories, humor<br>• Cue: attitudes and expectations about the pastor, church, Bible, God; note-taking outline<br>Some Use:<br>• Structured Modeling: sharing personal examples, practical "how to" instructions from presentation or Bible<br>Little or None:<br>• Consequence (how well they learned)<br>• Inquiry (figuring it out for themselves)<br>• Spontaneous Modeling |
|---|---|

| Traditional Lecture class (College or Seminary) | Significant Use:<br>• Identification: illustrations, stories, familiar vocabulary<br>• Inquiry: exams, raising questions in class, out-of-class assignments and reading<br>• Consequence: comments on assignments, course grades, answers to questions in class<br>• Cue: attitudes about teacher, subject, course, repeated concepts, summary outline of subject; taking notes<br>Some Use:<br>• Structured Modeling: practical "how to" instructions from class or reading<br>• Spontaneous Modeling: answering student questions |
|---|---|
| Adult Class Using Variety of Teaching Methods | Significant Use:<br>• Identification: illustrations, stories, familiar vocabulary, advance organizer<br>• Inquiry: in-class individual or group tasks (case study, problem-solving)<br>• Consequence: teacher evaluation of in-class small group work, answers to questions in class<br>• Cue: attitudes about teacher, subject, course, repeated concepts (advanced organizer), taking notes<br>• Structured Modeling: videotape, practical "how to" instructions from class or reading<br>• Spontaneous Modeling: role play |

In standard teaching situations, what Avenues of learning tend to be most common? Table 5.8 outlines the use of all six Avenues within three distinct educational settings: (1) a Sunday morning sermon[11] or adult Sunday school lecture, (2) a traditional lecture-oriented college or seminary class, and (3) an adult class involving a variety of learning activities. If our teaching purpose is to develop initial awareness or to convey new information quickly, then a session-long lecture may be a viable method. But if our complete goal is to nurture holistic growth, then we must use comprehensive teaching methods. Employing several Avenues promotes lifelong learning and retention.[12]

## Try It Out

1. Now that you have a better understanding of the learning Avenues, try your hand at the exercise below. Identify (circle) which one (or two) *main* Avenues of Learning provide the *major* learning potential *for students* for each teaching method listed below. Good teaching methods use many Avenues at once, but the genius of each method can usually be identified with one or two Avenues. If you are not familiar with the name of a method, move on to the next one. Assume that each method is done well for the fullest benefit to the learner. The first three have already been done. Use the abbreviations below.[13]

Information-Processing Learning Family
    **ID**       Identification Avenue
    **IQ**       Inquiry Avenue
Conditioning Learning Family
    **CN**     Consequence Avenue
    **CU**     Cue Avenue
Social Learning Family
    **ST**     Structured Modeling
    **SP**     Spontaneous Modeling

| | | | | | | |
|---|---|---|---|---|---|---|
| (ID) | IQ | CN | (CU) | ST | SP | **Advance organizer** |
| ID | (IQ) | CN | CU | ST | SP | **Agree-disagree statements** |
| ID | (IQ) | CN | (CU) | ST | SP | Student **answers** a teacher's question |
| ID | IQ | CN | CU | ST | SP | **Case study** |
| ID | IQ | CN | CU | ST | SP | **Chairs arranged** differently in class |
| ID | IQ | CN | CU | ST | SP | Teacher **demonstration** |
| ID | IQ | CN | CU | ST | SP | Teacher plays **"devil's advocate"** |
| ID | IQ | CN | CU | ST | SP | Class **discussion** of a moral dilemma |
| ID | IQ | CN | CU | ST | SP | Students attend a **drama** production |
| ID | IQ | CN | CU | ST | SP | **Drill and practice** of a new skill |
| ID | IQ | CN | CU | ST | SP | **Field trip** |
| ID | IQ | CN | CU | ST | SP | Receiving a **grade** on a term paper |
| ID | IQ | CN | CU | ST | SP | **Illustrations or examples** |
| ID | IQ | CN | CU | ST | SP | Teacher **interviews** a guest |
| ID | IQ | CN | CU | ST | SP | Student reads a **learning contract** agreement to find next assignment |
| ID | IQ | CN | CU | ST | SP | **Lecture** |
| ID | IQ | CN | CU | ST | SP | **Memory devices** |
| ID | IQ | CN | CU | ST | SP | Teacher gives an **object lesson** |
| ID | IQ | CN | CU | ST | SP | **Praising** students |
| ID | IQ | CN | CU | ST | SP | Students work through a **programmed text** |
| ID | IQ | CN | CU | ST | SP | **Quiz or test** |
| ID | IQ | CN | CU | ST | SP | Teacher does a **role play** with another teacher |
| ID | IQ | CN | CU | ST | SP | Students participate in regular class **routines** (e.g., pledge of allegiance ) |
| ID | IQ | CN | CU | ST | SP | **Songs/Music** |
| ID | IQ | CN | CU | ST | SP | Teacher reads a **story excerpt** in class |
| ID | IQ | CN | CU | ST | SP | Writing a **term paper** |
| ID | IQ | CN | CU | ST | SP | Students read a **textbook** |
| ID | IQ | CN | CU | ST | SP | Viewing a **video excerpt** |

2. All good teaching methods utilize one or more Avenues of learning. Note that some teaching practices may have limited learning benefits, but

they have other motivational or social value (e.g., an "ice-breaker" activity; more will be said about this in the next chapter). Cite two additional teaching methods that have not been listed. Now identify the major learning Avenue that supports the effective use of each method you listed.

3. Complete the following sentence: "To encourage student learning, the next time I teach I will be sure to . . ."

## Key Concepts and Issues

Avenues of learning
    and Levels of learning
    and teaching methods
    matched with age groups
direct modeling
example, role model, hero, mentor
evaluating mass media
peer ministry
Social Learning Family
Spontaneous Modeling
Structured Modeling
verbal modeling
symbolic modeling
youth ministry and adult workers

Part **3**

---

*Preparation for Learning*

# Sensitivity to Student Motivation

**Able and Willing**
**Willing to Learn**
**Six Factors in Student Motivation**
**Application: Learning Styles and Motivation**
**Conclusion**

"Are you ready?" This familiar phrase provokes various images because of its diverse usage. For instance, this common query is usually heard when a family is about to leave for church. It's used by two auto mechanics who jointly attempt to remove an engine from a car. And it's repeated by an impatient child who is helping her mother bake, and is about to pour the milk into the mixing bowl. Likewise we probably remember shouting, "Ready . . . set . . . GO!" when playing games in our childhood.

At a more complex level, being ready is also critical to the teaching-learning process. Teaching requires extensive preparation. When instructors begin class, we expect them to be ready to teach. But there's more to preparation. What about student readiness? As prepared teachers, do we assume that our students are equally ready to learn? Since we value teacher readiness, why don't we similarly prize learner preparedness?

---
### Try It Out
---

What does it mean for students to "be ready to learn"—to be able to participate in any given learning activity or assignment (e.g., class discussion, research paper, quiz)? What "entry characteristics" should teachers expect students to have? For example, it's obvious students need sufficient reading skills and vocabulary. But what kind of thinking skills, attitudes, physical abilities, or dispositions are necessary? Using an instructional setting with which you are familiar, jot down a number of different factors that teachers must assume about students' readiness to learn.

A conscientious teacher must be concerned about factors that affect the student's receptivity to teaching. What blessings and burdens do students bring to class? How might these affect their participation? Do they have the requisite knowledge and skills for today's lesson? In this chapter, and the next three, we'll look at pertinent issues of the students' readiness. Our effectiveness pivots on how well we understand our students' entry characteristics.

## Able and Willing

Readiness means that students must be both *able* and *willing* to engage in learning. The term "able" refers to whether students are capable of successful participation. "Willingness" speaks of their motivation.

Two different kinds of ability are in view. First, *maturational ability* is critical. Have students sufficiently grown up, as they should? This initial category is primarily relevant for those who teach children and young teens. We of course do not expect newborn babies to intelligently take part in Bible studies or to recite verses. At some point in the future we can anticipate that, but appropriate timing is the focus here. We don't expect toddlers to paint pictures without some blues, reds, or greens ending up where they shouldn't be. Coordination hasn't fully developed in young children. So we let them paint to their hearts' delight within their present level of physical maturity, using smocks to cover their clothing and plastic sheets to cover the floor. Similarly, during class discussions at youth meetings, we shouldn't expect all junior high students to engage in adult reasoning. Some attain their adolescent growth spurt later than others. So sensitive teachers keep this in mind when discussion questions are prepared; they shouldn't overfrustrate these late bloomers.[1]

The second element relates to a student's ability based on *prior learning*. In other words, the first category is a factor of human development, the second, a factor of experience. For instance, it is impossible to teach people how to study the Bible before they can read. As a parallel point to consider, language teachers tell us that once a person has learned one foreign language, it's much easier to learn another one. Whenever we teach, we make assumptions about what students are capable of doing. Whether consciously or not, we imagine what prerequisites our students have, then we plan a lesson built on this understanding. Obviously we must continually ask: Do we have valid assumptions about what our students already know and what they can do? If we plan our teaching too much beyond their present abilities—usually labeled as "teaching over their heads"—then our students will not be ready to learn. This factor of prior learning expresses just one dimension of how teaching must be geared to the level of capability of the child, youth, or adult.

In practice, it's very difficult to draw a hard line between these two elements of prior learning ability and maturational ability. Are toddlers able to build with wood blocks just because their physical ability has matured? Isn't their success with these blocks also based on their experiences—on their trial-and-error play, as well as their observations of older children who correctly use these blocks? Our purpose, therefore, is not to make these distinctions too finely, but to make it easier to diagnose learning problems. Suffice it to say that, except in situations involving special education learners, virtually all student "ability" difficulties either relate to prior learning inadequacies (e.g., reading skills required to study the Bible) or a combination of prior learning and maturational development (e.g., young teens using adult reasoning).

In short, improving our understanding of students' current abilities aids our assessment. Through various classroom exercises (e.g., informal quizzing, problem-solving exercises), we gain invaluable information about our learners. Appropriate lesson planning requires an accurate assessment of students' ability levels. Thus, matters of prior learning are specific to the subject being learned and must be assessed by the teacher on a student-by-student basis. In the case of the Corinthian believers, Paul was discouraged that they were not prepared to advance toward the next step of maturity: "I gave you milk, not solid food, for you were not yet ready for it. Indeed, you are still not *ready*. You are still worldly. For since there is jealousy and quarreling among you, are you not worldly? Are you not acting like mere men?" (1 Cor. 3:2–3; cf. Heb. 5:11–12).

The next three chapters offer an overview of some basic concepts of students' maturational capabilities (see Table 6.1).[2] A word of caution, though: developmental rates vary for each student. Consequently, for the best results, each teacher must ascertain individual student patterns of growth and preparedness. Now let's turn to the topic of motivation.

### Table 6.1
## Chapters on Readiness for Learning

| | |
|---|---|
| "Willing" | Motivation—Chapter 6 |
| "Able" | Physical Growth and Ability—Chapter 7 |
| | Cognitive Growth and Ability—Chapter 8 |
| | Personality Growth and Ability—Chapter 9 |

## Willing to Learn

"Jim is the most unmotivated student I've ever had in class!" Although the name may change, most teachers have made similar judgments about unwilling learners. We've felt frustrated by those who don't pay attention or even by those who overtly resist our teaching. But what do we mean by the word "unmotivated"? Looking at the concept from another angle, we usually consider anyone who persists at a task as being "motivated." Consequently, even including a negative sense, all students are motivated in some way (e.g., they persist in talking to their neighbor, doodling, watching TV, and not doing their homework). On the one hand, students may lack motivation to pay attention because the subject doesn't seem relevant. On the other, they may fail to be attentive because they're bored by certain teaching activities. If we want students to expend reasonable effort in our class sessions, then we must comprehend the complex arena of student motivation. We must master the issue of "willing"—the main subject of this chapter.[3]

---

### Try It Out

---

1. What are the major student motivational problems you face in teaching? Make a list of a half-dozen frustrations you have recently experienced, based on your students' barriers to learning.

2. Keep this list handy as you read the rest of this chapter. Next to these items write down practical strategies that might be used to address each motivational barrier.

---

### *What Hinders Motivation?*

Most teachers know that barriers to learning exist, but perhaps few recognize that these same barriers can significantly affect student motivation.[4] Our classes consist of many students. Like any other part of their unique personalities, each brings his or her own bundle of interests and aims to class. No lesson—no matter how good it is—can meet *all* the expectations of each student for the whole session. The larger the class, the greater the potential barrier. For that matter, individual student interests sometimes demand greater flexibility than is realistically possible. In addition, teaching in academic settings includes the pressure of scores and grades, mostly involving evaluative and competitive comparisons with classmates. Moreover, expectations to attain certain academic standards can easily erode a student's natural desire to learn.

Think about certain conflicting scenarios. Our culture encourages us to desire pleasurable recreational experiences, yet many learning tasks involve complex concepts, requiring patience and sustained concentration. This entertainment perspective, nurtured within our culture—particularly through the media—tends to develop a mindset that seeks excitement, fun, and lots of laughs. It's difficult to incorporate these elements in our teaching in *every* educational activity—in some cases it is not even possible. Let's face it, learning does involve work. Given this entertainment atmosphere, students may expend only a minimal amount of effort before giving up and turning their attention elsewhere. Today's students have a number of distractions—both good and bad—to keep their minds off the learning task at hand. Combine these facts with the tendency to sin (which we all have) and the need to tap into students' motivation may become the most critical element of the teacher's task—from the human point of view. As Hendricks says, "The longer I teach, the more convinced I am that a person's MQ—his Motivation Quotient—is more important than his IQ" (1987, p. 125).

### Designed to Be Curious

Yet we must not look only at the down side of the situation. God has made us as creatures of curiosity. We all have a strong, built-in desire to learn. The key, then, is to discern viable areas of curiosity, matching these with God's truth. Notice, for instance, how the customary religious practices of the Jews naturally prompted children's learning about God. Exodus 12:25–27 commands:

> When you enter the land that the LORD will give you as he promised, observe this [Passover] ceremony. And when your children ask you, "What does this ceremony mean to you?" then tell them, "It is the Passover sacrifice to the LORD, who passed over the houses of the Israelites in Egypt and spared our homes when he struck down the Egyptians."

Motivation to learn is an inherent characteristic of being human. Like any other, it must be developed to its fullest capacity.

We may ask, "Why do students exert any effort in a learning task?" It will help us analyze what's going on inside the student, to look at the "intrinsic" factors of learning. Such factors identify the way learners feel about the total educational scene. For example, teachers may ask, "Because of their past experiences with this class (or other classes), were my students eager to come to my class today?" "Did they participate well in a group setting, or were they indifferent toward the group, or did they follow their own interests?" LeBar (1989) called these the inner factors of learning. And she raised parallel questions for the instructor to ponder: "Are their personal psychological needs for security, affection, recognition, new experiences, freedom from guilt, being met by the class?" (p. 34).

Whether we know it or not, students develop positive *and* negative learning attitudes. Consequently, their willingness to participate is directly affected. In cases in which positive learning experiences do not occur, student motivation is often a primary reason. The teacher's purpose, then, is to *gain* and *sustain* student interest and effort throughout the learning process. On the one hand, if this significant purpose is neglected, some teachers answer questions that learners aren't even asking. We have all encountered this experience. At such times, student cries of "irrelevance" are justified. On the other hand, when teachers fulfill this purpose, they can tap into student motivation. For example, most instructors have some degree of control over teacher competence and enthusiasm, how the topic is taught, teacher expectations of students, and teacher-student relationships. The following section presents one helpful model of student motivation that incorporates several important factors for teaching.

## Six Factors in Student Motivation

"One of the logical reasons why ineffective and unmotivated learning so frequently occurs is because of the lack of motivation planning on the part of many instructors" (Wlodkowski 1985, p. 58). With this testimony in mind, Wlodkowski's theory of motivation sets out to help teachers with such planning concerns. The main points of motivation complement lesson planning by asking six basic questions (see Table 6.2; the key concept of each question is printed in italics; Wlodkowski 1985, pp. 66–67). "If each of these questions is adequately answered by the instructor (and integrated into the learning sequence with appropriate activities)," claims Wlodkowski, "learners will have an excellent chance of being motivated to learn throughout the learning sequence" (p. 67). These half-dozen questions associate with the three major phases of a teaching session: at the start, during, and at the end of class. Each of the six concepts is described below. A summary chart of teaching strategies from these concepts is presented at the conclusion of this section.[5]

### Table 6.2
### Wlodkowski's Six Questions about Student Motivation

**Emphasis on the Beginning of the Lesson:**
- What can I do to establish a positive learner *attitude* for this learning sequence?
- How do I best meet the *needs* of my learners through this learning sequence?

**Emphasis on the Main Part of the Lesson:**
- What about this learning sequence will continuously *stimulate* my learners?
- How is the *affective* experience and emotional climate for this learning sequence positive for learners?

**Emphasis on the End of the Lesson:**
- How does this learning sequence increase or affirm learner feelings of *competence*?
- What is the *reinforcement* that this learning sequence provides for my learners?

*Source:* Wlodkowski (1985, pp. 66–67).

### Attitudes

The first two factors of attitudes and needs relate to the beginning of the lesson. At this point, instructors are concerned with how students' attitudes can specifically work with or hinder their learning. Wlodkowski defines an attitude as a "combination of a perception with a judgment that often results in an emotion that influences behavior" (1985, p. 73). We want our students to have positive attitudes about four items: (1) the subject matter, (2) the learning environment, (3) themselves as learners, particularly their level of confidence in participating in class activities, and (4) the teacher. When students develop negative attitudes about any one of these areas it can spell trouble for effective learning. Mager (1984, pp. 55–65) addresses six corollary problem areas: pain (inflicted by the teacher), fear and anxiety, frustration, humiliation and embarrassment, boredom, and physical discomfort. By identifying which areas are problematic for students, we can then plan to help them move forward in their learning.[6]

### Needs

If what students are learning is not viewed by them as relevant to their interests, needs, ability levels, or goals, then they can remain aloof, becoming uninvolved. For "attitude," the first factor addressed above, we as teachers were dealing with issues about which students are largely *unaware*. In this second category, teachers attend to their students' felt needs—needs *known* to students. Through a variety of needs assessment techniques (e.g., individual interview, group conversation, questionnaire, or even a self-evaluation inventory) we come to know our students, what interests they have, what passions they hold. (In this respect, the general developmental needs of our students are spelled out in chapters 7, 8, and 9.)

Relevance is the key word. We must incorporate worthwhile content, examples, and exercises. In the classroom, we need to become adept at finding common ground, appropriate points of contact with our students. Table 6.3 outlines points of contact used by Jesus, Peter, Stephen, and Paul. Each example complements its respective setting.[7]

### Table 6.3
## Points of Contact in Teaching

| Passage | John 4 | Acts 2 | Acts 7 | Acts 17 |
|---|---|---|---|---|
| Teacher | Jesus | Peter | Stephen | Paul |
| Audience | Samaritan woman | Religious Jews at feast of Pentecost | Sanhedrin | Greek philosophers |
| Point of Contact | Water to living water | Old Testament quotes | Moses, the Lawgiver | Altar "To an Unknown God"; Paul quotes local philosopher |

At Michigan State University, one professor—a religious person, though not a Christian—asked students to provide background information about themselves on a card at the first session. On the card, among other things, one student listed that he was a faculty member of a seminary. The professor must have recognized that this student was very familiar with the Bible, because a couple weeks later, he illustrated a point in class by discussing how God had directed Gideon to select his army, as recorded in the Book of Judges. Following a study of the Book of Jonah, students in another class at a Christian college summarized the major concepts from each chapter as a chorus using a contemporary tune. One student played the piano as the whole class sang the verses recorded in Table 6.4.

### Table 6.4
# The Story of Jonah

(To the tune of the "Gilligan's Island" theme)

When Jonah heard a message from
   The Lord his God on high,
      He fled from God to Tarshish far,
To all he said good-bye, to all he said good-bye.

While on the ship a storm came up,
   The sailors were afraid,
They wondered what could be the cause
   Of this tempestous wave, of this tempestuous wave.

Jonah said, "I am the one,
   To blame for this array,
If you will cast me off this ship,
   The storm will go away, the storm will go away."

As soon as he was thrown off board,
   A giant fish came up,
And swallowed him completely up,
   For three days in his gut, for three days in his gut.

While Jonah was inside the fish,
   He surely wasn't bored,
He prayed sincerely from his heart,
   "Salvation's from the Lord!" "Salvation's from the Lord!"

As soon as Jonah recognized
   This truth within his heart,
The fish coughed him upon the shore,
   With one gargantuan barf, with one gargantuan barf

God told him, "Preach in Nineveh,
   Repent or be destroyed."
And when they did, he got so mad,
   He sulked and was annoyed, he sulked and was annoyed.

God grew a plant that gave him shade,
   To teach him of his love,
God can be mad and merciful,
   Because of who he was, because of who he was.

How we sequence a lesson and its educational activities can tap into our students' interest by using "psychological" as well as "logical" ordering. "Logical" ordering proceeds from foundational matters to particular concerns, from theory to practice. For instance, an instructor might begin a study of the Book of Jonah by surveying the history of the Assyrian nation and the role of Israel's prophets. Then, the story is chronologically unfolded. Chapters 1 to 4 would be detailed in an ordered progression.

By contrast, consider the value of "psychological" instructional ordering. This approach contemplates the best ways to secure and sustain student motivation. For example, the teacher might delay a treatment of Assryian history until the second or third session. Perhaps it could be covered at the end of the series. In the first session, students could be confronted with the basic message of the book: developing godly compassion for those outside of the kingdom of God. The teacher may actually begin with the key issue of the final chapter: "Have you ever been angry? Have you ever been angry *at God?*" This technique of lesson ordering challenges students to identify with the prophet Jonah as the entry point to studying the book's significant message. Relevant information about Nineveh, the Old Testament prophets, and Jonah subsequently arises through a more inductive study of the text.[8]

One widely used psychological ordering framework is the "Hook, Book, Look, Took" approach (Richards 1970). Every lesson or series of lessons should have these four basic components. The *Hook* segment helps students focus on the lesson topic in some interesting and pertinent manner. That is, the point of departure is with the learner. In the *Book* section, the main subject is investigated and explained. Next, application of the subject is broadly explored in the *Look* segment. What are the general implications for today? Finally, the lesson theme is privately addressed in the *Took.*[9] "What will *I* personally choose to do?" Figure 6.1 visually portrays the general movement of this four-part framework.[10]

One other principle of psychological ordering is commonly used. Some educational activities can be fun; others take concentrated effort and persistence. The Premack Principle (1965) suggests that we can use one activity to help with the other. Specifically, frequently occurring behavior can be used to reinforce less frequent behavior. So the teacher announces, "As soon as we get our science unit done, then we'll go out to the park to play some games," or, a parent says, "You can eat your dessert *after* you finish your vegetables." In sum, we use what students want to do to help them persist at activities they need to do.

We can also help students sustain their effort to learn by allowing them to make choices in their learning based on their own interests and knowledge. Such choices include selecting a topic to study (from certain options), and deciding what form their projects might take (e.g., a recorded interview, a newspaper column, or an art composition). By providing

**Figure 6.1**
# Movement of a Lesson

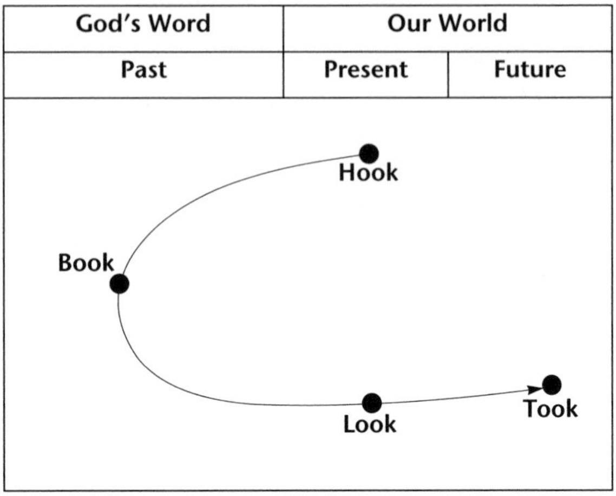

| God's Word | Our World | |
|------------|-----------|--------|
| Past | Present | Future |

these opportunities for self-directed learning, we help students develop habits of lifelong learning.[11]

### *Stimulation*

The next two factors, stimulation and affect, pertain to the main part of the lesson. A common complaint of students is that class is boring. How do we respond to this widespread problem? The "stimulation" factor addresses this topic. Since this concern applies throughout the whole lesson, all motivational strategies we use must encourage student effort to learn. Also, remember that a particular strategy that works for some learners may not for others. The primary strategy for stimulation, then, focuses on the students' *active involvement* in the lesson.

Sometimes students fail to learn because they are not fully listening (i.e., attending) to the lesson. The concentration span of individuals varies. Some remain at a task for hours; others give up after only a short time. For some, the classroom may be too warm, for others too cold. Still others may be distracted by emotional pain (e.g., from a recent argument with a close friend). In light of the need for learner participation, teachers must offer adequate *response* opportunities. If students know they have an opportunity to make a comment, or that they might be called on to answer a question, their state of alertness heightens. Various methods include visual and auditory material (e.g., diagrams, charts, music, movies) and participatory activities (e.g., role plays and simulations). Changing the pace of the lesson, including breaks and even planned physical movement (e.g., the teacher conducts class from different places in the classroom or students work in new groups), helps avoid the routines that make teaching flat and lifeless. One reason that the "Try It Out" sections are incorporated in each chapter is to break up the routine, providing an opportunity for reader participation.

To sustain students' curiosity and receptivity, teachers can employ unpredictable and novel class practices like humor, interesting personal stories, puzzling questions, and captivating dilemmas. Vary the level of questioning from simple memory tasks to complex evaluation by including each of Bloom's six cognitive categories (see chapter 2). Exercises in which students match their skills against appropriate challenges, either individually (e.g., an educational board game) or on a team (e.g., athletic sport) can intensify concentration and effort. For these kinds of activities, time appears to pass quickly. When genuine student participation exists, boredom often evaporates.

### Affect-Emotions

This fourth factor, affect, highlights the emotional climate of the classroom, along with the emotional experiences in learning. How students feel influences their receptivity to learning. Students come to class in particular moods, both positive and negative—the exhilaration of having done well on a test, the anticipation of tonight's pickup basketball game, the disappointment of missing a special event because of finances, the pain from being criticized in a conversation just before class.

These kinds of moods are natural and normal. Though we may not be able to directly change every mood, we can indirectly influence the emotional responses of our students primarily through our own moods, words, and actions. We can also help our students realize that their life doesn't have to be governed by their moods. It's important, therefore, that we come to our teaching while at our best. Our own emotional mood sets the initial tone for the classroom atmosphere. We can encourage or discourage students from entering class activities through our own personal mood.

In addition to what *we* do as teachers, students are affected by the particular learning activities they experience. For example, the use of small learning groups often plays an important role in developing receptive "affect" responses in students. Furthermore, stories and illustrations that include both emotional aspects and relevant subject matter help students relate more holistically to the subject. Jesus modeled this technique by employing parables full of emotion. For example, when the woman found her lost coin, she called together her friends and said, "Rejoice with me; I have found my lost coin" (Luke 15:9). Use of such vivid imagery summons us to think *and* feel.

## Try It Out

Imagine that you are in a Bible study group learning more about God's character. Today's topic is God as Creator. The group leader reads the sentence below. Reflect on the first thoughts and feelings that surface in your imagination, concerning the One who made trees arrayed with such color.

> It was warm and bright and the trees were in full color, magnificent, explosive, like permanent fireworks—reds and yellows, oranges, some so brilliant that Crayola never put them in crayons for fear the children would color outside the lines (Keillor 1987, p. 133).

Jot down one thought or feeling about the Creator prompted by this creative author.

---

Music moves us. We have all participated in a church service in which music set the tone for expectant worship. God made us so that music reaches deeply into our souls to soothe, to comfort, to excite, to activate us. Some instructors begin class with a chorus or hymn; others encourage students to complete assignments in which music plays a central role.

The kind of learning community we teachers facilitate in our classrooms also affects our students' receptivity to new ideas and skills. Developing friendship and trust among learners contributes to a supportive emotional climate. A variety of experiences can build this team atmosphere, such as group projects, drama, role play exercises, simulations, and field trips.[12]

### Competence

The final two categories, competence and reinforcement, focus on the end of an activity or of the lesson itself. We want to be sure learners increase their sense of confidence and mastery in what they have learned. Our purpose, then, is to provide appropriate feedback. We must make our students aware of their own progress, so they gain a sense of satisfaction from it. For example, Paul praised the Thessalonian believers for their exemplary evangelistic efforts:

> The Lord's message rang out from you not only in Macedonia and Achaia—your faith in God has become known everywhere. Therefore we do not need to say anything about it, for they themselves report what kind of reception you gave us. They tell how you turned to God from idols to serve the living and true God (1 Thess. 1:8–9).

Such encouragement is always welcome. If our learners feel that they are making progress, a measure of competence will result.

Many teachers use games, both for recreation (during a rainy recess) and educational value (e.g., taking turns, winning and losing, learning strategies). A dilemma arises when adults play individual games with children (e.g., checkers or most board games). How can we help them improve their skills without frustrating them because of our superior abilities? Some adults purposely play poorly and "let" the children win. This may work in some cases, but in general, it's based on a form of deception. The principle of "handicapping"—a concept widely used even in adult sports—is preferable. This "level playing field approach" to games of strategy between those of unequal ability allows both contestants to play to the best of their ability, yet does not overly frustrate the "weaker" opponent.[13]

One additional issue needs to be addressed: evaluating student progress. How can it be given so as to tap into student motivation? Constructive criticism, if couched within a good teacher-student relationship, helps students improve their skills. For example, a teacher may offer these balanced comments to a student about a term paper: "I see that you have put a lot of time into this report. I can tell by the number of sources you cite and the number of original ideas you include. Now, what needs attention is how the paper is organized. You have excellent ideas but they don't seem to fit together well. Is there a unifying theme that ties all these ideas together? Let's talk about it."

A parent might guide a child with these words when inspecting the newly mowed lawn: "You sure are growing up. I can trust you with using the lawn mower in a safe way and that makes me proud. Now remember our purpose. We don't want to just move the mower over the lawn, but we want to cut all the grass. Can you see the long grass pieces by the sidewalk? If you put the wheels about here, you'll be sure to get them. Let me show you." Affirmation (with specific steps for improvement) can keep a focus on confidence and mastery, rather than inadequacy and failure.

Helping students see their progress can be done through various evaluation strategies, but these must be structured to support, rather than discourage, student motivation. In some cases even quizzes and exams can have a positive effect on student interest. Progress can also be determined by students themselves. For instance, during the first day of a class on Bible study methods, the teacher might give students a Scripture passage to study. They are to spend a half-hour analyzing it and jotting down their findings. The teacher then collects their written record of findings and the class discusses the passage. Then, near the end of the course, the same exercise is given with a new passage and the same amount of time. Since learning tends to be incremental over time, students are typically surprised and encouraged to see their own progress, based on the two sets of Bible study notes. Self-evaluation can be a very helpful tool for students' sense of competence.

### Reinforcement

For the factor of competence, our focus relates to matters of *intrinsic* motivation. In many of the learning activities we do (because of the value or enjoyment associated with doing the activity), a sense of confidence and mastery is developed. For reinforcement, we look at *extrinsic* motivation. In these instances we participate in activities not necessarily for the activities' sake, but rather, for the outcome of the exercise. For example, we may have worked at a boring summer job during our teen years not so much for the work itself, but for the paycheck. So, even in a Christian learning situation, we can tap into students' goals to encourage them to participate in the learning activities we plan. For example, for many students higher grades have become an important extrinsic motivator. In more informal settings learners value participation because of the social benefits and personal attention it brings.

We must use extrinsic motivators wisely. They should be used like temporary training wheels on a bike: to help students begin moving when they face difficult learning tasks. But they can become harmful to students, too. For example, many students have made high grades their most important personal value. In extreme cases, students actually learn very little—except how to work the system to get an "A." Although we may provide extrinsic motivators for a time, we need to balance these efforts with an emphasis on student competence, primarily through intrinsic motivation. We must eventually take the "training wheels" off.[14]

---

### Try It Out

Wlodkowski (1985) outlines sixty-eight motivational strategies to be used within this six-factor framework (see Table 6.5).

### Table 6.5
## Wlodkowski's Summary of Motivation Factors

| Major Motivation Factor | Purpose | Strategy |
| --- | --- | --- |
| **Attitudes** (Beginning Activities) | To create a positive attitude toward the instructor | *1. Share something of value with your learners. <br> 2. Concretely indicate your cooperative intentions to help students learn. <br> *3. To the degree authentically possible, reflect the language, perspective, and attitudes of your learners. <br> 4. When issuing mandatory assignments or training requirements, give your rationale for these stipulations. <br> 5. Allow for introductions. |

| Major Motivation Factor | Purpose | Strategy |
|---|---|---|
| | To build a positive attitude toward the subject and learning situation. | *6. Eliminate or minimize any negative conditions that surround the subject.<br>*7. Ensure successful learning.<br>8. Make the first experience with the subject as positive as possible.<br>*9. Positively confront the possible erroneous beliefs, expectations, and assumptions that may underlie a negative learner attitude.<br>10. Associate the learner with other learners who are enthusiastic about the subject. |
| | To develop a positive learner self-concept for learning. | *11. Encourage the learner.<br>12. Promote the learner's personal control of the context of learning.<br>*13. Help learners to attribute their success to their ability and their effort.<br>*14. When learning tasks are suitable to their ability, help learners to understand that effort and persistence can overcome their failures. |
| | To establish learner expectancy for success. | 15. Make the learning goal as clear as possible.<br>16. Make the criteria of evaluation as clear as possible.<br>17. Use models similar to the learners to demonstrate expected learning.<br>18. Announce the expected amount of time needed for study and practice for successful learning.<br>19. Use goal-setting methods.<br>20. Use contracting methods. |
| **Needs** (Beginning Activities) | To ensure that instruction is responsive to learner needs. | 21. Use needs assessment techniques to discover and emphasize the felt needs of learners in the learning process.<br>22. Use needs assessment techniques to discover and emphasize the normative needs of learners in the learning process. |
| | To relate instruction to important physiological needs. | *23. When relevant, select content, examples, and projects that relate to the physiological needs of the learners. |
| | To satisfy and respect safety needs within the content and process of the instructional situation. | *24. When relevant, select content, examples, and projects that relate to the safety needs of the learners.<br>*25. Use imagery techniques to help learners clearly remember specific problems or tasks that are relevant to the knowledge or skill being taught. |

| Major Motivation Factor | Purpose | Strategy |
|---|---|---|
| | | *26. Reduce or remove components of the learning environment that lead to failure or fear.<br>*27. Create a learning environment that is organized and orderly.<br>28. Introduce the unfamiliar through the familiar. |
| | To satisfy and respect belongingness needs within the content and process of the instructional situation. | *29. When relevant, select content, examples, and projects that relate to the love and belongingness needs of the learners.<br>*30. Create components in the learning environment that tell learners they are accepted and respected participating members of the group. |
| | To satisfy and respect esteem needs within the content and process of the instructional situation. | 31. Offer the opportunity for responsible attainment of knowledge, skills, and learning goals that relate to the esteem needs of the learners.<br>32. When appropriate, plan activities to allow the learners to share and to publicly display their projects and skills. |
| | To satisfy and respect self-actualization needs within the content and process of the instructional situation. | 33. Provide learners with the opportunity to select topics, projects, and assignments that appeal to their curiosity, sense of wonder, and need to explore.<br>34. To the extent possible, and when appropriate, provide opportunities for self-directed learning.<br>35. Challenge the learners. |
| **Stimulation** (During Activities) | To maintain learner attention. | 36. Provide frequent response opportunities to all learners on an equitable basis.<br>*37. Help learners to realize their accountability for what they are learning.<br>*38. Provide variety in personal presentation style, methods of instruction, and learning materials.<br>39. Introduce, connect, and end learning activities attractively and clearly.<br>*40. Selectively use breaks, physical exercises, and energizers. |
| | To build learner interest. | *41. Relate learning to student interests.<br>*42. When possible, clearly state or demonstrate the advantages that will result from the learning activity.<br>*43. While instructing, use humor liberally and frequently. |

| Major Motivation Factor | Purpose | Strategy |
|---|---|---|
| | | *44. Selectively induce parapathic emotions.<br>*45. Selectively use examples, analogies, metaphors, and stories.<br>46. Selectively use knowledge and comprehension questions to stimulate learner interest.<br>47. Use unpredictability and uncertainty to the degree that learners enjoy them with a sense of security. |
| | To develop learner involvement. | *48. Use disequilibrium to stimulate learner involvement.<br>49. Selectively use application, analysis, synthesis, and evaluation questions and tasks to stimulate learner involvement.<br>*50. Make learner reaction and active participation an essential part of the learning process.<br>51. Introduce minor challenges during instruction.<br>52. Create opportunities and conditions for the flow experience. |
| **Affect** (During Activities) | To encourage and integrate learner emotions within the learning process. | *53. Selectively emphasize and deal with the human perspective of what is being learned, with application to the personal daily lives of the learners whenever possible.<br>*54. When appropriate, relate content and instructional procedures to learner concerns.<br>*55. Selectively relate content and instructional procedures to learner values.<br>*56. When appropriate, deal with and encourage the expression of emotions during learning.<br>*57. When appropriate, help learners to directly experience cognitive concepts on a physical and emotional level. |
| | To maintain an optimal emotional climate within the learning group. | *58. Use cooperative goal structures to develop and maximize cohesiveness in the learning group. |
| **Compe-tence** (Ending Activities) | To increase learner awareness of progress, mastery, achievement, and responsibility in learning in a manner that enhances the learner's | *59. Provide consistent feedback to learners regarding their mastery, progress, and responsibility in learning.<br>*60. When necessary, use constructive criticism.<br>*61. Effectively praise and reward learning.<br>62. Use formative evaluation procedures to measure and communicate learner progress and mastery. |

| Major Motivation Factor | Purpose | Strategy |
|---|---|---|
| | confidence, self-determination, and intrinsic motivation. | 63. Whenever possible, use performance evaluation procedures to help the learner realize how to operationalize in daily living what has been learned. |
| | | 64. Acknowledge and affirm the learners' responsibility and any significant actions or characteristics that contributed to the successful completion of the learning task. |
| **Reinforcement** (Ending Activities) | To provide extrinsic reinforcers for learning activities that because of their structure or nature could not induce learner participation or achievement without positive reinforcement. | *65. Use incentives to encourage participation in learning activities that are initially unattractive. <br><br> *66. Consider the use of extrinsic reinforcers for routine, well-learned activities, complex skill building, and drill-and practice activities. |
| | To help learners to be aware of the positive changes their learning behavior has produced. | *67. When learning has natural consequences, help learners to be aware of them as well as their impact. |
| | To affirm and to continue learner motivation for significant units of learning. | 68. Encourage or provide a reinforcing event for positive closure at the end of significant unit of learning. |

*Can also apply to other time phases.
*Source:* Wlodkowski (1985, pp. 254–57).

1. Think back over your recent teaching experiences—lessons you have taught, group studies you have led, or a few particular child-rearing experiences. Identify two or three  motivational strategies that you have used in the past. Match your example with the particular strength identified in Table 6.5. From the table, write down the specific number(s) of the strategy in the appropriate box on the left side.

|  | Past Teaching | Future Teaching |
|---|---|---|
| Beginning Activities<br>Attitudes |  |  |
| Needs |  |  |
| During Activities<br>Stimulation |  |  |
| Affect/Emotions |  |  |
| Ending Activities<br>Competence |  |  |
| Reinforcement |  |  |

2. Then, in the column on the right, from the table identify two or three new motivational strategies that you could try—strategies that are *not* found in the adjacent box to its left. Write the numbers in the appropriate boxes. On a sheet of paper, plan how you can specifically use one strategy for each box with your students (i.e., six total strategies). Using a particular strategy just once may not immediately solve all of the motivational problems you currently have, but over a period of time you should see some positive change.

## Application: Learning Styles and Motivation

Through repeated educational experiences—both good and bad—everyone cultivates personal learning preferences. Some people like to discuss theories, while others would rather work with practical ideas. Some prefer to make an oral presentation on a subject, other learners would rather write a term paper. Certain learners want to study in a quiet room, while others are never bothered by background noise.

Educational research helps us understand these individual preferences or "learning styles" (Dunn et al. 1989; Bonham 1988). Keefe (1983) places the various models within four basic categories.

1. Cognitive style models: focusing on modes of perceiving, thinking, problem-solving and remembering

2. Affective style models: focusing on personality traits related to attention, motivation, and needs

3. Physiological style models: focusing on biologically based responses in aural and visual capacities related to personal nutrition and health

4. Multidimensional models: models combining more than one of these other factors

One *multidimensional* learning style model that includes all three major emphases was developed by Dunn and Dunn (1978, Dunn et al. 1988). It employs five categories with twenty-one different factors that affect learning:

1. Environmental: sound, light, temperature, design
2. Emotional: motivation, persistence, responsibility, structure
3. Sociological: self, pair, peers, team, adult, varied
4. Physical: perceptual, intake, time, mobility
5. Psychological: global versus analytic, hemispherity, impulsive versus reflective

For instance, in the physical category "visual" (perceptual) learners retain information best by picturing it, while "manipulative" (mobility) learners prefer more "hands-on" involvement. In the sociological category "dyadic" (pair) learners work best with a partner, rather than alone (self) or in a group (team).

A popular *cognitive* learning style model was developed by Kolb (1984). It reduces all options to four individual learning patterns. There are four quadrants with two perpendicular axes (concrete versus abstract, active versus reflective). The foursome, as adapted for the teacher by McCarthy (1987; Kolb's terms are in parentheses), include:

1. *Imaginative or Innovative Learner* (Diverger): emphasis on group activities to explore many ideas through a variety of means.
2. *Analytical Learner* (Assimilator): emphasis on facts, logical soundness of ideas, and organized presentation of information.
3. *Commonsense Learner* (Converger): emphasis on practical and relevant-to-life uses for ideas and theories.
4. *Dynamic Learner* (Accommodator): emphasis on "hands-on," trial-and-error, and results-oriented experimentation in which learners are free to select activities from various options.

Each pattern has its own optimum set of matched teaching methods. To work with these particular student interests, McCarthy suggests that teachers rotate through a four-part cycle in their teaching, incorporating each of these four emphases. This permits students to learn in their most productive mode, at least for a period of time.

Based on our personalities and experiences, we each develop certain *preferences* for how we like to learn. Learning styles research provides another resource for tapping into students' *willingness* to persist in learning. But how can we incorporate these insights into our teaching? Most of us work with a class of students. We can't develop ten to thirty lesson plans per session—one for each student. The major benefit of these models is to help us diagnose individual learning *difficulties*. By using learning style instruments we can pinpoint a student's particular preferences.[15] With results in hand, we can assess whether any of the student's preferred learning modes are present in our teaching. Obviously, no class session can match up with every learning style, but there ought to be some reasonable correspondence between the ways *teachers teach* and the ways *students learn*.

The primary benefit for our lesson planning is that we now have useful criteria for selecting our teaching methods. We can vary our instruction accordingly in order to feature as many learning modes as possible.[16] One final word of wisdom: research suggests that optimum learning results when students are challenged to employ *all* of their available capacities and not just those they *prefer* to use (Wlodkowski 1985, p. 180).

## Conclusion

The task before us is to work with the particular moods of our students as they come to us. We want to align our teaching with their motivation to increase participation in class activities. In deciding which teaching methods to use, therefore, we must keep in mind *two* critical factors. We select specific methods that either contribute to our students' *learning* or that encourage our students' *motivation* (or methods that do both at the same time). By intentionally working with their particular interests and dispositions, we can help our students become mature men and women of God.

## Key Concepts and Issues

able and willing

curiosity

Dunn and Dunn's and Kolb's learning style models

hindrances to student motivation

intrinsic and extrinsic motivation

learning styles/preferences

  cognitive styles, affective styles, physiological styles, multidimensional styles

maturational ability

motivation

Premack principle

prior learning

psychological ordering

Readiness for learning

relevance

response opportunities

selecting teaching methods: for learning and motivation value

Wlodkowski's time-continuum theory of motivation attitudes, needs, stimulation, affect-emotions, competence, reinforcement

L evels
E xtent
A venues
R eadiness
N ature

# Human Nature:
# Birthday Gifts
# for Growth and Learning

**One Sunday Morning . . .**
**Three Factors: Heredity, History, and the Here and Now**
**Created in God's Image**
**Patterns of Physical Development**
**Application: Students with Special Educational Needs**

The concepts of "willing" and "able" remind us to be concerned with our students' *readiness* for learning. The previous chapter explored issues of student motivation—the "willing" part of that pair. In this chapter and the next two, the "able" component is in view. Do students possess the requisite abilities to fully participate in our planned learning activities? As much as we can, we want to maximize their learning accomplishments.

To better grasp the significance of this subject, consider the following classroom scenario. Specifically note the range and types of student abilities.

## One Sunday Morning . . .

The clock registers 10:14 A.M. at Berean Church. Jill Sinclair leads her second-grade Sunday school class through a craft activity. She wants to show the children how God is with them every moment of the day. Robby, first to finish, tries to help those next to him. Marilyn looks out the window, oblivious to the classroom noise; not even her classmates' voices or the rustle of paper and scissors disturbs her solitude. Scott, one of the youngest, is out of his chair again. This time, he runs around the table, tripping over the chair leg. When the class laughs at him (they have before), Scott bursts into tears.

Jill becomes angry and discouraged. As a first-year teacher, she has spent hours of study and preparation for this class. For a split second, she ridicules her own lesson subject. "How can *I* sense God's presence in this chaos?" she wonders.

What should she do? Jill's response depends on her perceived *abilities* of her six- to eight-year-old children, as well as on her understanding of each child's life situation. In addition, her reaction is contingent on her understanding of God and his dealings—both in her own life and in her students' lives.

## Three Factors: Heredity, History, and the Here and Now

Let's look at three children in Jill's class. Scott suffers from minimal brain dysfunction (MBD), a disorder of behavioral and cognitive functioning. This condition is often characterized by a heightened level of activity without detectable brain damage. It is commonly referred to as the "hyperactive child syndrome" (Elkind and Weiner 1978, p. 340). Scott's problem relates to a genetic deficiency.

Marilyn experiences severe emotional stress due to her home life. Her recently divorced mother lives with a boyfriend who verbally berates Marilyn. Marilyn is also a latchkey child; after school, she is alone until her mother gets off work. To cope, Marilyn spends hours daydreaming. In a world of her own, she plays with her imaginary friends. Marilyn's problem stems from the adverse effects of emotional and psychological abuse.

Both of Robby's conscientious parents are professional educators. They provide a healthy learning environment in the home. Robby loves to read. This is due, in part, to the fact that Robby's father and mother have read to him since the day he was born. Because of his advanced reading skills, Robby approaches most educational experiences with eagerness and confidence in his abilities.

Jill Sinclair brings her own background to class as well. At thirty-two, she desires to serve God and the church as a single woman. Jill likes to be in control of her circumstances. She likes to see results from her faithful preparation. Oftentimes, her class thwarts those desires. These personal trials raise soul-searching questions about her competence and her calling to teach. Should she serve in this teaching ministry? Or is God, in his omniscience, helping Jill develop patience? Is he teaching her flexibility?

These vignettes highlight three critical, interacting factors that are found in any educational setting.

1. *Heredity:* The first factor describes "at-birth," natural endowments (and limitations) related to human nature. They are fundamental to every classroom. This includes physical and psychological abilities; supernatural realities include sin tendencies and (for believers) spiritual regeneration at conversion. All gifts, natural and spiritual, are bestowed through the sovereign plan of God.
2. *History:* The second factor features matters related to background and past experiences. This includes previous learning as well as memories of people, places, and events. God's plan is also at work here, for his superintending activity over all creation affects each person's individual history.
3. *Here and Now:* The final factor emphasizes contemporary circumstances and learning contexts. What God is presently accomplishing takes on particular significance here, since it's the only factor teachers most often see (i.e., what is currently happening in their students' lives).

The potential for various combinations of these factors should remind us that *each learner is unique.* Awareness of these basic elements can help educators diagnose teaching-learning difficulties. They can also provide a relevant framework for educational planning. Each student comes to the classroom with a unique constellation of characteristics within the parameters of these factors. How well the teacher is able to teach largely depends on how well these factors are understood and addressed.

For example, there are a number of possible causes for a child's disruptive behavior:

1. *Heredity* (the child may have physical problems such as hyperactivity; a very young child may be frustrated by the lack of coordination skills necessary to use scissors)
2. *History* (the child may not have learned sufficient self-control; or, due to past abuse, the child may react to being touched by a classmate or by the teacher)
3. *Here and Now* (a bee may be chasing the child; spiritual warfare may be evident; or a student may experience an exciting, teachable moment)

No matter what the circumstances, God's sovereign activity reminds us that he is in control. Through all circumstances, he will bring glory to himself and he is good to his people. Romans 8:28 is the teacher's plumb line for keeping this bigger picture of teaching in perspective.

In this chapter and the next two, the emphasis is on how our students' *abilities* play a significant part in their learning, how their abilities influence their readiness for learning. Whatever human abilities we have are given to us by God ("Heredity"). Whether we fully develop and use these endowments largely depends on what has already occurred in our life journey ("History") and how we interact with our contemporary situation ("Here and Now"). Chapter 8 focuses on cognitive capacities, or how we develop in our *thinking abilities.* Chapter 9 outlines some key features of the self, or how we develop our *personality abilities.*

The remainder of this chapter touches on matters of "Heredity," with a concluding focus on the body that God has designed for us and related *physical abilities.* "Heredity" refers to the capacities God gives us at birth. In addition, for Christians, this includes the changes that take place in our nature at spiritual rebirth. Understanding these divine endowments helps us comprehend inherent possibilities and constraints for each learner. It would be foolish, for example, for us to pray that God would give us a third hand. It would be just as futile to request certain intellectual or spiritual gifts that God did not intend us to have.

## Created in God's Image

Basic to any Christian understanding of human nature is the crucial concept that everyone is created in the image of God (Gen. 1:26; James 3:9).[1] This distinction provides the potential to experience fellowship with God. Our uniqueness as "image-bearers" also made it possible for God to take on human form.[2] The incarnation of our Lord, the second person of the Godhead, affirmed the inherent value, goodness, and uniqueness of human nature, as originally ordained in the Garden of Eden (Gen. 1:31). Luke 2:52 records our Lord's own experience of growth on earth and the intricate processes of human development—from infancy to adulthood.[3] The manifold gifts and exceptional capabilities inherent in human nature are fully exhibited in the only perfect human,[4] the "last Adam" (1 Cor. 15:45)—Jesus Christ.

### Structure and Function

Hoekema (1986, pp. 68–73) suggests that being created in God's "image" encompasses both structural and functional dimensions. The *structural* dimension refers to our *hereditary capacities,* both material (e.g., muscular mobility of the body, brain) and immaterial (e.g., mind, will). The *functional* dimension refers to the *proper use* of these capacities according to God's purpose and will (e.g., speaking the truth in love rather than cursing). Thus, both "structural" and "functional" dimensions constitute the complementary features of our human nature.

Without the foundation of structure, there can be no function. And without proper functioning, people cannot fulfill their life purpose: to glorify God (1 Cor. 10:31). By way of illustration, a watch is created by its designer primarily to measure and register time. Secondarily, it functions as an attractive piece of jewelry. To use a watch for any other purpose than its designer intended (e.g., as a hammer or a toothbrush) yields poor results. Furthermore, it may permanently damage the watch, prohibiting it from fulfilling its legitimate purpose. Likewise, the structural endowments of humankind must be considered in accord with the functional purposes of the Great Designer.

### The Complexity of Human Nature

Our God, though existing as a trinitarian "being-in-fellowship," delights to incorporate diversity in unity throughout his creation. Besides his own being, we notice that "diversity in unity" is a primal characteristic of humans.

1. We are each singular and individual persons, yet we are made of immaterial (soul) and material (body) parts.
2. There is but one human race, though we were corporately created as male and female.[5]
3. We Christians live in this earthly realm, even though we're also citizens of the kingdom of God.
4. We exist as persons whose souls have been miraculously changed and are being renewed to new life eternal; yet we live in bodies that are undergoing decay toward death. We desire to live holy lives, yet we still sin.

Some of these tensions are only transitory. We need to change our myopic view to a wide-angle lens; we must shift from a ground level to a birds'-eye perspective. For example, the only way to get a sense of place and direction at a large shopping mall is to look at the mall directory. It details where each store is located. It shows the relationship of one store to another and of one elevation to the next. It also indicates where you are standing. When it comes to comprehending people—particularly who we are as teachers and learners—we must step back to see the larger picture. We must contemplate life from God's point of view. For instance, we can divide human history for Christians into four distinct periods of time (cf. Hoekema 1986, pp. 82–95; see Figure 7.1).

Augustine (b. A.D. 354), a scholar of the early church, offered the following famous phrases that pertain to these four historical periods to clarify humankind's relationship to sin. Though the phrases are a little tricky, they help us compare the distinctive feature of each of the four conditions.

A. Initial Condition: "able not to sin (and die)"
B. Fallen Condition: "not able not to sin"
C. Renewed Condition: "able not to sin"
D. Glorified Condition: "not able to sin"

Understanding these complementary categories assists our knowledge of human growth and learning. For example, for non-Christians, growth

### Figure 7.1
# Four Conditions: Christians in Transition

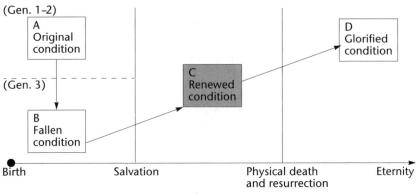

and learning take place in the fallen condition (B). For Christians, growth and learning occur in the renewed condition (C), with the realization that significant traces of our fallenness (Condition B, primarily relating to our bodies) remain until we enter the glorified condition (D).

### Try It Out

When we become Christians, we do not leave the human race. Even in the eternal state, we will still be human. Thus, some aspects of our nature remain the same, as we undergo transition from one condition to the next; other aspects of our nature change. That is, for the Christian, there is both *continuity* and *change* throughout our pilgrimage.

For each transition below (e.g., Condition A to Condition B), jot down one or two more specific *changes* that take place in human nature, and one or two more specific aspects that will *not* change. A few ideas have been included to get you started.

| Transition | Change | Continuity |
|---|---|---|
| Condition A → B | shorter life span | |
| Condition B → C | | babies conceived and born the same way (for believers and nonbelievers alike) |
| Condition C → D | new eternal bodies | |

There is evidence of both continuity and change in the transitions between each of the four conditions. Adam's or Eve's mind (Condition A) probably functioned in similar ways regarding knowledge and reasoning as it does for non-Christians (Condition B) and Christians (Condition C) today. Yet in some ways there are distinctions in mental processes, since non-Christian minds are now darkened toward God (Eph. 4:17–19), and Christian minds are being renewed (Rom. 12:2). With these transitions (from one condition to the next) certain changes take place, whether negative (e.g., from A to B) or positive (e.g., from B to C, and C to D).

Thus, Christians are *similar* to non-Christians in some ways (e.g., same physical body, same rational capabilities); yet we are *different* than non-Christians in certain *substantial* ways (e.g., the potential renewal that emerges from the power of the indwelling Holy Spirit). Metaphorically speaking, Christians live with one foot planted in both worlds: on the one side, with Condition B factors (e.g., a decaying body and continuing effects of our sinful dispositions) and, on the other, with Condition C factors (e.g., a mind being renewed; greater sensitivity to sinful actions). This thought is captured by Paul in 2 Corinthians 4:16: "Though outwardly we are wasting away, yet inwardly we are being renewed day by day." Believers must wait until the glorified state (Condition D) for a new kind of body (Rom. 8:20–23; 2 Cor. 5:1–4). [6]

## Patterns of Physical Development

"I praise you because I am fearfully and wonderfully made" (Ps. 139:14). As David contemplated God's creation of human beings (particularly the intricate and complex design of the physical body), he was overwhelmed with praise for God. No robotic machine can fully emulate all the mental faculties and motor skills God has given us. In the following section, key concepts about the marvelous gift of our bodies are discussed. Understanding the scope of our students' physical abilities and the various changes that occur helps us comprehend the inherent possibilities of, and constraints on, each student.

A study of our physical features also highlights the continuities and discontinuities of persons with the rest of God's creation. Some of our physical endowments are common to other creatures, such as the capacities to see and move. Other capacities are unique to humankind, like being created in the image of God. For example, we have received distinctive physical features like the twenty-eight subcutaneous facial muscles by which we are able to smile or frown (Cosgrove 1987, p. 30). Our vocal tract was designed specifically for the complexities of human speech (pp. 42–44).

An acorn will eventually become an oak tree, not an apple tree, strand of seaweed, or bird. The basic design is inherent within the seed, which will mature with proper nurture (e.g., sun, mineral-rich earth, water). In the same way, God has placed a design within the human seed. With appropriate nurturing, we will grow into mature adults. The word "growth" is best associated with the botanical sphere, conveying the imagery of progress dependent on the genetic code within the seed.[7] In each seed, both the *configuration* of the final adult form and the general *developmental pattern* (i.e., timing and sequence) toward that final form have already been determined. Within that configurational design there is great variability of form (e.g., height, weight, facial features, skin color, hair color, and eye color) and levels of physical ability.

In addition to this configuration, the maturational pattern deserves consideration. Both *sequence* and *time* are part of this pattern. Proper sequence dictates that adults must first be children. We experience fairly predictable bodily changes from birth to our senior years. These changes affect our mobility and capacity for action. For example, the onset of puberty around the age of twelve, a critical milestone of physical development, announces that adulthood (with all its potential) is just around the corner. This particular milestone involves both primary and secondary bodily changes. In addition, significant cognitive and personality factors emerge. It takes approximately fifteen to twenty years to reach the basic capabilities of adult functioning.[8]

As with the configurational design of the adult form, there is some variability in the timing of adult *functioning*. A positive, nurturing environment encourages human growth along "normal" chronology. But when growth has been slowed down, "abnormal" growth occurs. For example, a very negative and repressive environment may slow down growth so that some adult capabilities never reach optimum levels of functioning. This axiom is borne out by historical accounts of children who have grown up in wilderness settings or who have been deprived of human contact for long periods of time.[9]

## Application: Students with Special Educational Needs

In the class scenario described earlier, Scott's brain functioning was slightly dysfunctional. Some individuals are born with "slightly damaged equipment" (congenital in nature, either genetic or stemming from problems during prenatal development). Others may have their physical parts adversely affected *after* birth through severe accidents or disease (e.g., amputation of limbs, brain damage through drug abuse).

### Kinds of Physical-Structural Impairments

Some handicaps are more detrimental to human functioning than others. Table 7.1 lists the major categories of impairments that some learners face each day of their lives.[10] James Patridge, who lost both legs to a land mine in Vietnam, was able to race his wheelchair 180 feet, then crawl 60 feet on his chest before administering CPR to a one-year-old who had been pulled from a swimming pool (mentioned in chapter 1). For Scott, a student in Jill's class, medication would help him reduce his hyperactivity. In addition, early detection may prevent Scott from experiencing negative self-attitudes of failure and alienation, resulting from his disruptive behavior. Other handicaps (such as extreme mental retardation) set more permanent limits on intellectual functioning.

### Table 7.1
## Categories of Physical-Structural Disorders

**Communication**

- Speech disorders (e.g., speech that is difficult to understand, stuttering)
- Language difficulties (e.g., delayed language acquisition)

**Physical Health**

- Orthopedic handicaps (e.g., limited use of limbs, cerebral palsy)
- Health problems (e.g, asthma, diabetes, cystic fibrosis)

**Sensory**

- Visual impairment (blind: full or partial)
- Hearing impairment (deaf: full or partial)

**Mental Disorders**

- Limited intellectual functioning with varying degrees of impairment (usually three categories are used: educable mentally retarded—EMR; trainable mentally retarded—TMR; and severely or profoundly retarded)

*Source:* Adapted from Gage and Berliner (1992); Newman and Tada (1987); Seifert (1991).

Regardless of the particular disorder, our students are always capable of learning. As teachers, it's important to treat our students with respect and dignity—handicapped or not. All are fully human; all are vitally significant. Students will follow our example of how we relate to students with special educational needs. In the end, it is critical to realize that we value people, *not* on the basis of their function in society but because *all persons have been created in the image of God*—a distinctively Christian value.

In working with students, then, we need to know exactly how ready they are to learn. A professional assessment provides helpful information to guide appropriate educational experiences. Since Congress passed Public Law 94–142 in 1975, greater attention and resources have been focused on such special educational needs.[11]

---

### Try It Out

---

Many of us have experienced the "blind walk" activity in which one person with sight leads around a person who is blindfolded. This exercise is typically done in interpersonal or group dynamics classes to present the concept of trust. But this exercise also serves as an awareness activity to help sighted people understand in some measure how a blind person lives. In light of the kinds of disabilities identified in Table 7.1, can you think of educational experiences that would help students become more sensitive to persons with special needs? Jot a few ideas down; then try one out in the near future.

### We All Experience Some Limitations

All human bodies are subject to abnormalities in prenatal development, disease, aging, and eventually death and decomposition (Gen. 3:19; Rom. 5:12–14). Our years on this earth are limited. [12] The debilitating consequences of the curse have significantly affected our physical-structural capacities. From a biblical perspective, having unmarred bodily parts and functions is not an ultimate value. The critical issue is that, whatever our abilities, we should determine to bring glory to God. Although we may be limited by *structural* defects, we must strive to *functionally* demonstrate the dynamic work of God in our lives.

In a fallen world, God sovereignly allows a wide range of functional and dysfunctional bodily members for his own purpose (cf. Exod. 4:11; John 9:1–3). Yet regardless of the seemingly inequitable conditions of individual God-given capacities, each believer is called to confront stewardship responsibilities. The parable of the talents encourages believers to fully utilize what *has* been given, not to dwell on that which has *not*. Furthermore, this parable suggests the fair principle of God's assessment: each person is judged personally, based on what he or she started with—never in comparison with others who start out differently (Matt. 25:14–30; John 21:21–22).

In conclusion, despite these wonderful bodily endowments, Paul reminds us that we currently "groan inwardly" as we await "the redemption of our bodies" (Rom. 8:23). For ultimately our physical bodies will be changed. They are but temporary housing (cf. 2 Cor. 5:1–2). We will be clothed with immortality in glorified bodies (1 Cor. 15:52) as we enter a new state of existence (2 Pet. 3:13).

## Key Concepts and Issues

able and willing

continuity and change

   initial condition, fallen condition, renewed condition, glorified condition

development pattern—sequence and timing

Heredity, History, and the Here and Now

human nature

created  in the Image of God

physical development

physical-structural impairments/handicaps

    communication, physical health, sensory, mental disorders

Readiness for learning

special education

structural and function dimension

**L** evels
**E** xtent
**A** venues
**R** eadiness
**N** ature

# Developmental Changes
# in Our Thinking

**Qualitative Changes in Thinking**
**Thinking about Others**
**Growth in Moral Thinking**
**Application: Children and Conversion**

Children and adults think very differently—that's obvious. But have you ever wondered why? Is it just because children haven't been around long enough, that they don't know enough yet? Or is something else going on? To start this chapter, let's interview some children, teens, and adults, and compare their responses and insights.

Do you remember the choruses below? These two songs were once commonplace in children's ministry; some churches may still be using them. Read the words and try to summarize the main point of each chorus. What did the writer intend to say?

> Deep and wide, Deep and wide,
> There's a Fountain flowing deep and wide,
> Deep and wide, Deep and wide,
> There's a Fountain flowing deep and wide.
> —Herbert G. Tovey

> Climb, climb up sunshine mountain, Heav'nly breezes blow;
> Climb, climb up sunshine mountain, Faces all aglow.
> Turn, turn from sin and doubting, Looking to the sky;
> Climb, climb up sunshine mountain, You and I.
> —E. Pate

Compare your interpretations with the comments in Tables 8.1 and 8.2.[1] Notice the variation in responses, particularly between those of children's and those of teens' and adults'. In general, children's interpretations represent rudimentary perceptions and simple word pictures of *literal* reality. Teen and adult insights reveal more sophisticated, *figurative* connotations. You may wish to conduct your own interviews and see if these same findings are confirmed in your sample. Be sure to include one or two children, teenagers, and adults.

### Table 8.1
## Interpretations of "Deep and Wide" Chorus

#### Children

6 yrs. "It's a fun song about a big ocean."

9 yrs. "This is a fun song with motions. The 'deep' is about a waterfall falling off a rocky hill and everyone is looking; and the 'wide' is the ocean."

10 yrs. "Uh, it's talking about a spider—I don't know."

#### Teens

13 yrs. "This song doesn't mean much of anything, just a lot of motions."

15 yrs. "God is infinite, He is everywhere. God is so pure (the fountain)."

16 yrs. "That's probably the fountain of spiritual water, maybe the Holy Spirit."

#### Adults

42 yrs. "This is a good action song to get everybody loosened up. The word, 'river,' should be substituted for 'fountain,' because a river flows more so than a fountain."

45 yrs. "I take it as God's gracious nature and mercy, the fountain being the blood."

60 yrs. "It speaks of the love of God as being immeasurable. But even a good Buddhist could sing the same thing. It's not particularly a 'Christian' song."

### Table 8.2
## Interpretations of "Climb Up Sunshine Mountain" Chorus

#### Children

6 yrs. "I am climbing up a ladder to the sun. My face gets nice and warm from the sunshine."

7 yrs. "It means to climb up to Jesus, to Heaven by doing the right thing."

9 yrs. "I see a person climbing a mountain. He is carrying a stick because it is a rocky mountain. But he is singing a song and thinking of faces of all those people he knows."

**Teens**

13 yrs. "We are all climbing up this mountain where there is all this sun. And because [of this] . . . , the heavenly breezes are there to cool us off. When we climb we are to leave our sins behind and stop worrying."

15 yrs. "You are in the presence of God and all the sins don't matter. It's just peace and love and all that."

16 yrs. "It means that maybe if you shed light on your problems, they tend to go away or you see how small they can be."

**Adults**

23 yrs. "It talks about where Heaven is, you and I, where Christ is, I guess. Where God is. I don't know."

45 yrs. "It's figuratively speaking—it's like going to Heaven, a transit from earth to heaven; faces aglow because of the glory of heaven. We'd have turned from sin here on earth."

53 yrs. "I grew up in the church and this was a cute song with fun motions. I think it is a positive song, if not strictly theological."

The comments in Tables 8.1 and 8.2 illustrate how we tend to think at various age levels. The Bible verifies age differences in cognitive ability. Paul states, "When I was a child, I talked like a child, I thought like a child, I reasoned like a child. When I became a man, I put childish ways behind me" (1 Cor. 13:11). Paul implies that, for children, it is quite appropriate to talk, to think, and to reason like children. That is, *childlikeness* is not the same as *childishness*. The former speaks of acceptable behavior for children; the latter refers to unacceptable conduct, according to Paul's last phrase. Much more is expected of adults.[2]

## Qualitative Changes in Thinking

Though it's obvious that children and adults think differently, how can we best account for these variations? We know that, in the maturation process, a person's knowledge base expands—that there is a *quantitative* change. But we may not be aware that the *logic* of how that person thinks also changes—that there is an increase in complexity or a *qualitative* change. Based on the pioneering work of Piaget,[3] four general levels of qualitative reasoning have been identified. We all grow through these levels from birth to young adulthood.

A simplified illustration of Piaget's findings is described below, using the game of "Monopoly." Picture in your mind several people playing this game, people representing various cognitive stages. Contrast how each participant approaches the game.[4]

*Sensorimotor Period* (approximately birth through two years): Small children place houses, hotels, and dice in their mouths. They chew on the "Get out of jail free" card.

*Preoperational Period* (approximately two through seven years): Preschoolers play "at" "Monopoly," but intuitively make up their own rules. They can't understand the instructions. They have difficulty playing in turn. They can't exchange amounts of money (rents owed and money possessed). Generally, they fail to comprehend the goals of the game.

*Concrete Operational Period* (approximately seven through eleven years): School-aged children understand the basic instructions of the game—they are able to follow the rules. But they can't deal with hypothetical transactions. For example, they have difficulty with abstract concepts like mortgages, loans, and complex bargaining with other players.

*Formal Operational Period* (approximately eleven years and up): Teens and adults are no longer tied to concrete and tangible rules. They are able to engage in the complex, hypothetical transactions unique to each game.[5]

The point is that everyone understands and views life differently at various ages. The adult who is insensitive to this fact will not be able to work effectively with young children or teens.

One seminary student remembers how his mother wisely explained an important abstract concept in concrete terms that were more appropriate to his developmental level.

In about fourth grade I began to struggle with the word "love." I knew what "like" meant—I like my dog, my teachers. But this girl meant more to me, it must be "love." One day I asked my mom about how I could know if I was in "love." She gave the perfect "concrete" example that clearly established in my ten-year-old mind what true love was. She said, "Love is when you look forward to talking to a person as much as you like to look at Christmas toy catalogs." Oh, I didn't know it was that serious. Immediately I knew I wasn't in love, or even close.[6]

**Figure 8.1**

## Quantitative and Qualitative Mental Growth

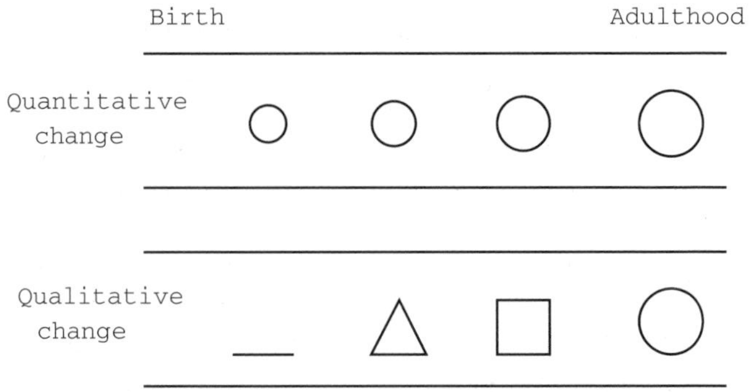

It's clear, then, that children do *not* think exactly like adults. Figure 8.1 portrays in a symbolic manner the difference between *quantitative* and *qualitative* change in cognitive capacities. Two series of shapes have been placed on a continuum, beginning with birth (on the left) and moving toward young adulthood (on the right). In the first row of symbols, the increasing circle size suggests that our understanding of previous information is proportionally enlarged. In the second row, the changing geometric shapes (from line to triangle to square to circle[7]) imply that each new stage of thinking introduces significantly new dimensions for processing information. Each stage represents a fundamentally different way of thinking. The technical definitions for this four-stage theory of qualitative cognitive development, advanced by Piaget, are provided in Figure 8.2.[8]

**Figure 8.2**
# Piaget's Stages of Cognitive Development

## ▬ *Sensorimotor Period* (birth–18 months/2 years)

Infants explore their world primarily through their sensory perceptions and motor activities—what Piaget called "practical intelligence." During these early years they develop various concepts (e.g., cause and effect, space and time, object permanence, a sense of self) and abilities (e.g., intentional behavior, symbolic representation of physical actions, rudimentary communication skills).

## △ *Preoperational Period* (approx. 2–7 years)

Toddlers and preschoolers begin to explore the world on a symbolic level: mental images, drawings, dreams, make-believe play, gestures, and language. Children imitate the activities of adults and thus learn to adjust to the world. In the latter part of this period, children's concepts are still fuzzy and somewhat confused—what Piaget calls "semilogical." For example, young children believe everything has a reason and a purpose, and that the whole world shares the same feelings and thoughts as they do.

## ☐ *Concrete Operational Period* (approx. 7–11 years)

School-aged children are capable of true "operational" thinking using concrete objects to organize and classify them mentally. Children can now master four mathematical operations: addition, subtraction (i.e., reversal of addition), multiplication, and division (i.e., reversal of multiplication). But thought is mainly limited to their own concrete, physical experiences.

## ◯ *Formal Operational Period* (appearing at approx. 11 years)

A new world of mental operations is open to adolescents: thinking about thoughts and ideas, not just concrete, physical objects. The beginnings of full adult reasoning powers become available so that adolescents can now consider abstract and hypothetical concepts, inductive and deductive logic, and the generation and testing of hypotheses.

*Source*: Piaget and Inhelder (1969); Pulaski (1980).

New ways of thinking appear at each age level. The change may be compared to shifting gears in a car with a manual transmission. The ratio of each gear differs to provide increased potential for power and speed. To move the engine to a desired upper level, the driver shifts to the subsequent gear. An appropriate order is followed: first, second, third, fourth, and overdrive.[9]

### Practice Increases Performance

In Piaget's research, a significant distinction is made between *capability* and *performance*. Although children and adults have the *capability* of a certain thinking level (the focus of Piaget's research), they may not regularly *perform* at that level. For example, just because someone owns a car does not mean that person can use that car to its greatest potential. This inability may be due either to a lack of training and experience, or because current circumstances do not demand or allow full use. If driving is restricted to the city, the driver may never use the overdrive gear. Full performance comes through regular practice in diverse settings.

The same is true with cognitive development. Although some adults have the potential to use complex levels of thinking (formal operations), they may actually employ a less sophisticated one (e.g., concrete operations). A similar point is suggested in Hebrews 5:14: "But solid food is for the mature, who by constant use have trained themselves to distinguish good from evil." The author held high expectations for his audiences' *capability*: "by this time you ought to be teachers" (v. 12a). But their *performance* was substandard: "you need someone to teach you the elementary truths of God's word all over again. You need milk, not solid food!" (v. 12b). Their performance indicated the poor stewardship of their capabilities.

Vygotsky (1986; cf. Tharp and Gallimore 1988) articulated a similar distinction but with a different twist, using the concepts of "assisted" and "unassisted" performance. Unassisted performance refers to what a student is able to do *without* the help of a teacher or others. A test usually evaluates this area of performance. Assisted performance is what a student is able to do *with* certain prodding and assistance from others. For example, consider this dialogue between a father and daughter (young Allison cannot find her shoes).

Dad:     Did you take them into the kitchen?
Allison:  Not in the kitchen.

Father:    Did you have them when you were playing in the den?

Allison:    Huh, I think in the den.

Allison has some information stored, but it's her father's questioning strategy that provides some organization for retrieval of that information. As she gets older, Allison may only need a single prompt from her dad (e.g., "Where was the last time you saw your shoes?") and she will conduct the interrogation strategy on her own. Later, she won't even bother her dad but will ask herself where she last saw her shoes.

Vygotsky suggests that the child's learning potential is in the region between the child's individual capacity and the capacity to perform *with* assistance, what he calls the "zone of proximal development" (ZPD). The ZPD is

> the distance between the actual developmental level as determined by individual problem solving and the level of potential development as determined through problem solving under adult guidance or in collaboration with more capable peers. The zone of proximal development defines those functions that have not yet matured but are in the process of maturation, functions that will mature tomorrow but are currently in an embryonic state. These functions could be termed the "buds" or "flowers" of development rather than the "fruits" of development (Vygotsky 1978, p. 86).

Employing this distinction, Tharp and Gallimore (1988) suggest that "*Teaching consists in assisting performance through the ZPD. Teaching can be said to occur when assistance is offered at points in the ZPD at which performance requires assistance*" (p. 31).

## Figure 8.4
## Progression Through the ZPD and Beyond

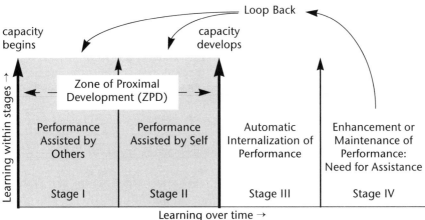

*Source*: Adapted from Tharp and Gallimore (1988, p. 35, Fig. 2.1).

Learning in this region of potential capacity involves the changing relationship from guided to internalized performance, involving four possible stages (see Figure 8.3). In Stage I, the teacher's or parent's task is providing sufficient assistance (e.g., through directions or modeling) for the child to accomplish the task. For example, Grace faces a bewildering array of puzzle pieces. The teacher may ask, "Which part of the puzzle would you like to start with?" And with follow-up praises and prods the puzzle is completed. On another occasion Grace may ask, "Which part do I use next?" Here, Grace provides clues to what kind of assistance is needed. In another setting in which David is stumped at solving a problem, a parent might say, "Okay, what else could you try?" When full responsibility for completing the task is taken on by the student, Stage I is completed.

Stage II does not imply that performance is internalized yet. The distinctive feature of the second phase is self-directed speech, in which the child accomplishes the task by prompting herself with comments previously supplied by adults, whether in spoken words or just in thought (e.g., "Go slow," "One at a time," "Be careful"). When a particular task can be accomplished "without thinking," the child has emerged from the zone of proximal development into Stage III, the developmental stage for that task—it is now developed. Here, task accomplishment becomes automatic (as in tying shoelaces or a bow); no real thought is necessary. "For every individual, at any point in time, there will be a mix of other-regulation [Stage I], self-regulation [Stage II], and automatized [Stage III] processes" (Tharp and Gallimore 1988, p. 38).

Stage IV involves a recurring loop back through previous stages either for improving and enhancing performance (e.g., learning to skate backwards), or for renewal of capacities once learned but now lost (e.g., relearning mathematical skills not used during the summer months). In the latter case, a child may only need to go back to Stage II—she can prompt herself regarding math computations. But if some assistance is needed, Stage I is involved. "In all these instances, the goal is to reproceed through assisted performance to self-regulation and to exit the ZPD again into a new automatization" (p. 39). In providing guidance for the child, "the adult graduates the assistance to the child's performance level: The more the child can do, the less the adult does" (p. 43).

## Try It Out

As teachers, we may actually hinder the full use of God-given mental abilities in our students. This occurs, for instance, when we give them the "right answers" at moments when they should think through the questions themselves. We circumvent their growth process. And we cannot assume that just because someone correctly recites a doctrinal statement that this assures full comprehension of its meaning. Several implications of these concepts could be drawn for teaching ministries with children and teens. Suggest some ideas for how to encourage their thinking with the following activities:

1. Question and answer exchanges

2. Bible memorization programs[10]

---

As Paul illustrates in 1 Corinthians 13:11, our students must move beyond childlike reasoning, especially in understanding God's word. Listen to the reflections of one high school student, following a later rereading of Herman Melville's novel, *Moby Dick:* "When I read this as a kid I thought it was just a neat whaling story: how to harpoon, the dangers of the sea. Now it seems different. Why is the Captain so obsessed with this whale? Does it have some special meaning?" (Sprinthall and Sprinthall 1990, p. 112).

Similarly, adults may assume they understand the primary messages of Scripture when, actually, they have only a cursory awareness. They may have regularly attended Sunday school as children. They may be acquainted with many Bible stories. Yet their comprehension of those stories is often based on elementary levels of thinking. They can recite verses and provide perfect definitions of key doctrines, but as adults, they may be unable to verbally defend their faith using Scripture. Furthermore, their lifestyle may exhibit little evidence of these divine truths. According to Paul, their "childlike" thinking remains, which for adults signifies "childish" perceptions.

Church leaders and teachers must help adult members upgrade their biblical comprehension at each new mental stage. This task is especially critical during the teen and young adult years. Throughout high school and college, young people are often forced to think about their faith from an adult perspective, and we teachers must prepare them for this challenge.

### Bible Versions and Cognitive Growth

One implication of cognitive development theory pertains to Bible versions. Selection of a Bible version should be based on relative reading levels.

---

### Try It Out

How accurately can you discern various reading levels? Daily newspapers are usually geared at about an eighth-grade reading level. Table 8.3 lists translations of Romans 12:16 from some common Bible versions.

1. See if you can guess:
   a. the reading level of each translation
   b. which Bible version is represented
   Clue 1: Reading levels range from third to the twelfth grade.
   Clue 2: The following five Bible versions are represented:

   International Children's Version (ICV)
   King James Version (KJV)
   New American Standard Version (NASV)
   New International Version (NIV)
   New King James Version (NKJV)[11]

2. Which Bible translation would you recommend as best for the public reading of Scripture? Why?
3. Which Bible translation would you recommend as best for:
   a. Youth? Why?
   b. Children who can read? Why?

---

**Table 8.3**

# Translations of Romans 12:16

A. Be of the same mind toward one another; do not be haughty in mind, but associate with the lowly. Do not be wise in your own estimation.
B. Live together in peace with each other. Do not be proud, but make friends with those who seem unimportant. Do not think how smart you are.
C. Be of the same mind one toward another. Mind not high things, but condescend to men of low estate. Be not wise in your own conceits.
D. Be of the same mind toward one another. Do not set your mind on high things, but associate with the humble. Do not be wise in your own opinion.
E. Live in harmony with one another. Do not be proud, but be willing to associate with people of low position. Do not be conceited.

---

One prominent contribution of the Protestant Reformers was their unswerving support of Bible translations in commonly spoken languages.[12] Today there are many excellent Bible versions suited to the varying mental abilities of children, youth, and adults.

In light of this overview, two areas are significantly influenced by cognitive development theory: *social perspective taking* and *moral thinking*.[13] To these implications we now turn.

## Thinking about Others

To sincerely love, we must be empathetic. We have to walk in other people's shoes—a process of social perspective or role-taking. Picture a mother resting on the sofa, suffering from an escalating headache.

Young Benji (age four) enters the room, vigorously beating the drum he received for his recent birthday. Benji's mother tells him that she has a headache, and asks him to stop playing the instrument immediately. Trying to relieve his mother's pain, the four-year-old proudly suggests that he play her a "pretty song." Her response is even more forbidding. Obediently, the youngster stops. Yet Benji fails to understand why his mother doesn't enjoy the drum sounds as much as he does. He leaves the room bewildered.

The more an individual can take the role of others, the quicker that person will accept others' perspectives. Summarizing the research literature, Hoffman (1977) proposes four phases of the development of social cognition when the "sense of other" emerges (notice the close connection with Piaget's theory in terms of similar concepts and approximate age ranges).

1. *At birth:* Babies view the world as extensions of themselves. Self and others are conceptually inseparable.
2. *During infancy:* Toddlers begin to recognize that others exist on a permanent basis, separate from themselves.
3. *During the childhood years:* Children start to realize that other persons have their own thoughts, feelings, and values distinct from their own.
4. *During adolescence:* Youth recognize that each person's thoughts, feelings, and other internal states are influenced by unique personal circumstances.

Although adults have the potential to reach fourth-level maturity, some habitually function at only the second or third level. These adults assume that others generally think as they do; that others solve problems the way they do. Since we are commissioned to share God's love, we must not underestimate our need to be "other-oriented," even if the other person does not solve problems or view life the way we do. To fail to do so may result in forfeiture of genuine ministry to others.

As a negative case in point, we may falsely presume that what a troubled friend needs is our good advice. In reality, what she needs is a listening, sympathetic ear. A husband may attempt to show love to his wife by buying her something special. After all, he reasons, *he* feels loved when *he* receives a gift. But his wife may prefer other expressions of love: an elegant dinner and quiet conversation, attending a play, or seeing a movie. We cannot assume that what meets *our* needs will necessarily meet the needs of *others*.[14]

In America, our tendency toward ethnocentrism (or cultural self-centeredness) intensifies the problem. For example, for the most part, we believe we need only one language, English, to adequately communicate with almost everyone. Yet most of humanity does not share this viewpoint. In many parts of the world, people must know two or three languages or dialects to speak with others in a neighboring town. Communicating in a foreign language forces individuals to think in thought forms that are unlike their own mother tongue.

A major goal of Christian teaching centers on helping students gain a divine perspective—to look at life the way God sees it. God's perspective includes the widest vantage point of all perspectives. By increasing our role-taking ability to become as empathetic as possible, we begin to live more compassionately in a sinful world. The incarnation of Christ represents God's ultimate role-taking posture. In love, he became one of us. Through this strategy Jesus became our sympathetic High Priest whom we can boldly approach (Heb. 4:15).

We grow in our social-thinking ability the more we experience and accept perspectives different from our own—within, of course, the parameters of a scriptural worldview. Therefore, we should promote activities that facilitate mature social thinking: role-playing exercises; developing friendships with those of another socioeconomic status; going to locations that provide diverse cross-cultural contexts; learning a foreign language; and sharing our faith with persons of different religious backgrounds.

---
### Try It Out
---

Listed in Table 8.4 are most of the "one another" verses from the New Testament.

1. Write one specific command from this list that was broken, based on your recent experiences. For example, have you observed a grumbling tongue? An unforgiving spirit? Gossip? Failure to encourage or thank someone?

2. Pick one or two verses that indicate areas of responsibility that may be lacking in your life. Ask God to provide you with the opportunities to personally apply these commands or to observe them being obeyed by other Christians.

---

## Growth in Moral Thinking

Can genuine moral development exist apart from God's divine work of regeneration? An affirmative response is indicated by the classic case of the rich young ruler (Luke 18:18–23). He had a respectable track record of moral behavior, a record that Jesus never challenged (though he may have been a little suspicious about it). The ruler had obeyed the law's "horizontal" (or moral) requirements. However, such obedience did

**Table 8.4**

# New Testament "One Another" Passages

Accept one another. (Rom. 15:14)
Be devoted to one another. (Rom. 12:10)
Be kind and compassionate to one another. (Eph. 4:32)
Be patient, bearing with one another. (Eph. 4:2; Col 3:12–13)
Carry each other's burdens. (Gal. 6:2)
Clothe yourselves with humility toward one another. (1 Pet. 5:5)
Confess your sins to each other. (James 5:16)
Don't grumble against each other. (James 5:9)
Do not lie to each other. (Col. 3:9)
Do not slander one another. (James 4:11)
Do what leads to peace and mutual edification. (Rom. 14:19)
Encourage one another. (Eph. 4:32; 1 Thess. 4:18; Heb. 3:13)
Forgive one another. (Eph. 4:32; Col. 3:13)
Have equal concern for each another. (1 Cor. 12:25)
Honor one another. (Rom. 12:10)
Live in harmony with one another. (Rom. 12:16; 15:5)
Love one another. (John 13:34)
Offer hospitality to one another. (1 Pet. 4:9)
Pray for each other. (James 5:16)
Serve one another in love. (Gal. 5:13)
Speak to one another with psalms, hymns, and spiritual songs. (Eph. 5:18–20;
    Col. 3:17)
Stop passing judgment on one another. (Rom. 14:13)
Spur one another on toward love and good deeds. (Heb. 10:24)
Submit to one another. (Eph. 5:21)
Teach and admonish one another. (Col. 3:16; Rom. 15:14)

not necessarily mean that "vertical" (or faith) obligations to God were satisfied. In other words, the "moral" domain does *not* fully equal the "faith" domain. This is apparent from the ruler's original motivation. By coming to Jesus, he acknowledged a spiritual void. Furthermore, moral growth does not deny God's involvement by any means. For moral maturity, even for the non-Christian, results from God's gifts of common grace. For example, we all possess his gracious gift of conscience (Rom. 2:15), a moral capacity to sense right and wrong.[15]

### *Content and Rationale*

In discussions of Christian morality within the evangelical church, we have tended to focus on the "right" answers with little concern for the reasoning behind those answers. Yet Scripture affirms that *why* we do (rationale) *what* we do (content) is just as significant (cf. Matt. 6:1–18). How people make choices about moral matters continues to interest social science researchers.[16] Kohlberg's (Kohlberg, Levine, and Hewer 1983) research into the psychology of moral judgments suggests that as we mature physically from childhood to adulthood, the reasons for our actions must also mature. The difference between these two concepts of "content" and "rationale" can be illustrated through the following interview responses:

**Interview #1—Daniel is six years old**
Interviewer: Daniel, should people tell lies to each other?
Daniel:       No. (Regarding *content* Daniel claims that lying is wrong.)
Interviewer: Why is it wrong to tell a lie?
Daniel:       Because if I get caught telling a lie, my parents will punish me. (*Rationale:* here Daniel attempts to avoid discipline.)

**Interview #2—Ruth is twenty-six years old**
Interviewer: Ruth, should people tell lies to each other?
Ruth:         No. (The same *content* as Daniel's response.)
Interviewer: Why is it wrong to tell a lie?
Ruth:         Because if I get caught telling a lie, my parents will punish me. (The same *rationale.*)

Ruth's response to the first question is appropriate. But her second response seems out of place for a twenty-six-year old. As we grow, although our beliefs and values, which include content (e.g., "Do not lie"), may not change much, our reasons why these beliefs and values are held *do need to change* (rationale). When teens and adults continue to use child-appropriate reasons they significantly hinder their growth in moral thinking.

### Aligning Lenses of Concern

What are appropriate reasons in moral decision-making at each stage of development?[17] Young children tend to exclusively consider their own needs and concerns. Then, in late childhood and the early teen years, in addition to personal concerns, adolescents attend to the approval of their peers. Finally, in adulthood, an additional third lens of concern emerges: being able to live by abstract moral principles. Thus, with each new stage of growth, we can potentially increase both the quantitative and qualitative factors that are necessary to evaluate each moral issue we encounter. But only with the complex, cognitive capabilities of adulthood are we able to hold in tension *all three* lenses of concerns in moral decision-making.[18] Figure 8.4 outlines the development of these emerging lenses from childhood through adulthood. The mature believer, then, should have an appropriate and balanced concern for self, others, and universal moral principles—all three being viewed within a divine perspective.

Teens and adults encounter problems when they focus exclusively on the concerns of "self" and "others," without regard for universal moral principles. For example, how might the "Golden Rule" be understood when consideration is restricted to just one or two lenses of concern? Table 8.5 lists these restricted perspectives, followed by scriptural illustra-

**Figure 8.4**

# Lenses of Moral Growth

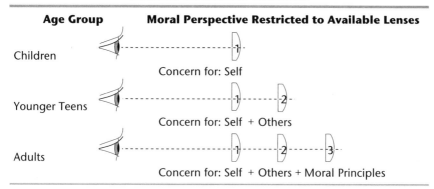

| Age Group | Moral Perspective Restricted to Available Lenses |
|---|---|
| Children | Concern for: Self |
| Younger Teens | Concern for: Self + Others |
| Adults | Concern for: Self + Others + Moral Principles |

*Note:* 1. With each new life phase, a new lens capability emerges.
2. Teachers must customize God's truth so it can be understood within the students' lens capability.

*Source:* Adapted from Kohlberg (1981); Lickona (1983); Ward (1989).

tions of each view. Remember, it is normal for children and young teens to focus on self and others, respectively, due to their limited cognitive capabilities. But these restrictions do not apply for mature teens and adults.

The examples in Table 8.5 indicate that, although actions might be perceived by others as being good, what may be an appropriate rationale for a child may be totally inappropriate for a teen or adult. Another implication: the number of lenses of concern we regularly consider in our decision-making affects our interpretation of Bible passages and understanding of moral messages. A pastor may preach a sermon on the "Golden Rule," emphasizing universal moral principles, but members of the congregation will comprehend the message within their own thinking patterns, as illustrated in Table 8.5.

**Table 8.5**

# Lenses of Moral Growth Focusing on "Self" and "Others"

**Exclusive Focus on Me**

*Perspectives appropriate for children:*

"I will do what I like to do since everyone else would do the same thing if they were in my shoes."

"Let's make a deal: I will do this for you if you do this for me."

*Scriptural case of inappropriate adult perspectives:*

John 12:3–8: Judas claimed that the money used to purchase expensive perfume should have been given to the poor. He wasn't concerned about the poor but about the disciples' treasury since he regularly stole money from it.

Mark 7:9–13: Jesus castigated the religious leaders for the deceptive practice of "dedicating" their possessions to God ("Corban") so they could set up a life estate for themselves while avoiding the obligation to provide for the needs for their aged parents (dedicated property could not be used for secular purposes) (cf. also I Tim 5:8).

### Exclusive Focus on Self and Others

*Perspectives appropriate for younger teens:*

"If everybody in the group does it, then I will do it too."

"I try to put myself in your shoes and do what would be best for you--whether the action itself is right or wrong."

*Scriptural cases of inappropriate adult perspectives:*

Matt. 6:2: Jesus claimed that the religious leaders gave to the poor, not to please God, but to show off and to build up a reputation among the people.

Acts 4:36–5:11: Ananias and Sapphira, apparently in order to copy the example of Barnabas and to gain the acclaim of the early church, pretended to give the full proceeds of a sale, when they had actually kept back a part.

Our goal as educators, then, is to help teen and adult believers align all *three* lenses of concern as they make moral decisions.[19] Table 8.6 provides some examples related to finances. Ideally, harmony is possible among the three lenses because God's truth is not ultimately opposed to our concerns for ourselves, for others, or for universal moral principles. Even in difficult situations, we can experience the harmony of God's truth among the three lenses. Compare the example of Daniel's three companions (Dan. 3) and Peter and John (Acts 4:1–31). Just as an optometrist aligns various lenses to help us see clearly, so we need to align all three lenses of concern to gain a clear perspective on God's truth.

## Application: Children and Conversion

More thought needs to be given to our theological understanding of the child's salvation experience. The evangelical church's standard, for the most part, has been the adult "crisis" conversion model. We have often valued examples of people who dramatically shift allegiances from a secular to a Christian culture (just look at the types of public testimonies we honor in public). We employ this model because it is typically presented in the New Testament. Yet virtually no guidelines exist in the New Testament for how children—those who grow up in the church—should come to faith. The experience of Timothy, reared in a Jewish home, is the only explicit biblical reference to an individual who received childhood nurture (2 Tim. 1:5; 3:14–15).

Although children, like any other age group, must make a conscious, age-appropriate decision to place their faith in God, the ideal is for a child to grow up developing "Christian" character *before* and *after* a per-

**Table 8.6**

# Aligning Three Lenses of Moral Growth with God's Truth

Peter claimed that Ananias and Sapphira were free to keep their money or give it for the needs of the saints, but by claiming to give more than they actually did they lied to the Holy Spirit. (Acts 5:3–5)

Believers who benefit from those teaching God's word should financially support these teachers. (Gal. 6:6; 1 Tim. 5:17–18)

"Do not be deceived: God cannot be mocked. A man reaps what he sows." "Whoever sows sparingly will also reap sparingly, and whoever sows generously, will also reap generously." (Gal. 6:7 and 2 Cor. 9:6)

God's grace was manifest in the sacrificial giving of the (mostly Gentile) Macedonian believers (Philippi, Thessalonica, and Berea) that, despite their poverty, they made a generous contribution for the poor in Jerusalem. (2 Cor. 8:1–5, cf. Rom. 15:26; Acts 24:17)

Based on Christ's example of gracious self-less giving, Paul urges the (mostly Gentile) Corinthian believers to complete the generous commitment they had previously made to collect additional money for the poor in Jerusalem. In the future, these Jewish saints may be able to help the Corinthians in their need. (2 Cor. 8:6–15; 9:5; cf. Rom. 15:26, Acts 24:17)

God loves cheerful givers. (2 Cor. 9:7)

sonal decision is made for salvation in Jesus Christ.[20] In other words, even prior to a public decision for Christ, parents and teachers should encourage children to develop virtuous character qualities.

We need to view salvation as encompassing many developmental phases over time. It is not just a "one-time" decision, nor is it several totally distinct "conversions." Rather, like any significant commitment, there is both a point of original commitment as well as subsequent affirmations. Given age-level differences, these follow-up decisions represent, in some sense, fresh and new choices. As a biblical case in point, we can be fairly certain that the faith expressed by young Timothy did not suffice for Timothy as an adult. To use an illustration, age-level commitments (and subsequent affirmations) for Christ cannot be compared to the dispassionate and mundane renewal of a driver's license every few years. It is far more comparable to a growing and healthy marriage relationship.[21]

Listen to the concerns of one mother as she anticipates what lies ahead for her two children who just received Jesus Christ as Savior. Her daughter is five and her son is three.

> While I was as touched as any mother would be at this momentous occurrence, doubts cast a shadow on the delight of my joy. *They're so young. Will this decision stick? When she's twelve, will she even remember this moment?*

*When he hits sixteen, will he pull away in defiance, negating the reality of what happened here?* How could I help them recall this moment with the sincerity and unswerving commitment only a child could bring to it? (Morgan 1991).

The immediate family is not alone in this responsibility. The nuclear family and the church family must work together in supporting this important spiritual journey. By cooperating with God's grace operating in children and teens, we can corporately participate in nurturing growth toward an "adult" faith. Table 8.7 suggests several occasions when children, teens, and young adults might be publicly recognized.[22] In this way, we provide them with spiritual milestones so that their journey does not become stagnant.[23] Positively stated, these growth markers express respect for developmental distinctives.

## Table 8.7
## Corporately Nurturing Faith in Children

| Phase | Minimum Age | Preparation/ Instruction | Ceremony |
|---|---|---|---|
| One "Family" Reception | Part 1: During first year | Parenting class for parents and grandparents | Infant baptism or Parent/ Child Dedication |
| | Part 2: Near age of accountability | Church leaders interview child and parent | White carnation placed at front of auditorium |
| Two: "Family" Presentation | Start of elementary school | Church orientation class for child and parents | Child baptism or First communion |
| Three: "Family" Affirmation | Start of high school | Doctrine or Catechism class | Adult baptism or Public testimony |
| Four: "Family" Commissioning for Service | Start of college or career | Vocational class perspectives | Commissioning/ Laying on of hands |

*Note:* Although *minimum* ages are given and children or teens may be taught in a class setting, progression through these phases is dependent on the initiative of the child or teen.

Four major life phases are linked with five public ceremonies. Each phase relates to significant times of potential spiritual commitment. Each phase includes a preparation class for instruction. In every phase the teacher's complementary purpose is twofold: to help participants realize their respective *private* commitments; and to help them understand the aims and events of the *public* ceremony. The latter includes roles for church leaders, parents, children, and teens. Even the congregation plays an important part. Since church traditions vary as to when baptism should occur, this important event will be included in all three of the first phases.[24]

In Phase 1, *"Family" Reception,* the child is initially received by the church family for corporate nurture through an infant baptismal or a parent-child dedication service.[25] At the ceremony, the congregation is challenged to encourage and support the parents as they commit themselves to disciple the child. This life phase concludes when the child personally accepts Jesus Christ as Savior.[26] At that time, a white carnation is set on the pulpit or platform just as the red rose had earlier announced the physical birth. The "second" birth of the child is thus symbolized.

*"Family" Presentation* is the motif of Phase 2. Following a preparation class for family members, the child is presented to the church "family" in a special way. The significant spiritual milestone here can be indicated by childhood baptism and/or the child's first participation in the Lord's Supper—the family meal. Following the ceremony, the child is encouraged to become involved in ministry and to begin exercising his or her spiritual gift(s).

Phase 3, taking place sometime in midadolescence, focuses on *"Family" Affirmation.* The necessity for some kind of "affirmation" of faith during adolescence stems from the new cognitive capacity (formal operations) now available—full adult thinking. For example, some churches withhold key responsibilities of membership from children (particularly voting privileges) until the midteen years for related reasons. Why not formalize this important rite of passage and link it with an intensive period of instruction?[27] Thus, the teen becomes a member of the church in full standing, with all its rights and responsibilities. At this special ceremony, teens publicly indicate their faith in God through believers' baptism or personal testimony. Continuing responsible ministry involvement is encouraged.

In preparation for this milestone, teens are challenged to transform their "childhood" understanding of basic doctrine into "adult" forms of comprehension. Remember that young people are radically changing how they think. They possess new high-technology equipment: the capability of "abstract" adult reasoning. They may claim they already know what we are teaching them from the Bible—but we must always remain somewhat skeptical. At this time, it is important for us to guide teens to *convert*[28] their biblical "childhood" data into "adult" data. Youth who have been reared in the church do not need a lot of new information. Rather they need

- to be challenged to think for themselves
- to reflect on the implications of their Bible knowledge
- to dialogue with peers and adults to crystalize their views
- to act out their "adult" beliefs

In Phase 4 young adults commit themselves, in a public manner, to serving the Lord, regardless of the specific vocation they will enter. Diligent study of God's truth and intentional personal reflection precedes this moment: the *"Family" Commissioning for Service* ceremony.[29] Each of these corporate services yields blessings for the entire membership. Not only are first-time participants challenged to grow, but every ceremony offers an occasion of faith reaffirmation for each member.[30]

In this chapter we have described normal patterns of development for growth in our thinking capabilities. Children learn best when we work at their level of capability. Notice how God works with us, regarding the trials he allows in our lives: "No temptation has seized you except what is common to man. *And God is faithful; he will not let you be tempted beyond what you can bear.* But when you are tempted, he will also provide a way out so that you can stand up under it" (1 Cor. 10:13). God knows just the right amount of trial commensurate with our ability. Can we do any less in working with our students? Yet, too often, students are not fully employing the cognitive skills they have. Inhibited cognitive growth is evident through shallow thinking. As teachers, we must encourage our students to move beyond the sometimes painful barriers that so easily limit their full potential to become mature, intelligent adults.

## Key Concepts and Issues

aligning lenses of concern in moral decision-making

assisted and unassisted performance

capability and performance

childhood conversion and cognitive thinking

childishness and childlikeness

content and rationale

corporate ceremonies for nurturing children's faith to adulthood

ethnocentrism

Kohlberg's theory of moral thinking

moral thinking

Piaget's theory of cognitive development

    sensorimotor, preoperational, concrete operations, formal operations

quantitative and qualitative change

Readiness for learning

reading levels and Bible versions

"sense of other"

social perspective taking

Vygotsky's zone of proximal development

**L** evels
**E** xtent
**A** venues
**R** eadiness
**N** ature

---

# Mapping Our Personality Growth

---

**Features of Personality**
**Patterns of Personality Growth**
**Application: How Willing and Able Are Students?**
**Conclusion**

Our students are constantly "coming and going." They portray the ebb and flow of human development. Specifically, they "come" to us as persons with distinctive personality characteristics, talents, and learning histories. And they are "going"—moving forward in their spiritual pilgrimage. Since they share several common traits of being human, we can predict many of the experiences they will face. Yet, as their teachers, we must always appreciate the uniqueness of their private journey on the road of life.

This chapter looks at the developing self. What are the key aspects of personality? Multiple theories have been espoused concerning patterns of personality development; a few of the more prominent proposals are analyzed here.

## Features of Personality

Various terms describe the immaterial part of our being: the soul,[1] the self, and the personality represent three common terms. Each refers to the synthesis of all characteristics that uniquely constitute a person, aside from the body. Each individual has a variety of capabilities, clustered into faculties, that typically include the mind, the will, and the emotions. In this section, we look at two broad components of personality: *identity* and *temperament*.

### Identity

"Who am I?" Whether we know it or not, we constantly confront this question from childhood to adolescence to adulthood. A famous wood carver was once asked how he knew what to cut from the wood block, as he carved a life-sized statue. He said that he cut away whatever did *not* belong and left what *did*. Throughout life, everyone participates in the same task: we determine what should belong to our identity and what should not.

We enter life as "undifferentiated" infants; we sincerely believe that the world is an extension of ourselves. Personality growth involves a life-long "differentiation" process. As believers, we strive to balance the competing tensions of *clinging* to mature facets of self while *letting go* of immature and sinful aspects.[2] Jesus notes this struggle when he says, "If anyone would come after me, he must deny himself and take up his cross and follow me. For whoever wants to save his life shall lose it, but whoever loses his life for me and for the gospel will save it" (Mark 8:34–35).[3]

The essence of personality development, then, is creating a sense of who we are, distinct from those with whom we live, work, and play (parents, relatives, church members, teachers, etc.). This task is never easy and is ever-present. In light of these facts, it should be reassuring to realize that a Christian perspective on personality development incorporates additional help in this complex and important task. We need not grow alone. As we are obedient to the revealed truths of Scripture, as we are responsive to other believers, each of us grows in a unique *partnership with God*. Notice the interchange between the personal pronoun, "I," and Christ, regarding Paul's testimony of his own personality growth: *"I have been crucified with Christ and I no longer live, but Christ lives in me. The life I live in the body, I live by faith in the Son of God, who loved me and gave himself for me"* (Gal. 2:20). On the basis of this mysterious union with Christ each believer grows toward maturity. And, again, our growth as persons also takes place within a community of believers—the body of Christ—who aspire to love and guide us in righteous living (Col. 3:12–17).

Our self-image plays a significant role in our sense of identity. In developing a healthy self-image, Hoekema challenges us to avoid two extremes. "Man's self-image is sometimes inordinately high (in the form of sinful pride) or excessively low (in the form of feelings of shame or worthlessness)" (1986, p. 104). In response to the first extreme of sinful pride, God "helps us cultivate true humility. This includes, among other things, an honest awareness of both our strengths and weaknesses, so as to give us a realistic image of ourselves" (p. 106).

In response to a "woe is me" perspective stemming from the second extreme, Hoekema suggests that three interwoven concepts lay a foundation for developing a positive self-image: God's forgiveness, our daily growth through the sanctifying work of the Holy Spirit, and our status as new creatures who live in a new era of life. Hoekema cautions: "The Christian self-image is never an end in itself. It is always a means to the end of living for God. . . . It delivers us from preoccupation with ourselves and releases us so that we may happily serve God and love others" (p. 111).[4]

### Temperament

Temperament includes the inclinations that significantly influence how a person feels and acts.[5]

Buss and Plomin (1984) suggest that temperament can best be described in light of three broad concepts: emotionality, activity, and sociability. "Emotionality equals distress, the tendency to become upset easily and intensely" (p. 54). This distress is differentiated into two aspects that affect behavior: fear and anger. Activity includes three distinct factors: tempo (pace and activity), vigor (force of physical movement and volume of vocalizations), and endurance (a measure of time) (Ratcliff 1993, p. 18). Sociability is the preference to be with others over being alone. Buss and Plomin (1984, p. 63) list five intrinsically social rewards that motivate our sociability: presence of others, sharing an activity, attention, responsivity, and initiation. Combinations of these broader three elements (emotionality, activity and sociability) yield diverse personality types that we observe every day in our interaction with others.

We often forget that Paul and Barnabas experienced a serious interpersonal conflict, noted in the latter part of Acts 15. Their debate focused on John Mark. Paul thought John was unqualified for their second missionary trip since he had given up so easily on the first journey (see Acts 13:13). On the other hand, Barnabas saw potential in Mark. For him, Mark was well worth the risk. Ironically, Barnabas had spotted the same potential in Paul years earlier (Acts 9:26–27).

Who was right? In such cases, conflict is amoral. Neither right nor wrong exists. Each position portrays a direct consequence of alternate perspectives. Besides perspectives, spiritual gifts play a part in such struggles. Paul's gifts were more task-oriented and Barnabas' were more people-oriented. These men resolved this stressful dispute by organizing *two* missionary teams (Acts 15:39–40). That is, they agreed to disagree; they agreed to get on with God's work, although their strategies were different.

---

### Try It Out

---

How do we deal with conflicts among colleagues (or students dealing with students)? Are there effective ways to handle disagreement?
   A. Consider a few conflict-resolution *strategies*:
      1. Attack opponents as trouble-makers.
      2. Defend oneself at all costs and eventually come out on top as the winner.

3. Completely withdraw from the conflict and quit, if necessary.

4. Outwardly give in to opponent's demands, but inwardly retain anger and hurt.

B. Which of these strategies predominantly describes your approach to dealing with conflict over things that matter to you? Why do you tend to use this strategy? Have you tried alternate means?

---

Various personality or social style instruments[6] help us comprehend the attention we give to either "task concerns" or "people concerns." In addition to these emphases, some individuals possess a more "take charge" manner ("tellers"), while others prefer to come at problems by raising tough questions ("askers"). Thus, four basic patterns of personality styles emerge: analytical (beaver), driver (lion), expressive (otter), and amiable (golden retriever). This popular four-factor temperament theory suggests guidelines for improving our working relationships. Understanding temperament patterns (of ourselves and others) steers us away from unnecessary conflict. The relationships between these four types are diagrammed in Table 9.1.

### Table 9.1
## Motivational Patterns of Temperament

**Emphasis on Task—Controls Emotion**

| | Analytical: How? | | Driver: What? | | |
|---|---|---|---|---|---|
| | Strengths: | Weaknesses: | Strengths: | Weaknesses: | |
| "Asks" | • Industrious | • Critical | • Strong-willed | • Pushy | "Tells" |
| | • Persistent | • Indecisive | • Independent | • Severe | |
| | • Serious | • Stuffy | • Practical | • Tough | |
| | • Exacting | • Picky | • Decisive | • Dominating | |
| | • Orderly | • Moralistic | • Efficient | • Harsh | |
| | Amiable: Why? | | Expressive: Who? | | |
| | Strengths: | Weaknesses: | Strengths: | Weaknesses | |
| Slow-er Pace | • Supportive | • Conforming | • Ambitious | • Manipulative | Faster Pace |
| | • Respectful | • Unsure | • Stimulating | • Excitable | |
| | • Willing | • Pliable | • Enthusiastic | • Undisciplined | |
| | • Dependable | • Dependent | • Dramatic | • Reacting | |
| | • Agreeable | • Awkward | • Friendly | • Egotistical | |

**Emphasis on Relationships—Emotes**

*Source:* Adapted from Merrill and Reid (1981); Phillips (1985).

The college class at First Church has its share of ups and downs, like other classes. Personality clashes are part of its landscape, even among the leadership team. For example, Johann and George don't see eye to eye. George thinks Johann doesn't listen, and that he makes decisions too quickly. Johann thinks George doesn't stand up for his convictions; he's too sensitive to people's opinions. Whenever there's a problem to resolve,

George insists on convening a task force to study the issue first. Johann thinks committees are a waste of time; "committee accomplishment" is an oxymoron, he says. From this single case, it's not difficult to see how particular conflicts, even among believers, can run deep.

The four-part temperament grid explains why Johann (a strong *lion*) tends to offend others. He focuses on *what* needs to be done. People like him overturn any opposition to finish the job. We need such people to move us into action—to move beyond talking to doing. Their ability to make quick decisions is especially critical in times of emergency.

Amiable *golden retrievers,* like George, exhibit the exact opposite motivation. They sensitively determine *why* we do the job we do. They make sure all opinions are considered; they're cooperative and loyal. These types of people model good teamwork. But, in conflict, they would rather switch than confront. And that approach expresses both positive and negative features.

Expressive *otters* are more alert to *who* is involved. They like to be with people. They are great motivators. They encourage us. We need their kind words, their hopeful spirits, and their helpful affirmation. One downside is that they let important details fall through the cracks. Finally, analytical *beavers* want to know *how* the job will get done. They are our critical mindset. They ask the tough questions. We need their quality-control emphasis. But they can tend to be too critical and very slow to make decisions. To help us look at the four styles from another angle, Table 9.2 contrasts the differences in humorous form.

### Table 9.2
## Four Different Perspectives

*Getting on an elevator:*

The Driver walks up, gets on the elevator, pushes the button, and the door closes.

The Expressive lets others in, says "always room for one more," and "come in, you're going to be late; we'll wait for you."

The Amiable will wait in line, but if it's late, will take the stairs.

The Analytical will get on the elevator, but if it's crowded, he will count the number of people, and if the number is over the limit, will make someone get off.

*Shopping for groceries:*

The Driver is an impulse shopper. No list. They are sometimes almost through the checkout line when they walk back to get two items they forgot.

The Expressive can tell you where everything is in the store, whether you ask or not.

The Amiable is prepared, has a list, and gets the task done as quickly as possible.

The Analytical brings coupons and a calculator to make sure they're getting the best deal.

*Hanging wallpaper:*

The Driver says, "Come over Saturday and help me wallpaper. And bring the paste." He starts in the middle of the living room. The patterns don't match. He says, "So what, that's what drapes and pictures are for."

The Expressive has the wallpaper in the closet with the paste. It's on a list of things to do. He never gets around to it.

The Amiable starts in the corner of the guest bedroom, gets finished, and cleans up his tools.

The Analytical starts in a closet or in the garage to be sure the pattern is going to match. He gets it exactly right before he starts on the living room.

*Reading a newspaper:*

The Driver reads mainly the headlines. Good luck if they get to the paper before the rest of the family. They'll scatter it and you'll never find some of the sections.

The Expressive will first read the obituaries to see if they know anyone. Then it's Ann Landers, and human interest stories.

The Amiable looks over the entire paper. They cut and save interesting articles and sometimes entire issues.

The Analytical calls the newspaper if they find an error. They also are great at spotting coupons in ads and can tell you where the sales are in town.

Source: Unknown.

This four-part framework offers teachers one model for knowing what holds the attention of different learners. For example, the driver needs to know what the main purpose of the lesson is (early on) as well as how the lesson fits in with personal goals; the expressive student relishes stories and illustrations; the amiable learner appreciates personal remarks about the teacher's own experiences; and the analytical person requires appropriate, factual substantiation for general statements or principles.

Figure 9.1 suggests the distinctive emphases that teachers from each style contribute. Ultimately, we need the benefit that every person offers. We need all styles providing balanced direction. If we understand our own tendencies, it is easier to prevent potential interpersonal frustrations. We also curtail unnecessary conflicts by realizing how our words and actions are often misunderstood through a different set of perceptions. Furthermore, as we understand the personalities of others, we put ourselves in their shoes. We look beyond our private viewpoints. By checking any selfish reactions, we begin the reconciling process of working toward mutually agreeable solutions.

## Try It Out

Review the four extreme ways to resolve conflict and match them with their respective behavior style:

(1) Attack opponents as trouble-makers.

## Figure 9.1
# Complementary Teacher-Leader Styles

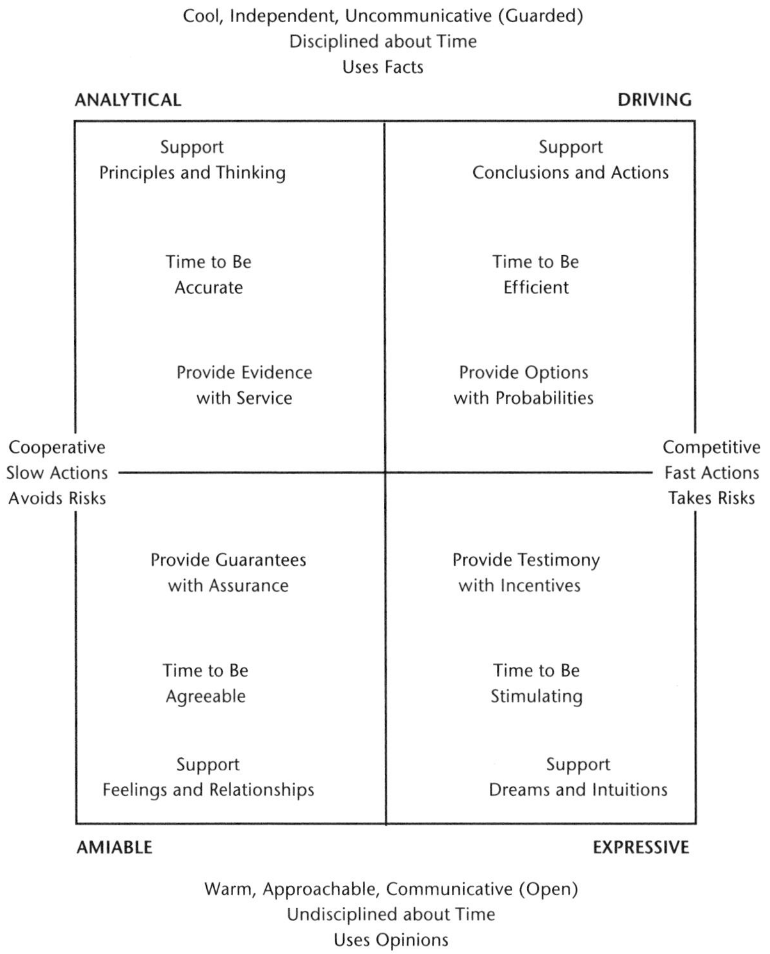

Cool, Independent, Uncommunicative (Guarded)
Disciplined about Time
Uses Facts

| ANALYTICAL | DRIVING |
|---|---|
| Support Principles and Thinking | Support Conclusions and Actions |
| Time to Be Accurate | Time to Be Efficient |
| Provide Evidence with Service | Provide Options with Probabilities |

Cooperative — Slow Actions — Avoids Risks ——————————— Competitive — Fast Actions — Takes Risks

| | |
|---|---|
| Provide Guarantees with Assurance | Provide Testimony with Incentives |
| Time to Be Agreeable | Time to Be Stimulating |
| Support Feelings and Relationships | Support Dreams and Intuitions |

| AMIABLE | EXPRESSIVE |
|---|---|

Warm, Approachable, Communicative (Open)
Undisciplined about Time
Uses Opinions

*Source*: Adapted from Gangel (1989, p. 24).

(2) Defend your viewpoint at all costs and come out as the winner.

(3) Withdraw completely from the conflict or quit.

(4) Outwardly give in to opponent's demands, but inwardly avoid resolution.

_____Beavers—Analyticals?

_____Golden retrievers—Amiables?

_____Lions—Drivers?

_____Otters—Expressives? [7]

Since we can observe characteristic traits in young infants (Goldsmith 1983), is temperament given to human beings at birth?[8] It appears that, just as God assigns natural talents to everyone (as well as spiritual gifts to Christians), he also provides each individual with a unique temperament. But there is a balance: on the one hand, temperament is largely grounded in our inherited nature; on the other hand, how we express our temperament is influenced by our experiences. For example, to what extent is our temperament influenced by environmental factors? As believers—though we have different inclinations—we each must still "keep in step with the Spirit" (Gal. 5:25) so that we avoid such unnecessary conflicts.

## Patterns of Personality Growth

In this final section, a few analytical tools are discussed that help us understand diverse patterns of development, primarily within American culture. These various theories offer a broad map of our students' journeys—both where they've been and where they're going. Since sufficient commonality among human beings exists, it is possible to identify issues and concerns that most persons experience at some point in time.

But certain cautions should also be raised. First, these theoretical patterns are not blueprints. They are broad, not precise. Also, they are not meant for everyone, but for most people. Third, each pattern tends to be culture-specific; so our focus aims at the predominant culture within the United States and Canada.[9] As you read about each pattern, keep your particular students in mind. Identify specific areas or needs that they have, in light of each theory.

### Needs to Be Met along the Journey

It's obvious that basic needs affect learning. In fact, the more basic the need the more impact it makes. For example, it's hard for students to concentrate on taking a test when they are very hungry. And it's next to impossible to focus on any school work if a life-threatening situation is disturbing learners (e.g., an earthquake, a fire). Certain basic needs must be met before students are receptive to learning—especially concentrated thinking. This fundamental idea has been formally organized by Maslow (1968, 1987) into a theory specifying a hierarchy of needs (see Figure 9.2).

The eight need-stages (Hamachek 1990, pp. 57–61) can be viewed chronologically or sequentially: people grow through different stages, beginning at the base; each stage is dominated by a particular set of needs. Before a higher stage emerges and becomes dominant, the peak of the previous stage must be passed. Maslow's theory can also be used as a practical tool to analyze a point in time in the learner's life. In this way teachers are encouraged to make sure the deficiencies of lower needs are

## Figure 9.2
# Maslow's Hierarchy of Needs

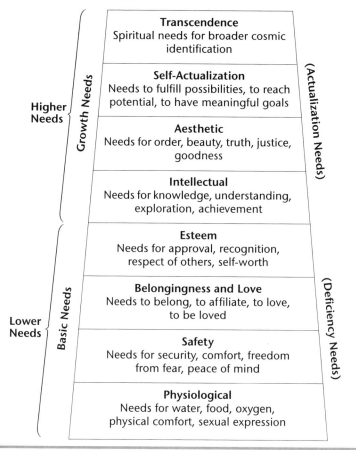

*Source:* Hamachek (1990, p. 58).

met, in order for students to attain greater growth at the higher needs. For example, when students don't feel accepted or safe it is difficult to attend to needs of knowing or self-actualization. If students are making progress at these higher growth stages, they will most likely continue in that direction.

### Crises along the Journey

Life involves trials and conflicts. James 1:2 encourages us to welcome trials because, by going through them successfully, we can mature. Erikson (1963) posited that everyone confronts eight particular sets of psychosocial crises over their lifespan, from infancy to old age (see Table 9.3[10]). According to Erikson, if a person does not resolve each crisis in a positive manner, that particular challenge continues to hinder subsequent personality growth.

### Table 9.3
## Erikson's Psychosocial Stages

| Period | Psychosocial Crisis | Resulting Virtues or Vices |
|---|---|---|
| Infancy: | Trust vs. Mistrust | Hope vs. Withdrawal |
| Toddlerhood: | Autonomy vs. Shame & Doubt | Will vs.Compulsion |
| Preschool: | Initiative vs. Guilt | Purpose vs. Inhibition |
| School Age: | Industry vs. Inferiority | Competence vs. Inertia |
| Adolescence: | Identity vs. Identity Confusion | Fidelity vs. Repudiation |
| Early Adulthood: | Intimacy vs. Isolation | Love vs. Exclusivity |
| Middle Adulthood: | Generativity vs. Stagnation | Care vs. Rejectivity |
| Later Adulthood: | Integrity vs. Despair | Wisdom vs. Disdain |

Source: Erikson (1963, 1982).

Both therapists and educators utilize these Eriksonian concepts to guide the growth of clients and students.[11] For example, the popular term "identity crisis" depicts the specific crisis that adolescents face. By understanding how pivotal it is for this age group, youth workers are better prepared to assist teens through this critical transitional period.

### Tasks along the Journey

What does it take to be recognized as an adult? In some cultures a person is not fully recognized as an adult until his or her first child is born. These so-called rites of passage—recognized transitions from childhood to adulthood—arise in every culture. One familiar tradition within Jewish culture is the "bar mitzvah" or "bath mitzvah" ceremony, recognizing the former child—now adult at age thirteen. Several less formal rites of passage into adulthood include obtaining an initial drivers' license, registering to vote, taking a full-time job, and getting married.

### Table 9.4
## Havighurst's Developmental Tasks

*Developmental Tasks of Infancy and Early Childhood* (0-6 yrs.)
1. Learning to walk
2. Learning to take solid foods
3. Learning to talk
4. Learning to control the elimination of body wastes
5. Learning sex differences and sexual modesty
6. Forming concepts and learning language to describe social and physical reality
7. Getting ready to read
8. Learning to distinguish right and wrong and beginning to develop a conscience

### Developmental Tasks of Middle Childhood (6-12 yrs.)

1. Learning physical skills necessary for ordinary games
2. Building wholesome attitudes toward oneself as a growing organism
3. Learning to get along with age-mates
4. Learning an appropriate masculine or feminine social role
5. Developing fundamental skills in reading, writing, and calculating
6. Developing concepts necessary for everyday living
7. Developing conscience, morality, and a scale of values
8. Achieving personal independence
9. Developing attitudes toward social groups and institutions

### Developmental Tasks of Adolescence (12-18 yrs.)

1. Achieving new and mature relations with age-mates of both sexes
2. Achieving a masculine or feminine social role
3. Accepting one's physique and using the body effectively
4. Achieving emotional independence of parents and other adults
5. Preparing for marriage and family life
6. Preparing for an economic career
7. Acquiring a set of values and an ethical system as a guide to behavior—developing an ideology
8. Desiring and achieving socially responsible behavior

### Developmental Tasks of Early Adulthood (18-30 yrs.)

1. Selecting a mate
2. Learning to live with a marriage partner
3. Starting a family
4. Rearing children
5. Managing a home
6. Getting started in an occupation
7. Taking on civic responsibility
8. Finding a congenial social group

### Developmental Tasks of Middle Age (30-65 yrs.)

1. Assisting teen-age children to become responsible and happy adults
2. Achieving adult social and civic responsibility
3. Reaching and maintaining satisfactory performance in one's occupational career
4. Developing adult leisure-time activities.
5. Relating oneself to one's spouse as a person
6. To accept and adjust to the physiological changes of middle age
7. Adjusting to aging parents

### Developmental Tasks of Later Maturity (65 yrs. and up)

1. Adjusting to decreasing physical strength and health
2. Adjustment to retirement and reduced income
3. Adjusting to death of spouse
4. Establishing an explicit affiliation with one's age group
5. Adopting and adapting social roles in a flexible way
6. Establishing satisfactory physical living arrangements

Source: Havighurst (1972).

For each of six stages, from infancy to later adulthood, Havighurst (1972) identified six to nine "developmental tasks" (see Table 9.4). "A developmental task is a task which arises at or about a certain period in the life of the individual, successful achievement of which leads to his happiness and to success with later tasks, while failure leads to unhappiness in the individual, disapproval by the society, and difficulty with later tasks" (1952, p. 2). Although some of the particular tasks outlined by Havighurst may be dated, the concept is still a profitable one. Beyond mastering specific subject matter, we must help our students prepare for their complex roles in society. We teachers must continually ask: "What does it take for our students to become godly men and women?" To this end, you may wish to revise and adapt Havighurst's outline to make it more appropriate for your own context.[12] For example, in her book on learning, Beechick (1982, pp. 146–48) employs Havighurst's developmental task concept to identify nineteen "spiritual developmental tasks," from preschool through adulthood (see Table 9.5).

## Table 9.5
# Beechick's Spiritual Developmental Tasks

### Spiritual Developmental Tasks of Preschool
1. Experiencing love, security, discipline, joy, and worship
2. Beginning to develop awareness and concepts of God, Jesus, and other basic Christian realities
3. Developing attitudes toward God, Jesus, church, self, Bible
4. Beginning to develop concepts of right and wrong

### Spiritual Developmental Tasks of Elementary School Years
1. Receiving and acknowledging Jesus Christ as Savior and Lord
2. Growing awareness of Christian love and responsibility in relationships with others
3. Continuing to build concepts of basic Christian realities
4. Learning basic Bible teachings adequate for personal faith and everyday Christian living, including teachings in these areas:
   a. prayer in daily life
   b. the Bible in daily life
   c. Christian friendships
   d. group worship
   e. responsibility for serving God
   f. basic knowledge of God, Jesus, Holy Spirit, creation, angelic beings, Heaven, Hell, sin, salvation, Bible literature, and history
5. Developing healthy attitudes toward self

### Spiritual Developmental Tasks of Adolescence
1. Learning to show Christian love in everyday life
2. Continuing to develop healthy attitudes toward self
3. Developing Bible knowledge and intellectual skills adequate for meeting intellectual assaults on faith
4. Achieving strength of Christian character adequate for meeting anti-Christian social pressures
5. Accepting responsibility for Christian service in accordance with growing abilities
6. Learning to make life decisions on the basis of eternal Christian values
7. Increasing self-discipline to "seek those things which are above"

*Spiritual Developmental Tasks of Maturity*
1. Accepting responsibility for one's own continued growth and learning
2. Accepting biblical responsibilities toward God and toward others
3. Living a unified, purposeful life centered upon God

*Source:* Beechick (1982, pp. 146-48).

---

## Try It Out

Reflect on the spiritual developmental tasks identified in Table 9.5.

1. What is particularly helpful about the chart?

2. What improvements would you make?

3. Is a chart on "spiritual developmental tasks" a helpful resource? Explain.

---

## Application: How Willing and Able Are Students?

This section concludes the four-chapter series on "readiness for learning." The purpose was to highlight prominent factors that affect students' receptivity to learning. By appropriating these factors we help students become more effective learners. Chapter 6 focused on the "willing" component; various features of student motivation were recognized. Chapters 7–9 treated the "able" component and responded to the question, "What abilities do our students bring with them to the learning situation?"

**Figure 9.3**
# Willing and Able Diagnosis Framework

| | | Able | |
|---|---|---|---|
| | | No | Yes |
| Willing | No | **Level 1**<br>Believers in the Book of Hebrews | **Level 3**<br>Jonah the prophet |
| | Yes | **Level 2**<br>Young boy with his lunch | **Level 4**<br>Tabernacle craftsmen |

*Source:* Adapted from Hersey and Blanchard (1982).

These two concepts of *able* and *willing* form a two-by-two matrix that helps teachers diagnose the student's relationship to a particular learning task or experience (see Figure 9.3).

Level 1: *Unwilling and Unable*—Students are not confident or competent in a given skill or task. Various inadequacies arise here. Students may be uncertain or insecure about what is expected of them. They may doubt that they can successfully grow in this area. The writer to the Hebrews addresses believers who fit this category. He accuses them of being "slow to learn" (5:11). Their choice to refrain from growing (i.e., being unwilling) caused them to remain as infants in the faith (i.e., being unable). This consequence was both tragic and unnecessary because these immature believers had ample time to become teachers.

Level 2: *Willing but Unable*—Students are confident and receptive, but lack the specific capacity or training that is required. For example, although he was unable to feed the large crowd that had been listening to Jesus, a young boy was willing to share what he had. Of course, the Lord miraculously multiplied his lunch of five barley loaves and two fish (John 6:9).

Level 3: *Able but Unwilling*—Students are competent, yet feel insecure about some aspect of a given task. Their reluctance occurs for a number of reasons. The story of Jonah comes to mind. This capable prophet intentionally abandoned his divine calling. In an unusual manner, God challenged Jonah to reconsider his attitude and actions. Even though he eventually preached God's message to the citizens of Nineveh, Jonah's recurring unwillingness caused him to miss the greatest Gentile revival recorded in the Old Testament.

Level 4: *Willing and Able*—Students are ready and equipped for the skill or task. They may require only a minimum amount of coaching. Once Moses had received the plans from God, Bezalel, Oholiab, and other skilled craftsmen—who were eager and willing—began to build the tabernacle in the wilderness (Exod. 36:2).

---

### Try It Out

---

Think about your previous experiences as a teacher. Identify at least one of your students for each of the first three categories below. In light of the particular ideas offered to enhance "Readiness for Learning" in Chapters 6–9, devise one appropriate strategy to help each student you identified. How could you enable them to become better learners?

| Level | Proposed Strategy |
|---|---|
| 1. Unwilling and Unable | |
| 2. Unable but Willing | |
| 3. Unwilling and Able | |

## Conclusion

Knowing where our students have come from and where they are going can help us better serve them. Aleshire (1988) urges us to heighten
our sensitivity to often-hidden issues:

> Attending [to the needs of people] is an important dimension of ministry
> because people often express their needs indirectly and sometimes not at
> all. They do not always say, "Here is my need." They do not always even
> know their needs. Paying attention to people provides the information re-
> quired for articulate expressions of ministry (p. 15).

Recognizing that biblical education is always a two-way street, we teachers
must regularly assess our own teachability. How are we growing? Are we
fully utilizing all of God's gifts and opportunities? What victories—as well
as roadblocks—can we spot in our own pilgrimage? Complacency is not an
option. Figuratively speaking, we may have the potential of an eight-cylin-
der engine, but only be running on three or four cylinders. With Paul as our
model, we must press on to full maturity: "Not that I have already ob-
tained all this, or have already been made perfect, but I press on to take
hold of that for which Christ Jesus took hold of me" (Phil. 3:12).

## Key Concepts and Issues

able and willing matrix

Buss and Plomin's theory of temperament
      emotionality, activity, and sociability

driver, expressive, amiable, analytical

Erikson's stages of psychosocial crises

handling conflict

Havighurst's developmental tasks

identity formation

Maslow's hierarchy of needs

personality development

Readiness for learning

self-image

soul, self

task-oriented and people-oriented

temperament

# Part 4

# Purposes in Learning

# The Goal: Christian Maturity

**The Aim of All Learning**
**Four Themes of Christian Maturity**
**Application: Learning Dispositions Through Spiritual Disciplines**
**Conclusion**

So far we have looked at four major aspects of learning: Levels, Extent, Avenues, and Readiness. These represent common categories typically included in books on learning theory. But a Christian view includes more. We must consider the *Nature* of learning, particularly the essence of learning from God's eternal perspective. The final two chapters center on this critical topic. In the final chapter, God's call for his children to be lifelong learners is analyzed. For Christians, learning is a never-ending process of change and growth.

The learning process must have a final product. Too many works in Christian education are long on technique, but short on *teleios* (Greek, for "purpose"; related to the Greek word for "mature"). What are we aiming at? What should the end "product" look like for believers? That's the subject of this chapter.

## The Aim of All Learning

We need to focus attention on what we ultimately must learn: what the purpose of life is all about. Packer (1973, p. 29) confronts the vital issue of the purpose for our teaching and learning:

What were we made for? To know God. . . . What is the "eternal life" that Jesus gives? Knowledge of God. "This is life eternal, that they might know thee, the only true God, and Jesus Christ, whom thou has sent" (John 17:3).

What is the best thing in life, bringing more joy, delight, and contentment, than anything else? Knowledge of God. . . . Once you become aware that the main business that you are here for is to know God, most of life's problems fall into place of their own accord.

Our Lord summarized all the Old Testament commands by quoting Deuteronomy 6:5: "Love the Lord your God with all your heart and with all your soul and with all your mind. This is the first and greatest commandment" (Matt. 22:36–38). The Westminster Catechism states it this way: "What is the chief end of man? To love God and to enjoy Him forever." Joy (1985) asserts that "God's relationship with humans is one of intimate bonding, and that all human intimacies are 'rehearsals' for the ultimate reunion of humans with their creator" (p. ix).

If these statements reflect our ultimate purpose in life, then our primary focus for all learning necessitates getting to know God better. All that we do as teachers—all of our planning, all of our praying, all of our teaching—must contribute to this basic aim. During the final moments with his disciples before his arrest, Jesus reminded them that they had to continue to nurture this special relationship. "Whoever has my commands and obeys them, he is the one who loves me. He who loves me will be loved by my Father, and I too will love him and show myself to him" (John 14:21).

At the heart of our relationship with God is the degree of trust in him. "And without faith it is impossible to please God, because anyone who comes to him must believe that he exists and that he rewards those who earnestly seek him" (Heb. 11:6). We can either rely on what God has promised in his word, or we can trust our "sight"—what we see and believe about our circumstances in this physical world. "Now faith is being sure of what we hope for and certain of what we do not see" (Heb. 11:1). Our Lord honored such faith in his reply to Thomas' lack of faith: "Because you have seen me, you have believed; blessed are those who have not seen and yet have believed" (John 20:29). We recognize the existence of both spiritual reality and material reality (cf. 2 Kings 6:16; Matt. 14:30). In fixing our eyes on the unseen (2 Cor. 4:18), we march to the drum of kingdom priorities (Matt. 6:31–34).

Lewis and Demarest (1987, p. 122) note that "The comprehensive purpose of special revelation [i.e., the Bible] is the reestablishment of the *full communion of sinful people with God*" (emphasis added). Houston (1989, p. 56) comments that "Many people have an internal division between what they think and what they do, between belief and action. In fact, many religious people see their faith as a set of beliefs they agree to, rather than as a living relationship with God." We hinder our dynamic fellowship with God when we predominantly focus on anything other than experiencing full communion with God.

## Four Themes of Christian Maturity

Although this *vertical* focus—Communion with God—is the most central component of our ultimate purpose, it's not the exclusive one. For after our Lord described the "first and greatest commandment," he added: "And the second is like it: 'Love your neighbor as yourself' [Lev. 11:44]. All the Law and the Prophets hang on these two commandments" (Matt. 22:39-40). Our Lord refused to separate these two dimensions of our responsibility. Besides our focus on God, we also hold an imperative for *horizontal* responsibilities. That is, we have "earthly" duties—three to be exact.

### Figure 10.1
## Four Themes of Christian Maturity

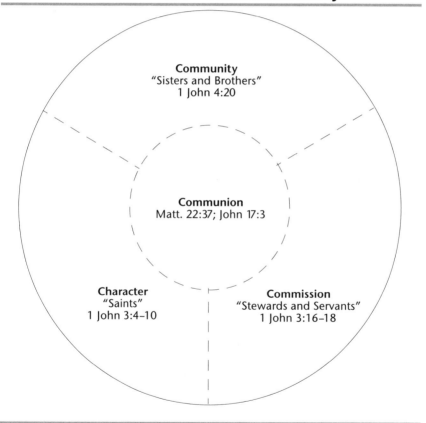

The model of Christian maturity that is advanced in this chapter features four basic themes that resonate throughout all of Scripture. More precisely, there is one main theme, along with three corollary ones (see Figure 10.1). *Communion* with God, just described as our ultimate purpose, highlights our primary *vertical* responsibility. Our three remaining duties (all *horizontal* in nature) identify complementary themes of *Community, Character,* and *Commission.* These three emphases are evident in Peter's exhortation to the church in his first epistle: "You also, like living stones, are being built into a spiritual house to be a holy priesthood, offering spiritual sacrifices to God through Jesus Christ. . . . But you are a chosen people, a royal priesthood, a holy nation, a people belonging to God, that you may declare the praises of him who called you out of darkness into his wonderful light" (1 Pet. 2:5, 9).

We are a select people, bonded together in Christ Jesus. Reflecting and maintaining this unity of fellowship is the goal of *Community.* We are "living stones," who share the same "spiritual house." The second horizontal theme of *Character* emphasizes our sanctified walk and morality. We are a "holy priesthood" and a "holy nation." Our reputation should be morally distinctive from that of nonbelievers. Finally, we are responsible before God to use our talents and gifts to "declare the praises" of God and to serve his kingdom. That is, we have a *Commission.* To be physically healthy in this life, it's necessary that we eat a balanced diet from the four basic food groups (bread/cereals, fruits/vegetables, meats, and milk). Likewise it's essential for progress toward Christian maturity that we pursue balanced growth in four basic themes: Communion, Community, Character, and Commission. These four themes are evident, in preliminary ways, back in the Garden of Eden. And they remain as viable ideals throughout all eternity. As Lewis and Demarest (1990, p. 103) affirm, "God is now retrieving from the fallen world a people to share his *fellowship, values,* and *work*" (emphasis added). In the following section, all three horizontal themes are analyzed.[1]

### Community: Pursuing Love and Unity

A significant and corporate element of fellowship permeates Scripture. Peter describes believers as "a spiritual house" and "a chosen people." This Community focus is verified in commands that are *plural* throughout the epistles of the Greek New Testament. Specifically, the word "you" represents the second-person plural pronoun. The inspired authors wrote to the believers as a *group,* not as individuals. But our individualistic orientation, as American Christians, often causes us to misread these "you's" as directed to a particular believer—as a *singular* pronoun. A better way to read such exhortations, however, is to use the Southern "you all."

"Family" is the predominant metaphor in the New Testament that illustrates our common relationship in Christ. Consequently, we actually assume the roles of family members: "Do not rebuke an older man harshly, but exhort him as if he were your father. Treat younger men as brothers, older women as mothers, and younger women as sisters, with absolute purity" (1 Tim. 5:1–2; see also Matt. 12:48–50). Furthermore, the New Testament identifies two distinguishing "trademarks" of the church: love for one another and unity among the members.

> *Love:* "A new commandment I give you: Love one another. As I have loved you, so you must love one another. *All men will know that you are my disciples* if you love one another" (John 13:34–35).

> *Unity:* "My prayer is not for them alone. I pray also for those who will believe in me through their message, that all of them may be one, Father, just as you are in me and I am in you. May they also be in us so *that the world may believe* that you have sent me" (John 17:20–21).

God provides supernatural resources to implement these ideal truths. Believers are indwelt by the Holy Spirit who unifies us (Eph. 4:3). And he produces the fruit of love in us (Gal. 5:22).

> The ultimate foundation for all community is found, not in the creatures, but in the ultimate nature of things, in the triune Creator. The final reason for families staying together is not legal agreement enforced by state or church, but demonstration of Trinitarian love and grace. And schism in the church is scripturally sinful (1 Cor. 12:25), not only because of the hurt to many members, but also because it violates their unity in Christ's body and its unity in Him with the Father and the Spirit (Lewis and Demarest 1987, p. 286).

The theme of Community urges us to befriend our brothers and sisters in Christ. Among other matters, this entails valuing the uniqueness of each person, appreciating our distinctives, and sensing pressing needs to be met. In order to do this we must move beyond the limited way we tend to look at faith and life. Such acceptance of others is difficult if we are narrow-minded. Thus, an important goal of Christian education centers on gaining this divine perspective: to look at life the way God sees it, the widest vantage point of all perspectives. The incarnation of Christ represents God's ultimate role-taking posture. In love, he became one of us. Through this strategy Jesus became our sympathetic High Priest whom we can boldly approach (Heb. 4:15). Consequently, by increasing our role-taking task of empathy, we likewise live more compassionately among believers in a sinful world.

One way we exhibit Community is to be persistent in our generous forgiveness of others (cf. Matt. 18:21–35). Forgiveness is the lubricating oil of relationships. Such liberality should never be interpreted as compromising or cheap, for Christ's great sacrifice made our forgiveness possible and paves the way so that we may forgive others. In fact, if we are worshiping God (i.e., Communion) and we recall an interpersonal offense (i.e., Community), we are to promptly cease our worship and satisfy the offense (Matt. 5:20–26). Thus, as Christ demonstrated earlier, it is impossible to divorce our horizontal obligations from our vertical duty. "Our relationship with God can never be right when our relationship with other people is wrong" (Houston 1989, p. 150; cf. 1 John 4:21).[2]

### Figure 10.2
## Assessing Group Closeness

### What Is Said

| | | Topic (external to group) | Group | Personal (self-disclosure) | Relationship (exchange between two group members) |
|---|---|---|---|---|---|
| **How It's Said** | **Non-responsive** | "Interesting." Uh-huh. | "I don't care." "What name should we call our group?" | "How are you doing?" "Fine." | "Do you think we could maybe . . ." |
| | **Conventional** | tell a joke; quote a Bible verse | "One of the purposes of our group is to . . ." | "What we've got to think about is . . ." | "I appreciate your friendship." "I like . . ." |
| | **Assertive** | "God has a special concern for the poor." | "We ought to . . ." | "No way; I can't do that!" | "You always have the last word!" |
| | **Speculative** | "What do you think Jesus meant when he said . . . ?" | "How do we incorporate our diverse goals into our group aims?" | "How do I come across?" "Am I expecting too much of my kids?" | "Look at me; what do you see?" |
| | **Tentative** | "I get the idea that God has a special identification with the poor." | "It seems that one of the reasons we're a close-knit group is that . . ." | "Have you ever noticed that I'm usually the last one to share?" | "It seems that we both want the group's attention. Is that right?" |

*Source:* Griffin (1984) [Based on "Hill Interaction Matrix" (HIM)].

### Try It Out

1. Figure 10.2 displays a grid that can be used to evaluate closeness in groups or between two people based on conversation. The two axes are "What is said" and "How it's said" and yield twenty boxes. For each box, an illustrative comment is supplied. Familiarize yourself with each type of comment.

2. Consider your own groups and relationships with other believers. How would you rate the quality of fellowship? If there's a good amount of "personal" and "relationship" comments made at the "speculative" and "tentative" levels, a healthy closeness is evident.
3. Test the waters in one of your relationships or groups. Initiate more intimate conversation. The relationship may be ready to move to a deeper level of closeness.
4. What can you do to grow greater "Community" in your class? Jot down a few specific strategies.

### *Character: Pursuing Right Living*

Whatever is good and right must be defined by the character and commands of God: "Be holy, for I am holy" (Lev. 11:45; 1 Pet. 1:16). We are indwelt by the Holy Spirit who desires to produce the fruit of righteousness in our lives (Gal. 5:22–23). Freed from slavery to sin (Rom. 6:6–7), we are no longer under bondage to law but rather are under God's grace (Rom. 6:14). We are free to become slaves of righteousness (Rom. 6:18–19), to present our thoughts and feelings and the actions of our bodies as instruments of righteousness (Rom. 6:13) and as holy sacrifices, acceptable to God (Rom. 12:1).

As Christians, we have in fact been "created to be like God in true righteousness and holiness" (Eph. 4:24). Yet Paul also warns us that it takes great effort to pursue this godliness (1 Tim. 4:7b–8). Fortunately, this lifelong task is not left to us alone. Empowered by the Holy Spirit (Gal. 5:22, 25), we can grow in righteousness among the company of others who share the same pilgrimage (2 Tim. 2:22).

In particular, a theology of Christian Character highlights two central activities:

*Focusing on lifestyle habits*—We must develop and maintain a disposition to obey God, as evidenced in our self-control and participation in moral actions (through spiritual disciplines and personal habits) (e.g., 1 Cor. 9:24–27).

*Focusing on conscience*—We must nurture and be responsive to a sensitive conscience, the seat of our moral standards (e.g., Ps. 119:11; Rom. 14:22–23; James 1:22–25). We must also improve our moral reasoning and decision-making, in that our conscience is the locus of arbitration regarding moral decisions (e.g., Heb. 5:14).[3]

Willard (1988) states that we cannot expect to do what Jesus did, in his public life, unless we are willing to practice the disciplines of his private life, such as prayer, solitude, and fasting (cf. Matt. 4:1–2; Luke 5:16):

> Our mistake is to think that following Jesus consists in loving our enemies, going the "second mile," turning the other cheek, suffering patiently and hopefully—while living the rest of our lives just as everyone around us

does. . . . [We] completely ignore the need for character change in our lives as a whole. The general human failing is to want what is right and important, but at the same time not to commit to the kind of life that will produce the action we know to be right and the condition we want to enjoy. This is the feature of human character that explains why the road to hell is paved with good intentions. We intend what is right, but we avoid the life that would make it reality (pp. 5–6).

Olympic athletes, pursuing a gold medal, make a total commitment to a regimen of training so they can excel in a particular event. In 1 Corinthians 9:24–25 Paul refers to this kind of training as he explains his own regimen: "I beat my body and make it my slave so that after I have preached to others, I myself will not be disqualified for the prize" (v. 27; cf. 1 Tim. 4:7b–8). Does our worthy desire to be holy require less commitment and complete training? In chapter 2, we outlined the kinds of learning that are possible, as related to the affective, behavioral, cognitive, and dispositional domains. Learning to be holy necessitates holistic growth in each of these levels of learning. Nothing short of this comprehensive development will do.

## Try It Out

Two areas were outlined as essential for growth in Character.
1. Evaluate your *lifestyle habits.* Use the 4-T test:

> Thoughts
> Time
> Talents
> Treasure[4]

Identify two or three habits from each of the four categories above that are pleasing to God. Then reflect on at least one habit from each category that would not receive such a favorable heavenly commendation.
2. Consider the maturing of your *conscience.* How are you keeping your conscience sensitive to the leading of the Spirit? How are you improving your ability to discern between good and evil (cf. Heb. 5:14)?
3. What specific step would be most prudent at this point in your Christian walk to keep growing in Character in light of responses to either item #1 or #2?

### *Commission: Pursuing Service in His Kingdom*

One major purpose for our existence is to serve God, as Paul notes: "For we are God's workmanship, created in Christ Jesus to do good works, which God prepared in advance for us to do" (Eph 2:10). Christians have two specific worldwide mandates related to this service: one as fellow heirs of the kingdom of God and one as fellow human beings. These set the boundaries for knowing God's will for us as stewards on this earth.

*Our Commission as Disciple-Makers to All People.* Before he returned to heaven, our Lord commanded the apostles:

> All authority in heaven and on earth has been given to me. Therefore go and make disciples of all nations, baptizing them in the name of the Father and of the Son and of the Holy Spirit, and teaching them to obey everything I have commanded you. And surely I will be with you always, to the very end of the age (Matt. 28:18–20).

This command focuses on people and their eternal destiny. It's a call to help individuals come to a saving knowledge of God and present participation in the kingdom of God. We want to grow together so that our relationship with God moves toward its fullest potential. In this regard, this final theme of Commission has a dual emphasis both toward those outside the church and those within the church.

*Our Commission as Stewards of All the Earth.* Our obligation is not restricted to evangelism and discipleship. Although we have become citizens of heaven, we are still citizens of this earth. The "Discipling" commission did not supersede this "Stewardship" commission; it only put our ultimate beliefs and values in perspective. We still have a fundamental responsibility to care for all of God's creation. After our first parents were formed, God commanded them: "Be fruitful and increase in number; fill the earth and subdue it. Rule over the fish of the sea and the birds of the air and over every living creature that moves on the ground" (Gen. 1:28; cf. Gen. 9:1–3; Ps. 8:6–8).

As Christians, we are stewards along with non-Christians of the natural realm. We face together the tension between *conserving* and *consuming* what God has so richly provided for us. Willard (1988, p. 51) reminds us of this ecological stewardship:

> Perhaps our present tendency to have pets and zoos, to be fond of living creatures and domesticate them, and our amazing powers to train and control other creatures on the planet are but dim reflections of the divine intention for us. Our care about the extinction of species and our general feeling of responsibility and concern for the fate of animals, plants, and even the earth also speaks of this divine intention. Scientists talk easily and often of our responsibility to care for the oceans and forests and wild, living things. This urge toward such responsibility is, I think, only a manifestation of the *imago Dei* originally implanted in humankind and still not wholly destroyed.

In light of these significant responsibilities, we should restore the full meaning of the term "vocation." Based on the Latin, *vocatio* ("to call"), for centuries Christians have used the phrase a "calling from God." Unfortunately, we often restrict the meaning of the phrase to full-time, religious work.[5]

In God's eyes, however, there is no dichotomy of the sacred and secular. God has made each of us stewards of his grace and gifts. He will hold us accountable for our time, talents, and treasures (Luke 12:42–48). The parable of the talents in Matthew 25:14–30 stands as a prominent reminder of this comprehensive view of Commission. Growth in vocation involves competence and confidence in being stewards of God-given opportunities and capabilities.

We also represent light and truth to this world; as God's church we cannot condone actions of evil. We are the ambassadors of the King of Kings and we must represent kingdom values. "For you were once darkness, but now you are light. Live as children of light. . . . Have nothing to do with the fruitless deeds of darkness, but rather expose them. For it is shameful even to mention what the disobedient do in secret. But everything exposed by the light becomes visible, for it is light that makes everything visible" (Eph. 5:8–14). In faithfully serving God now we prepare ourselves for our ultimate destiny: to reign with God and serve him forever (Rev. 22:3–5).

---

### Try It Out

One area of Commission is portrayed by our spiritual gifts. All Christians have at least one spiritual gift, given by God (1 Cor. 12:7,11). Although these divine gifts are fully operational when given, we need to learn how to use them responsibly. For example, Paul encouraged Timothy to "fan into flame" his gift (2 Tim. 1:6). How are you currently using your spiritual gift?

1. What are you doing to regularly improve your gift? As a first step, study the following passages that identify the various spiritual gifts: Rom. 12:3–8, 1 Cor. 12:8–10, 28–30; Eph. 4:11–12; 1 Pet. 4:9–10. Then, get involved in a ministry through which your gift can be employed. If you have actually received a particular gift, God will confirm it through the benefits you bring to others, through the affirmation of mature Christian leaders, and through the witness of the Spirit in your heart, as you joyfully serve. Seek out those who ably demonstrate that particular gift and invite them to guide and encourage you in the use of your gift.

2. How can you help others to get involved in serving so they can identify their gifts?

---

## Application: Learning Dispositions Through Spiritual Disciplines

In the first half of his book, *The Spirit of the Disciplines,* Willard (1988) makes a case for the contemporary use of spiritual disciplines against common misperceptions. "Spirituality has thus come to be regarded by the world as those futile, self-torturing excesses of strange men and women who lived in far-off, benighted places and times" (p. 79). "The disciplines for the spiritual life, rightly understood, are time-tested activities consciously undertaken by us as new men or women to allow our spirit ever-increasing sway over our embodied selves. They help by assisting the ways of God's Kingdom to take the place of the habits of sin embedded in our bodies" (p. 86). Learning at the Dispositional Level requires habituation in the things that please God. A virtuoso practices hours on end so that music flows effortlessly from an instrument. Developing godliness requires the same kind of rigor (cf. 1 Tim. 4:8), so that our human instruments freely resonate with the music of God's holiness.

The purpose of a spiritual discipline is to shore up and strengthen particular areas of weakness of character. "The need for extensive practice of a given discipline is an indication of our *weakness,* not our strength. We can even lay it down as a rule of thumb that if it is *easy* for us to engage in a certain discipline, we probably don't need to practice it. The disciplines we need to practice are precisely the ones we are *not* 'good at' and hence do not enjoy it" (p. 138).

Based on his study of those that have stood the test of time throughout church history, Willard identifies fifteen particular disciplines[6] and arranges them into two general categories: disciplines of abstinence and disciplines of engagement. In practicing a discipline of *abstinence* "we abstain to some degree and for some time from the satisfaction of what we generally regard as normal and legitimate desires" in order to "bring these desires into their proper coordination and subordination within the economy of life in his Kingdom" (pp. 159–60). Seven particular disciplines are listed, including solitude, silence, fasting, frugality, chastity, secrecy, and sacrifice. By practicing disciplines of *engagement,* we attempt to "counteract tendencies to sins of omission" (p. 176). Of these there are eight: study, worship, celebration, service, prayer, fellowship, confession, submission. Such disciplines always stand as the means for such growth, not ends in themselves, a fact apparently forgotten by the Pharisees (cf. Matt. 6:1–18). Our purpose for such training in spiritual maturity must be different than theirs.

### Table 10.1
## Spiritual Disciplines and the Four Themes of Christian Maturity

### Communion

*Abstinence*

- Solitude—isolating ourselves from others to be alone with God.
- Silence—shutting out all the sounds of the world to listen to our inner thoughts and God's voice.

*Engagement*

- Prayer—conversing with God on a continual basis.
- Study—meditating on the Word of God.
- Worship—expressing the beauty, goodness, and greatness of God through words, rituals, and symbols, alone and with others.

## Community

*Engagement*

- Celebration—coming together to feast with God's people: to eat and drink, to sing and dance, and to share stories of God's working in our lives as a congregation.
- Confession—letting trusted others know our deepest weaknesses and failures, being completely transparent so God's provision for our need can be supplied through others.
- Fellowship—engaging in common activities of worship, study, prayer, celebration, and service with other believers.
- Submission—allowing the mature and wise ones of our fellowship to direct our efforts in growth to help us do what we like to do and refrain from what we don't want to do.

## Character

*Abstinence*

- Chastity—turning away from indulging in the sexual dimension of our lives so as to properly live as sexual beings.
- Fasting—avoiding food and sometimes drink to increase self-control over all our desires.
- Frugality—refraining from using money or goods we have merely to gratify our desires so as to help ourselves be free to see the needs of others.
- Sacrifice—forsaking the security of meeting our own needs with what we have so as to meet the needs of others.

## Commission

*Abstinence*

- Secrecy—not making known our good deeds and good qualities so as to enjoy our relationship with God independent of the opinions of others.

*Engagement*

- Service—using our goods and strength to actively and humbly promote the good of others and God's purposes in our world in order to please God and not others.

*Source*: Modified from Willard (1988, pp. 158–191).

---

## Try It Out

Table 10.1 lists the specific disciplines identified by Willard (1988, pp. 156–91). They have been arranged according to their respective focus on abstinence or engagement, as well as their particular contribution to the four themes of Christian maturity.

1. Identify two or three items from the list in which you perceive yourself to be fairly competent. In which areas would you be able to guide others in their growth?

2. Circle two or three items from the list that represent areas where you need more training and growth. What steps could you take to increase your degree of exercise and training for one of these areas?

## Conclusion

What is our ultimate purpose in life? What should all of our learning be directed toward? In this chapter, four themes of Christian maturity have been identified. This comprehensive approach provides a useful way to plan our lessons and to develop our curricula. *Communion, Community, Character,* and *Commission* must be balanced in harmonious synthesis. For Christians, *all* of our learning and teaching, no matter what context, must be directed toward these complex and complementary goals.

### Try It Out

Find a couple of your past lesson plans. Look them over. What parts of the lesson relate to each of the four themes of Christian maturity? Place the following abbreviations in the margin of your lesson plan:

> CMN (Communion)
> CTY (Community)
> CHR (Character)
> CSN (Commission)

Do you tend to overemphasize one or two areas? Is any area seriously neglected? Such an evaluation identifies the degree of balance in our teaching of scriptural values. One lesson may not emphasize all four, but the four themes ought to be evident within a series of lessons.

## Key Concepts and Issues

a model of Christian maturity
    Communion, Community, Character, and Commission
commission as disciple-makers
conscience
family as a metaphor
greatest commandment: Matt. 22:36–40

horizontal and vertical themes

lifestyle habits

love and unity

Nature of learning

quality of fellowship

spiritual disciplines: abstinence and engagement

spiritual gifts

stewards of the earth

training for godliness

vocation

weakness of character

**L** evels
**E** xtent
**A** venues
**R** eadiness
**N** ature

11

# A Lifelong Call to Change

"No!" That's one of the first words we learn. And we wear it out during our toddler years. It's a word that our parents don't intend to teach us, but we learn it nevertheless. "No" is a forceful word. It brings an abrupt halt to any activity. It's one thing for a child to say "no" to her parents. It's quite another thing to say "no" to our heavenly Father. But that's exactly what Peter said—three times no less—to God! Well, not to make excuses for this burly fisherman, but he was well known for his lack of tact and his inflexibility. Remember when he didn't want his feet washed by our Lord at the Last Supper? Now some might say, "But that was the 'old Peter.' All those events took place *before* our Lord's ascension into heaven. What about the 'new Peter'? What about his bold sermon on the Day of Pentecost in Acts 2? And don't forget his courageous reply to the religious leaders, 'We must obey God rather than men!'" (Acts 5:29).

Let's take a look at one of Peter's significant learning experiences, as recorded in Acts 10. The question might be raised, "Was the 'old Peter' that much different than the 'new Peter'?" This scriptural text indicates certain similarities. Recall that, in this passage, God wanted to teach Peter some important truths, and Peter's initial response was "No!" Was this man a *reluctant* learner? It appears that way. As we shall see, God was leading Peter through some thought-provoking experiences. God's purpose was to help him gain new insights about the kingdom of God. It was time for a change. It was time for an important step forward in the church's ministry.

What about us? Can learning about God's ways sometimes be difficult for us, too? We may feel anxious when we are stretched beyond our comfort zones. We may feel awkward and indecisive when the Holy Spirit provides us with new opportunities to grow. These are not enjoyable feelings. They may cause us to say "no" to God when he wants us to take a new step as his disciples. Sometimes, just like Peter, we balk at God's leading. Perhaps by studying Peter's example as a hesitant learner, we may gain valuable insights into our own pilgrimage as learners.

## Lunchtime in Joppa

Tremendous growth and vitality marked the early days of the church at Jerusalem. But success can breed jealousy. And eventually, the church became the target of persecution, following the martyrdom of Stephen. Christians scattered everywhere throughout the regions of Judea and Samaria (Acts 8:1). Shortly thereafter, Peter's itinerant ministry in Judea commenced (Acts 9:32). He traveled in a north-westerly direction from Jerusalem toward the Mediterranean Sea. In the town of Lydda, he healed a man who had been paralyzed and bedridden for eight years. This miracle launched the Spirit's reconciling ministry in the lives of many in Lydda and Sharon (9:35). Word about the miracle spread to Joppa on the coast. A request was made by the saints in Joppa for Peter to come to them in order to prevent a funeral service. But Tabitha, the kind and godly woman, had fallen sick and had died. Undaunted by this seemingly hopeless situation, Peter—by the power of God—raised her from the dead. This began a revival in the region and many believed in the Lord (9:42).

It was lunchtime one day in Joppa and Peter was famished. While waiting for final preparations by his host, Peter prayed on the flat rooftop. God had used him to bring about great revival in Judea. It is difficult to know for certain what Peter said, but perhaps he was praying for wisdom to guide the church's ministry due to the number of believers being added to the church. He may well have asked God to grant new evangelistic opportunities. Little did Peter realize what kind of door God would open!

Luke records that, as Peter prayed, "he fell into a trance" and saw something like a large sheet being lowered from the sky (10:10). All kinds of animals, reptiles, and birds appeared. Then a voice called out, "Get up, Peter. Kill and eat." Peter was so hungry he could have eaten anything . . . well, almost. For he responded, "Surely no, Lord!" What was the problem? Though he was famished, Peter's religious scruples prevailed. "I have never eaten anything impure or unclean." He knew that the law prohibited certain kinds of food (see Lev. 11:41–47). But the voice to Peter persisted. "Do not call anything impure that God has made clean." Peter had forgotten or didn't understand that Jesus had taken away those restrictions (see Mark 7:14–19).

Peter then experienced two "video replays" of this strange lunch spread—probably to make sure he didn't forget it. These visions left him perplexed; he wondered what they were all about (Acts 10:17,19). Perplexity is a good sign because it often leads to learning (based on the Inquiry Avenue of learning). While Peter was in this condition, some Gentiles arrived in Joppa looking for him.

Peter's bewildering rooftop experience represents only Part Two of this intriguing story of church history. God, the Master Teacher, was preparing Peter to guide the church toward a fellowship of *both* Jews and Gentiles united in one church. Bible students recall that Part One of the story took place a day earlier in Caesarea, just up the coast a little way from Joppa. There, God responded to the prayer of a God-fearing Gentile named Cornelius (10:1–8). An angel told him to speak with Peter. Cornelius immediately sent three men to Joppa; they arrived just after Peter's vision of the sheet.

Now Part Three unfolded. What timing! If this were a movie, we might wonder why God waited so long to get Peter ready. Remember that he received his vision the day *after* the angel visited Cornelius' house. The messengers were already on the road to get Peter, when he had his heavenly experience. These Gentiles had no clue about what was happening to Peter. And Peter had no idea that three men stood outside the gate. All that the Spirit told Peter was, "Simon, three men are looking for you. So get up and go downstairs. Do not hesitate to go with them, for I have sent them" (10:19–20). But this posed yet another problem. Tradition prohibited Jews from associating with Gentiles. It took nothing short of a direct command from God to prompt Peter to invite these strangers into the house as his guests. For the *first* time in his life he had invited Gentiles to be his guests! Peter probably experienced a very sleepless night.

The next day, Peter, the three men, and some Jewish believers set out for Caesarea. When they arrived, Cornelius' house was packed with relatives and close friends. At this time, Peter made the connection that the clean and unclean animals of the vision represented Jewish and Gentile people. "But God has shown me that I should not call any man impure or unclean" (10:28). But that's as far as it went. Some learning had taken place, but there was still room for growth.

Peter followed up with, "May I ask why you sent for me?" Isn't he a little dense—as we all are at times? Peter still had no idea that God wanted revival among the Gentiles, too. In response to Peter's question, Cornelius rehearsed his own story of the angelic visit. He then invited Peter to speak God's message to them (10:30–33). Finally, all the puzzle pieces fit. Peter confessed: "I now realize how true it is that God does not show favoritism but accepts men from every nation who fear him and do what is right"

(10:34–35). Peter had learned his lesson! God accepted all people into his kingdom—whether Jew or Gentile. What a remarkable day for the church! Then, to finish the story, Peter explained the Good News of Jesus Christ; the Holy Spirit came upon these Gentiles, astonishing the Jewish believers who had come along (10:45). Peter concluded, "Can anyone keep these people from being baptized with water? They have received the Holy Spirit just as we have" (10:47). The full acceptance of the Gentile believers was now complete.

In retrospect, we might ask, didn't Peter comprehend the Great Commission, as recorded in Acts 1:8? "But you will receive power when the Holy Spirit comes on you; and you will be my witnesses in Jerusalem, and in all Judea and Samaria, and to the ends of the earth." Didn't he get it? We can only conclude that all of the apostles understood it only as a commission for the *Jewish community.* How else can we interpret the fact that their early ministry efforts, recorded in Acts 1–9, were exclusively Jewish-oriented? Their Jewish culture simply blinded them to the full implications of Jesus' words. It was their custom; they were comfortable associating with Jews and avoiding Gentiles. So God took specific, explicit measures to open Peter's eyes.

But before we judge Peter too harshly, we need to realize that we all wear blinders to some extent. We all become accustomed to ways of thinking, feeling, and acting that are either just plain wrong, or at least very limited in scope. God wants us, like Peter, to comprehend the full liberating power of his gospel—to experience the abundant life and fully use all the gifts and abilities he has given us. But change often comes hard. It did for Peter and it does for us. We can either welcome change or resist it.

## Called to Be His Disciples

The heart of the Great Commission is to "make disciples" (Matt. 28:19). The word "disciple," translated from the Greek, originally meant "learner" or "student." By the time of the New Testament, the term had taken a more focused meaning: "followers of a great leader or movement. . . . Hence, in the Christian sense, a disciple of Jesus is one who has come to him for eternal life, has claimed him as Savior and God, and has embarked upon the life of following him" (Wilkins 1992, pp. 40–41). Being a follower of Jesus is a lifelong process.

"To learn is to change! Learning is changing!" (Leypoldt 1971, p. 27). We use the term "change" to designate the essence of learning. Put simply, learning is something that occurs through our experiences and interactions. Two restrictions apply. Any change based on maturation (natural processes like physical development) does not equal learning. Also, we don't include counterproductive changes, such as learning a repulsive habit. In this case, "learning" is one step forward and two steps backward. Consequently, it is imperative that we educators focus on learning toward biblical aims. Employing terminology used by James, "listeners" of the word are not true learners; "doers" of the word are (James 1:22–25). So, it's fair to say that if we aren't changing in some way—our thoughts, emotions, values, dispositions, actions—then we probably aren't learning.[1]

Our attitude about learning new things is directly affected by our previous experiences of learning—whether they were pleasant or painful. And, due to the pace of change in our contemporary society, the older we get, the more we want to hold on to traditional patterns. There is great comfort in adhering to our customs. We indeed have legitimate needs for security and comfort, yet we must align these values with the priorities of God's Kingdom. Changing habits can be a difficult and uncomfortable process. It takes time even for small changes. Every January, for instance, we have to learn to write the new year on our checks. Other changes, like new clothing styles, new addresses, and new jobs, require even more patience. But, as believers, even more sophisticated change remains. For, as pilgrims in progress, our comfortable ways of living must be regularly replaced by the patterns of new life in Christ. "You were taught, with regard to your former way of life, to put off your old self, which is being corrupted by its deceitful desires; to be made new in the attitude of your minds; and to put on the new self, created to be like God in true righteousness and holiness" (Eph. 4:22–24). A posture of openness toward God's teaching is a primary requisite for growth (cf. Prov. 1:1–7).

## What Have We Learned about Learning?

We have traversed the broad and complex territory of learning theory and practice. Within a Christian worldview, this subject contains both natural and supernatural elements. It was noted that Christian education involves changing toward conformity to Christ. This process includes human effort and the work of the Holy Spirit (2 Cor. 3:17–18). And, since learning is predominantly an internal process, we can never fully "see" learning take place; we often notice only its external effects (cf. John 3:8). Table 11.1 presents a summary list of the major learning concepts in this book.

### Table 11.1
### LEARN: A Summary of Factors

LEVELS OF LEARNING: "What can we learn?" (Chapter 2)
- Affective—Emotions and Attitude
- Behavioral—Physical Skills and Habits
- Cognitive—Knowledge and Intellectual Skills
- Dispositional—Values and Tendencies to Act

**EXTENT** OF LEARNING: "How well can we learn?" (Chapter 2)

- Distinction between Capability and Performance
- Degrees of learning within each Level (e.g., Cognitive Level: Awareness, Understanding [i.e, Comprehension, Transfer, Analysis, Synthesis, Evaluation], Wisdom)

**AVENUES** OF LEARNING: "In what ways can we learn?"

### *Information-Processing Learning Family: (Chapter 3)*

- Identification (e.g., instruction that "makes sense" through analogy, metaphor, parable, illustration)
- Inquiry (e.g., instruction that "doesn't make sense" through case study, puzzling event, discussion question)

### *Conditioning Learning Family: (Chapter 4)*

- Consequence (e.g, learning follows instruction through nonverbal, verbal, and written feedback, repetition)
- Cue (e.g., learned symbols precede instruction through familiar music, memory devices like advance organizers)

### *Social Learning Family: (Chapter 5)*

- Structured modeling (e.g, planned or "edited" instruction like demonstration, video, reading Scripture)
- Spontaneous modeling (e.g., "unrehearsed" instruction like Q & A, field trip)

**READINESS** FOR LEARNING: "Are we prepared to learn?"

### *Willing: Student Motivation—organizing instruction according to the learner's needs and interests (Chapter 6)*

- Motivational theories (e.g., Wlodkowski's Time Continuum Model: Before Lesson—Attitudes and Needs; During Lesson—Stimulation and Affect-Emotions; End of Lesson—Competence and Reinforcement)
- Psychological ordering of methods and Premack Principle (e.g., Richards' Hook, Book, Look, Took model)
- Learning Styles

### *Able: (Chapters 7-9)*

- Maturation—issues of natural growth (e.g., cognitive growth from concrete operations to formal operations)
- Prior or Prerequisite Learning (e.g., previous critical thinking skills learned from using case studies)

**NATURE** OF LEARNING: "What is the essence of learning?" (Chapters 10-11)

- Learning proceeds toward: Communion, Community, Character, and Commission.
- Learning involves change.
- Learning may be uncomfortable.
- Learning for Christians, as disciples, is our life-long calling.

> Learning for Christians is change facilitated through deliberate or incidental experience, under the supervision of the Holy Spirit, and in which one acquires and regularly integrates age-appropriate knowledge, attitudes, values, emotions, skills, dispositions, and habits into an increasingly Christ-like life.

## Try It Out

1. In Table 11.1, read the summary statement of learning (at the bottom of the table in the box). Identify which words specifically relate to each of the five features outlined in Table 11.1. Circle words in the summary, adding the respective *letter* of the acrostic "LEARN" to each word.[2]

2. Using the definition, reflect on the evidence of Peter's holistic learning experience previously discussed. For instance, identify specific changes he experienced in knowledge, attitudes, and so forth.

---

A more comprehensive understanding of learning provides a helpful analytical framework for diagnosing learning difficulties. For example, imagine that at a Backyard Bible Club you ask young LaVerne to explain a verse she can easily recite from memory. "I don't know," responds the third-grader. Your remedy to this problem depends on your diagnosis. Here are three possibilities.

1. **L**evel of Learning: LaVerne's tone of voice may be scornful. She's just plain *bored* (affective and dispositional level of learning). The youngster knows what the verse means, but she won't tell. She hasn't been challenged by the activities and has developed a "bad attitude" about the program. Part of the problem is that she feels coerced; her mother requires her to attend. Some positive attitudes and tendencies to participate need to be developed.

2. **E**xtent of Learning: LaVerne's tone of voice may be sincere. The third-grader really *doesn't* know the answer. LaVerne may only have an *awareness* degree of knowledge of the verse. She needs to move on to the next degree of comprehension.

3. **R**eadiness for Learning: LaVerne's tone of voice may be hesitant. This child could be *fearful* of giving the wrong answer (motivation). LaVerne has a good idea what the verse means, but doesn't want to risk being embarrassed, as she has been in the past. She needs to feel accepted. Her confidence must be strengthened.

With an increased understanding of learning—along with other factors related to student behavior—teachers have more options to accurately remedy learning problems.

## Application: Teaching with E's

An understanding of comprehensive learning principles also guides us in selecting appropriate teaching methods. After diagnosing what our students need to learn, we must determine the best strategy to move them in the right direction. To make it easier to use the six Avenues of learning in your lesson planning, the following design is offered as one model for teaching. Table 11.2 outlines a five-task framework. The relevant Avenues of learning (and sample teaching methods) are associated with each task. Although primarily the six Avenues are highlighted, note that concern for student readiness (motivation and developmental appropriateness of methods) must also be a consideration in lesson design.

## Table 11.2
# Teaching with E's

| Five Teaching Tasks (with Student Request) | Primary Supporting Avenues of Learning | Sample Teaching Methods | |
|---|---|---|---|
| | | In Class | Out of Class |
| **Emphasis** "What is most important?" | • Cue | Key terms, pictures, music repetition, reminders, advance organizer, memorize Scripture | Visit other settings where these selected "cues" are also present (e.g., youth conference) |
| **Example** "Explain it to me." | • Identification | Word pictures, analogies, good stories, illustrations, good books, guest speakers | Meet with respected "heroes" (of students) who value what is being taught |
| "Show me." | • Structured and Spontaneous Modeling | Verbal: testimonies, biographies Direct: demonstration, drama Symbolic: videos | Field trips to city mission, spend weekend at home with family exemplifying value |
| **Exercise** "Let me think it through." "Let me ask a question." | • Inquiry | Agree/disagree sheet, case studies, dilemmas, reflection papers on out of class experiences, small group discussions, play "devil's advocate" | Field trip: visit and discuss issues with others from diverse perspectives |
| "Let me try it again." | • Consequence and Cue | Role play; develop classroom culture or class routines that live out values | Work projects (e.g., remove graffiti, chores for "shut-ins"), One-week camping trip (and live out "classroom culture" during that week) |
| **Encouragement** "I need your affirmation." | • Consequence | Praise, affirmative comments, "catch them being good" | Whenever teacher sees students out of class, gives affirmative comments |
| **Evaluation** "What did I do well?" "Where do I need to improve?" | • Consequence | Quizzes, tests, (role play as assessment method); learning contracts; awards, prizes, penalties related to "classroom culture" policies; peer tutoring | Evaluation of tasks in work projects, Out-of-class personal projects with accountability partner |

The following discussion offers several examples to help visualize how these five teaching tasks can work. Imagine that we want to teach our students how to be more compassionate. What should we do? (Although a sequential order is followed below to explain the five tasks, in practice, they are much more interrelated.)

### Emphasis: What Is Most Important to Learn?

We can't teach everything. Teachers must make some judgments about what knowledge, values, skills, and dispositions are most important for students to learn. Then, we primarily use the Cue Avenue to focus students' attention on these matters, reminding them of its importance. Our purpose is for students to develop linkages between a word (or other symbol) and the concept we are teaching. It doesn't matter if it relates to a thought, an attitude, a value, or an action. Once the linkage is made, we can use the symbol to *remind* students about the connected appropriate thinking, decision-making, feeling, or action. For example, regarding the topic of compassion, we can have students memorize a verse like Ephesians 4:32. Then, to promote recall, we can have an oral or written quiz about the concept of compassion, distribute a handout summarizing it, have students read a discussion of it, draw students' attention to it by saying "this is important for you to learn," or by writing the word "compassion" on the blackboard as we present a lecture on the topic.

Other Avenues of learning also contribute to this learning process, but in a *secondary* way. We can *emphasize* compassion (1) when we praise or admonish a student's word or behavior (Consequence), (2) when we tell a story illustrating compassion (Identification), (3) when we ask a question about it (Inquiry), and (4) when we exemplify it in our own habits (Spontaneous/Structured Modeling) or by watching a movie that features compassion as a main theme (Structured Modeling).

### Examples: What Does It Look Like?

Once our students' attention is focused, they may ask, "What does 'compassion' look like?" We need to initially clarify the various facets of compassion. Our students' awareness of the concept of compassion must be taken to a deeper level of understanding and practice. As mentioned in chapter 5, based on Structured Modeling, we could use a variety of ways to exemplify compassion. Differing degrees of exposure could be employed for each of the three categories of modeling.

(1) *Verbal modeling*: Have students study relevant passages of Scripture; have respected peers or adults share experiences in which they offered or received compassion; read biographies of Christian servant-leaders who demonstrated compassion.

(2) *Direct modeling:* Have learners enact a drama to portray compassionate actions; visit a soup line at the City Mission; spend a day visiting with a family that is compassionate; watch a (live) play in which compassion is a major theme; or live with a mature Christian family (here or

in another country) for several weeks and observe their ministry of compassion.

(3) *Symbolic modeling:* Have students view television programs or movies that exemplify compassionate values, whether they involve Christians (e.g., World Vision specials) or not (e.g., "Ghandi" video).

In addition to these modeling avenues, use word pictures and analogies (Identification avenue) like "forgiveness is the oil that lubricates relationships." It is critical to use varied examples to help develop a comprehensive concept of compassion.

### Exercise: Let Students Try It Out

Next, we need to encourage our students to experiment with and *practice* compassionate words, feelings, and actions. Whatever we truly value will eventually evidence itself in outward acts. Habits of compassion develop through individual acts of compassion. Within the classroom we need to grow a compassionate community. Structure classroom routines and activities to guide student practice with other class members (e.g., peer tutoring, classroom chores that serve the whole class, group projects, peer mediators to help resolve conflicts). With guidance, the class itself can become a context in which to learn—a community of compassion.[3] Students can experiment with new modes of thinking and acting through role play (Inquiry Avenue).

Beyond the classroom, students could distribute clothes at a Salvation Army center, clean up the park, paint over graffiti on public walls, do some chores for a "shut-in" or widow from the church, or help repair a ministry facility in a needy area of town. Students could also serve on a short-term mission team to a Third World country.

If we wish to be characterized by compassion, then regular participation in compassionate acts offers proof of our convictions, since "faith without deeds is dead" (James 2:26). Our actions clarify how committed we are about being empathetic and merciful. God superintends our lives so that even unplanned experiences help our students become more compassionate. Even trials of life and the suffering they often entail can prompt growth (James 1:2–4) and can prepare us for ministry to others (2 Cor. 1:3–7).

### Encouragement: Students Need Our Affirmation

Learning can be difficult and frustrating. Students need a loving and supportive context in which they can feel free to take risks—to try out new things. Productive learning requires that students be given the freedom to fail. It seems that too often in class we give our attention to students only when they do something wrong. Current citizenship education programs focus on "catching them being good." This principle applies both to the teaching task of "encouragement" and to the final one of "evaluation." By our affirmation and praise we honor their efforts and actions.

For example, we notice that Yvone picks up Jerome's pencil. At the next opportunity, we privately thank her for her kindness, or we may wish to offer public praise. Even if we observe that Jimmy is *not* pulling Sharon's hair (a regular bad habit of his), we can acknowledge his self-control. We must work with students at their level of performance. *Any* feeble attempts by students that move in the direction of compassion must be affirmed by the teacher.

### Evaluation: Wise Guidance for Improvement

Finally, we teachers must give feedback about our students' thoughts, decisions, feelings, and actions in general—and those of compassion, in particular. This is the most critical phase of learning. Without this type of guidance our students have no way of telling if they are on the right track growing in Christian love. Without some measure of evaluation and accountability, our students' new patterns of living may lose hold in time, and temptation to stray is ever present. For example, we happen to overhear a conversation among classmates in which one student tells a joke that disparages another person (e.g., based on intellectual or athletic disabilities, race, or gender). Privately we confront the student, saying, "The joke may be funny, but it's not a very compassionate way of speaking." Giving helpful feedback to our students completes the learning process (cf. Rom 15:14; James 5:19–20).

## Conclusion

Human teachers play a significant role for students in the learning process. Yet we have tended to see our contribution *primarily* as dispensing new information, in relation to the first two E's of Emphasis and Examples. But we must acquire a more full-orbed perspective of our responsibility if we wish to facilitate the fullest learning possible. It must encompass all five E's, especially the latter three—those that tend to be given short shrift in much of our practice of education: Exercise, Encouragement, and Evaluation. For students can pursue additional information about the subject at hand through a variety of written and mediated sources. But these resources cannot provide *guided supervision* of the learning experience— the unique province of the teacher. If we truly wish to nurture mature attitudes and dispositions, along with knowledge and skills, it will require a more comprehensive approach to the task of teaching.

---

### Try It Out

Reflect on past lessons you have taught.

1. Which of the five "E's" do you give significant emphasis to in your lessons?

2. Which one of the five "E's" may need more attention in your lessons?

3. Jot down one idea within this particular "E" and try it out in your next lesson.

---

This particular five-task model of teaching is just one way of integrating various principles of learning.[4] If we can understand why a particular method works—what particular principle undergirds its effectiveness—it will be much easier to adapt any teaching method to better serve our teaching purposes. Knowing *why* we do *what* we do as teachers can help us pursue better learning and instruction. Granted, we can't explain everything about how learning and teaching work. As Paul said long ago: "I planted the seed, Apollos watered it, but God made it grow" (1 Cor. 3:6). That point reminds us of the purpose for devoting an entire book to the concepts and principles of the learning process. It can best be summarized by this timeless definition of Christian education:

> **Christian education is a reverent attempt to discover the divinely ordained process by which individuals grow in Christlikeness, and to work with that process (Harner 1939, p. 20)..**

## Key Concepts and Issues

a model of teaching: Teaching with E's

    Emphasis

    Examples

    Exercise

    Encouragement

    Evaluation

change

    openness to change

    resistance to change, painful experiences

definition of learning

disciples: following Jesus, listeners and doers

Nature of learning

Peter and resistance to change (Acts 10)

Table 11.1 (summary of concepts in book)

# Teaching Methods and the Six Avenues of Learning

Why does a particular teaching method work? Educational activities are based on a view of how students learn best. In the text, six basic principles or Avenues of learning have been described. Listed below are twenty-eight different teaching methods. One (or two) *main* Avenues of learning that provide the *major* learning potential for students for each teaching method listed are indicated. Good teaching methods use many Avenues at once, but the genius of each method can usually be identified with one or two Avenues. Each method is done well for the fullest benefit of the learner.

Information-Processing Learning Family
  **ID**    Identification Avenue
  **IQ**    Inquiry Avenue
Conditioning Learning Family
  **CN**    Consequence Avenue
  **CU**    Cue Avenue
Social Learning Family
  **ST**    Structured Modeling
  **SP**    Spontaneous Modeling

(ID) IQ    CN (CU)    ST SP    **Advance organizer**
ID (IQ)    CN CU    ST SP    **Agree-disagree statements**
ID (IQ)    CN (CU)    ST SP    Student **answers** a teacher's question
ID (IQ)    CN CU    (ST) SP    **Case study**
ID IQ    CN (CU)    ST SP    **Chairs arranged** differently in class
ID IQ    CN CU    (ST) SP    Teacher **demonstration**

| | | | | | | |
|---|---|---|---|---|---|---|
| ID | (IQ) | CN | CU | ST | SP | Teacher plays "devil's advocate" |
| ID | (IQ) | CN | CU | ST | (SP) | Class **discussion** of a moral dilemma |
| ID | IQ | CN | CU | (ST) | SP | Students attend a **drama production** |
| ID | IQ | (CN)–(CU) | | ST | SP | **Drill and practice** of a new skill |
| ID | IQ | CN | CU | ST | (SP) | **Field trip** |
| ID | IQ | (CN) | CU | ST | SP | Receiving a **grade** on a term paper |
| (ID) | IQ | CN | CU | ST | SP | **Illustrations or examples** |
| ID | IQ | CN | CU | ST | (SP) | Teacher **interviews** a guest |
| ID | IQ | CN | (CU) | ST | SP | Student reads a **learning contract** agreement to find next assignment |
| (ID) | IQ | CN | CU | (ST) | SP | **Lecture** |
| ID | IQ | CN | (CU) | ST | SP | **Memory devices** |
| ID | IQ | CN | (CU) | ST | SP | Teacher gives an **object lesson** |
| ID | IQ | CN | CU | ST | SP | **Praising students** |
| ID | IQ | (CN) (CU) | | ST | SP | Students work through a **programmed text** |
| ID | IQ | (CN) | CU | ST | SP | **Quiz or test** |
| ID | (IQ) | (CN) | CU | ST | SP | Teacher does a **role play** with another teacher |
| ID | IQ | CN | (CU) | ST | (SP) | Students participate in regular class **routines** (e.g., pledge of allegiance ) |
| ID | IQ | CN | (CU) | ST | SP | **Songs/Music** |
| (ID) | IQ | CN | CU | (ST) | SP | Teacher reads a **story excerpt** in class |
| ID | (IQ) | CN | CU | ST | SP | Writing a **term paper** |
| (ID) | IQ | CN | CU | (ST) | SP | Students read a **textbook** |
| ID | IQ | CN | CU | (ST) | SP | Viewing a **video excerpt** |

For further information on teaching methods, you may wish to consult a standard graduate text by Joyce et al. (1992). For book-length treatments from a Christian perspective, see Leypoldt (1967), Gangel (1972), LeFever (1985), McNabb and Mabry (1990), and Schultz and Schultz (1993).

# Unity in Diversity: Body, Soul, and Gender

Our uniqueness as humans issues from the fact that we have been created in the image of God (Gen. 1:26; James 3:9). In Chapter 7, we discussed the complexity of human nature and the characteristic of diversity in unity:

- We are each singular and individual persons, yet we are made of immaterial (soul) and material (body) parts.
- There is but one human race, although we were corporately created as male and female.

In this appendix, we give more detailed attention to these matters.

## Created as Body and Soul

Scripture uses a variety of terms that allude to differing aspects of essential human nature. The following terms come from Paul's writings (McDonald 1984, p. 678):

- *pneuma* (used 146 times as "spirit", e.g., 2 Cor. 7:1)
- *sarx* (used 91 times as "flesh", e.g., 2 Cor. 7:1)
- *sōma* (used 89 times as "body", e.g., Rom. 1:24)[1]
- *kardia* (used 52 times as "heart" as the seat of life, e.g., Rom. 1:24)
- various Greek words translated as "mind"; the most common term is *nous*, used as such 21 times, e.g., Eph. 4:17
- *psychē* (used 11 times as "soul", e.g., Rom. 2:9)

199

There is no question that persons function as *unitary* beings. The question is whether we are made up of distinct components that function harmoniously as one person. Human life cannot be reduced to just one substance—the material. For example, the purely materialistic view of human nature reduces an understanding of persons to what can be scientifically measured: physical acts and brain states, a naturalistic monism, understanding that persons are high-tech machines. Yet our Christian worldview incorporates both natural (or physical) and supernatural (or transcendent) realities (2 Kings 6:15–17). A traditional biblical understanding of humanity's structure delineates two basic aspects: material (i.e., based in physiology—the "body") and immaterial (i.e., not based in physiology—the "soul"[2]).

The tension Christian authors feel in discussing this subject is evident in the terms used to describe human nature, phrases like "minimal dualism" (Evans 1981, p. 313) and "contingent monism" (Erickson 1986, p. 538). Authors wish to identify two substances while indicating that these two substances normally function as one.

As Paul outlines in 1 Corinthians 15, God has made bodies appropriate for each level of existence on earth including those for fish and birds (vv. 38–39). Our physical bodies provide the vehicle through which we as souls can interact with this natural world. Paul reminds believers that we currently "groan inwardly" as we await "the redemption of our bodies" (Rom. 8:23). These perishable bodies will eventually give way to the imperishable "spiritual body" of the future (1 Cor. 15:42–43). At death, our souls live on although they become separated from the physical corpse. At the resurrection, our souls will be united with a new resurrection body.

Some contemporary evangelical authors are challenging this conception of personhood. How do we resolve the fact that persons function as holistic beings, yet biblically are described as made up of body and soul? Diverse responses have been offered to solve this age-old "mind-body" or "monism-dualism" issue.

Why is the debate important? One implication of the choice either for ontological monism or dualism affects what takes place after physical death. The significance and nuances of this particular issue are analyzed by Cooper (1989), Habermas and Moreland (1992), and Moreland (1993). A full review of the subject lies beyond the scope of the appendix, but, briefly, the implications are as follows.

*Ontological or substance dualism* holds that a person is made of body and soul (i.e., two constituent parts). After death, the soul continues to exist and is later united to a resurrection body. Thus, for a temporary period, persons are in a disembodied state.

*Ontological monism* sees a person as an indivisible unit (i.e., one constituent part). Thus, at death, the person ceases to exist. Then, immediately, or at a later time an individual is *recreated* as a glorified person. Thus, there is no continuity of existence.[3] As one author suggested, the quality of our earthly life is preserved in the memory of God and recreated, as a sequel to our present relationship with God, by an act of God (referring to Donald MacKay, as recorded by Farnsworth 1985, p. 140).

It is important to note that these two views cannot be mixed and matched— they are mutually exclusive. An ontological dualist holds to the *continuing* existence of the soul after death.[4]

## Created as Male and Female

According to Genesis 1:26, God made humankind in his image as male and female. Besides the perpetuation of the race for this life, the distinctive contribution of gender is the *social* character of humanity. "It is not good for the man to be alone" (Gen. 2:18). God is a trinitarian being in fellowship; humanity was created as a duality. Adam and Eve were both blessed by God and commanded to fill and to rule the earth (Gen. 1:28). And we are heirs together of life in Christ (Gal. 3:28) and God's grace (1 Pet. 3:7).

Although we exhibit some distinctive physiological features (e.g., reproductive glands, hormones, voices), we cannot be certain as to what extent our psychological differences result primarily from genetic structure or socialization. Scripture does present a few functional differences between the sexes, yet disagreement about their contemporary relevance is evident in the various interpretations offered. The primary points of contention among evangelical Christians relate to four passages and associated issues: (1) 1 Timothy 2:13 (cf. Gen. 2:18; significance of Adam's creation prior to Eve); (2) Genesis 3:16b (God's judgment at the fall regarding the "battle of the sexes" throughout life); (3) Ephesians 5:22–25 (headship in the marriage relationship); and (4) 1 Timothy 2:11–3:2 (potential restrictions in women's involvement in authoritative teaching in the church and participation as elders). How issues (3) and (4) are related to issues (1) and (2) is also a matter of discussion.

What are appropriate roles for men and women in church ministry? Based on differing understandings of the passages identified above, three main positions among evangelicals have emerged. They are arranged below from the least to the most restrictive position (Conservative Baptist Seminaries 1989, p. 5):[5]

- Egalitarian Position—All ministries of the church are open to all qualified men and women. Gender is not a relevant distinction for excluding a person from any office.
- Moderate Position—The office of elder alone is reserved for men. Women are to be encouraged to minister in any other office or ministry open to any other nonelder, assuming their qualifications and gifting are appropriate.
- Hierarchical Position—The office of elder (and usually of deacon) is reserved for men. Women are excluded from any ministry that includes public teaching to the corporate body or exercising authority over men. As a general pattern, men will be in authority over women and not visa versa.[6]

The issue of ministry roles represents a critical matter. We recommend continuing study. Since truth should always be balanced by love, we further suggest that, as we persevere in our efforts, we must serve one other and demonstrate the unity within Christ's body. Our growth toward maturity in Christ should seek to incorporate the fullest richness of our respective gender—not ignore or limit it— for we have been created as male *and* female.

All cultures outline certain gender-specific norms and roles, even though a wide range of human virtues can be actualized by both males and females. Scripture addresses these virtues, available to either gender, which represent mature humanity. Yet, realistically, we all live within a particular cultural context. Thus, we must balance the tension between *fitting in* our culture and *transforming* our culture. We honor both our ethnic and gender identity when we fully incorporate the good of our culture into our ways of thinking and acting. We honor our Christian identity to the kingdom of God when we critique the ideas and practices of our culture and become change agents when necessary. Ultimately, we anticipate the full realization of God's kingdom, when righteousness will be established on earth (2 Pet. 3:13).

# Notes

## Preface

1. House (1988) provides a helpful survey of the advantages of various schooling options for Christians—public, private, and home—written by their respective advocates.

2. This book is our third collaborative writing project. Our first joint effort was completed under Ted Ward's supervision at Michigan State University. We conducted parallel dissertation studies: Klaus investigated the moral dimensions of seminary curriculum (Issler 1984) whereas Ron studied the social dimensions (Habermas 1985). The second collaborative undertaking resulted in our first book: *Teaching for Reconciliation: Foundations and Practice of Christian Educational Ministry* (Baker 1992).

## Chapter 1: Why Worry about How We Learn?

1. Some texts provide practical exercises at the end of each chapter. The "Try It Out" exercises in this book, besides breaking up the chapter, offer an opportunity to work with a few ideas while reading the text. A few of them appear in each chapter. Some may wish to postpone doing these exercises until finishing the chapter.

2. For previous book-length discussions of learning theory from a Christian perspective see Boehlke (1962), Leypoldt (1971), Beechick (1982), and Barlow (1985). The reader may also wish to consult standard textbooks on educational psychology: Good and Brophy (1990), Dembo (1991), Seifert (1991), Gage and Berliner (1992), Biehler

and Snowman (1993), Lefrancois (1993), and Woolfolk (1993).

3. Material included in this book is taken from every source of knowledge: revelation, intuition, logic, experience, human authorities, and empirical research. Regarding the integration of Christianity and science, the book takes an eclectic approach, as developed by Moreland (1987). After describing five specific types, he prefers one that takes into consideration four of the five models:

An eclectic model of inte-gration . . . recognizes that sometimes [1] the two disciplines are concerned with two distinct realms, sometimes [2] they are noninteracting approaches to the same realm which provide answers to different kinds of questions, sometimes [3] theology provides an adequate worldview, consistent with the necessary philosophical presuppositions of science, and [4] sometimes they are interacting, competing approaches to natural phenomena. When theology and science relate in this last way, caution must be urged to guard against using God to merely cover our scientific ignorance. But when ultimate boundary conditions are being considered or cases where careful biblical exegesis seems to indicate that a gap should be expected, then God can be used to explain such cases. The objection that this involves a poor "God-of-the-gaps" strategy fails to be convincing (pp. 207–8).

The work of social science researchers will be cited to clarify how humans tend to learn. Almost all of these social science researchers are not evangelical believers. Yet "all truth is God's truth" (Gaebelein 1954; Holmes 1977) no matter *who* uncovers that truth. Whether the researcher is a believer or not, conclusions drawn from empirical research studies must be held tentatively, because additional data may clarify an interpretation or even contradict it.

In addition, the interpretive grid of social scientists affirms a purely materialistic view of human nature. Such a view reduces an understanding of persons to what can be scientifically measured: physical acts and brain states—a naturalistic monism. The Bible teaches a "conditioned" or "holistic" duality of the constituent elements of personhood. We are both body (material element) *and* soul (immaterial). See Appendix B for further comments.

From a Christian perspective, a major problem of social science research is that the people being studied are in a *fallen* condition. Even subjects who are regenerated are not "fully" human. Only in our glorified state will we truly manifest God's full design of humanity. Coupled with this problem is that the social science researchers themselves succumb to this same limitation. And faulty viewpoints, whether of believers or nonbelievers, likewise pertain. See Pazmiño (1988, chap. 6) for a discussion of the major views of integrating social science knowledge with Scripture. See Wilhoit (1991) for guidelines about how evangelicals can approach social science research.

4. "For instance, in spite of its long history and its estimable list of supporters, the [exclusive] notion of 'God as Teacher' fails, since in the end, human teachers do the teaching and the role of the human teacher must be explained. Is he a deluded puppet or merely a mechanical intermediary?" (Williamson 1970, p. 113).

5. See Habermas (1994b) for a concise overview of the biblical and theological foundations of Christian education, along with its brief history and future challenges.

6. Bible scholars who do not claim to have had a born-again salvation experience are able to understand the message of the Bible. The late Joseph Bayly related this story about one of his professors: "I remember studying under C. T. Craig, New Testament scholar and Revised Standard Version translator at Union Seminary the summer of 1942. The course was 'The Pauline Interpretation of the Gospel.' For the first few weeks Dr. Craig could not have been more clear in his understanding of the Pauline teaching if he had been teaching at Dallas or Wheaton.

"Then, at a critical point in the course, he said, 'Up to this time we've been studying what Paul actually said. Now we shall proceed to reinterpret his writings in the light of the twentieth century.' From then on he cut down what he had previously built. St. Paul was 'a child of his times'; cultural change necessitated a drastic revision of his ideas" (1982, p. 59; cited in Roberts 1984, p. 29).

7. For further study of this issue, see Fuller (1978).

8. See Gage and Berliner (1992, pp. 386–419) for a brief summary of the research literature on the advantages and disadvantages of lecturing, as well as suggestions for the effective use of lecture. Additional guidelines can be found in Habermas (in press) and Gangel (1974).

It may be difficult for college and seminary students to understand the need for using a variety of teaching methods. Students reason, "My professors primarily use the lecture method and I am able to learn very well from it. Why can't the people I teach learn like I do?"

What students fail to recognize is that formal education is a package deal and classroom time is only *one* element of the package—the most visible element, like the tip of an iceberg. Other elements significantly contribute to the effectiveness of classroom lecturing. Two factors work in the college or seminary student's favor: student motivation and all nonlecture student learning activities.

Motivation is intensified for the college or seminary student in light of working toward a degree, earning grades, and paying tuition for courses. Especially because they have paid tuition, highly motivated students sitting in a course with a very knowledgeable professor will often prefer a "bare bones" lecture. They have paid to hear the professor share his or her perspective. These students know they can listen to comments by other students outside of class, for free.

*Note:* This kind of highly motivated student may be a special case and some principles of learning (e.g., motivational considerations) are not as necessary as in other cases. Their case may be approaching an ideal—but only a small percentage of students seem to ever fit in that category. Nevertheless, it is a worthy aspiration to help all students become highly motivated, self-directed, lifelong learners.

Intensified learning for such students in academic settings results from a variety of elements: students spend much time out of class reading textbooks and writing papers; students study for hours, preparing for quizzes and exams, sometimes teaching themselves material that did not make sense to them during the lecture; and students receive substantial feedback on their learning through graded papers, tests, and so forth. In contrast, students in a typical church class are in a very different situation. They are not as motivated and usually don't do any out-of-class homework. Thus, within that one hour of class, teachers must tap into student motivation and help students learn the material. Any "homework" assignments must actually be done during class time—thus, the need for teaching methods that involve student participation.

9. For those familiar with Frankena's model for developing a philosophy of education, Frankena's box D (learning theory and teaching methods) is covered by the following LEARN elements: Levels, Extent, Avenues, some concepts in Readiness and Nature. Frankena's box B (which includes the nature of persons) fits with most of the elements of Readiness. See Habermas and Issler (1992, chaps. 1 and 19) for an introduction to Frankena's model.

10. Included in this category should be the concern that some students may come under the persuasion of one particular Christian leader, so that they are unreceptive to anyone else's teaching. Such cultlike narrowmindedness is inappropriate in evangelical churches. As Protestants, we have already renounced the idea that any one human being has the exclusive corner on God's truth. The teaching ministry of the Holy Spirit is available to all believers. One check on that kind of usurping authority is the need for a church to be led by a *group* of godly leaders.

11. See Moreland (1987) for an insightful apologetic tool to help students in their thinking about the critical issues of life. For matters related to Christianity and science, see Moreland (1989).

12. See Arnold (1992) for a comprehensive survey of the evil work of Satan and his demonic hoard, primarily based on Paul's letters.

13. "In the eighteenth century and much of the nineteenth, phlebotomy [bloodletting] held a position in therapeutics comparable to that of antibiotics today. For inflammatory diseases, such as pneumonia, phlebotomy was the traditional and generally accepted method of treatment" (King 1991, p. 192). In defense of this traditional practice, one nineteenth-century physician wrote: "the efficacy of bloodletting in the treatment of pneumonia, is not an error and a delusion; it has its foundation in nature and in truth . . . clear, intelligible, philosophical demonstration" (Bartlett 1848, p. 42).

14. Various methods were used to drain the blood, depending on the physician's training, skill, and background. Some doctors would cut a vein (called "phlebotomy") and let the blood pour into a bowl. Or they might heat a cup and then apply it to the cut to draw out the blood. And then, there was the more "mechanical" method—applying leeches! With this method, the doctor had to be skilled in locating a vein. To drain the required amount of blood (about twenty ounces), it took about twenty leeches. Or, to conserve leeches, the doctor could use just one leech by cutting off a part of it so the leech would not become fully engorged. But then the leech would die and it could not be reused (Copeman 1960).

Amazing as it may seem, in modern medicine, leeches are still used in particular situations. When a small part of the body (e.g., an ear or a finger) is being reattached, the arteries can be repaired, but the veins are too small to suture. The reimplanted part becomes engorged with blood and may be lost. In such cases, leeches remove the blood, which decreases the swelling and allows the veins to heal (personal conversation, Dr. Mary Wilder, July 17, 1991). For further information about this modern practice, see Gonzales (1978).

15. In addition to the fluids, there were four basic properties: heat, cold, moisture, and dryness. The four temperaments, a combination of these properties, were labeled after the names of the four humors—apparently sharing similar characteristics—in the order presented earlier: sanguine (hot and moist), phlegmatic (cold and moist), choleric (hot and dry), and melancholic (cold and dry) (Copeman 1960, 87–88).

# Chapter 2: What Can We Learn?

1. The word "conative" is related to the Latin *conatus,* which refers to "an effort to accomplish a desired end, endeavor, exertion, attempt" (Glare et al. 1968, p. 383). The term has been used in the past by some philosophers to refer to the faculty of volition and desire (OED 1971). Webster's defines "conation" as "the act or faculty of striving or making an effort" (Guralink 1984, p. 292). Lee (1985, p. 30, n. 50) hypothesized that conation is a discrete category for learning outcomes but judged the empirical data to be insufficient. Empirical researchers will probably never come to any conclusion about this as long as their worldview ignores the existence of the soul. For example, though Watson and Tharp (1989) provide helpful guidance in habit formation, they explain away the will: "The word *willpower* implies some entity, something in your psychological makeup, something that allows you to do hard jobs, overcome temptations, stick to your goals. But what is it— an electric current, some form of energy? It's just a word, a label we use when we want to describe how people deal with problems in self-direction" (pp. 7–8). Yet even Christian psychologist Bufford (1981) considers the concept of "self-control" to be a misnomer, p. 182.

2. Lee (1985, chap. 5) includes the concepts of feelings, emotion, attitudes, values, and love in his discussion of affective content.

3. A brief but readable discussion of the three-domain perspective is provided in a self-instructional text for Sunday school teachers developed by Ford (1978).

Lee (1985) slices the learning pie a little differently. First, he divides learning content into two main categories (p. xii): "structured" content (i.e., the actual teaching interaction itself) and "substantive" content (what we usually call the subject matter). For this "substantive" content, he identifies five different groupings, mainly composed of opposing pairs of learning outcomes, to total nine learning "contents" (p. 14): (1) product and process content; (2) cognitive and affective content; (3) verbal and nonverbal content; (4) conscious and unconscious content; and (5) lifestyle content. In his book, he devotes a chapter to each of these contents (except for conscious content).

Lee's "lifestyle" content is treated in chapter 9 of his book. This domain focuses on a holistic integration of all the discrete learning contents. We agree that the whole is greater than the sum of the parts. We have used the synthesis of the four themes of Christian Maturity (see chap. 10) to address this need for synthesis.

See Steinaker and Bell (1979) for their attempt to integrate the various domains into *one* taxonomic guide for teaching practice.

4. Gagne (1985) further divides the cognitive domain into three distinct areas: "verbal information" (the content—what we can tell others), "intellectual skills" (the rules we learn to govern our behavior, such as the rules of grammar), and "cognitive strategies" (how we work with the content we have learned through memorizing, retrieval, problem-solving, etc.).

5. This three-part continuum is suggested by Lee (1985, p. 159).

6. This bicycle illustration comes from a presentation Dan Stevens, an education professor, uses to explain the various categories of Bloom's taxonomy.

7. Both Lee (1985) and Ford (1978) use the term "knowledge," where this book uses

the term "awareness" or "recognition." This reflects the term used in Bloom's taxonomy for the most superficial level of cognition. "Knowledge" is such a good biblical term, however, that it would be improper to restrict it to such a narrow view of mental activity. The term can be used as a way of describing the whole of the cognitive level, while "awareness" captures the first level of the "knowledge" domain.

8. The term "application" refers to what the educational literature understands as "transfer of learning." On the one hand, transfer relates to the use of the concept with a new problem, but still working within the classroom. On the other hand, the broader view is concerned with a student's use of the concept beyond the classroom, in the student's life experiences in other kinds of settings. Hamachek (1990, pp. 473–75) suggests that teachers keep the following guidelines in mind to help such transfer to life experience: (a) connect in-school learning to out-of-school experiences; (b) teach for greater understanding of the "whys"; and (c) stress underlying principles, generalizations, and applications.

9. The technical terms for interference in learning theory are "proactive inhibition," when old learning persists and prevents new learning; and "retroactive inhibition," when new learning "erases" old learning.

10. A discussion of short- and long-term memory functioning is beyond the scope of this book. Standard educational psychology textbooks, such as Sprinthall and Sprinthall (1991), provide a useful introduction.

11. Taxonomies of the behavioral or psychomotor domain have been developed by Simpson (1966), Harrow (1969), Kibler, Parker, and Miles (1970), and Jewett and Mullan (1977).

12. For "Guided Response" (Phase 2), it is helpful, first, for the teacher to do a "task description" of the skill (Davis, Alexander, and Yelon 1974, chap. 5). Such an analysis identifies the various subskills that make up the larger skill. Then, the list of subskills can be arranged into the best teaching sequence.

13. "People making news," reported in *U.S. News and World Report* (June 16, 1986).

14. Hauerwas (1975) highlights the importance of developing dispositions: "All sides assume that the primary issue for moral behavior is the decision we make about particular situations and practices. As a result it is forgotten that what is at stake in most of our decisions is not the act itself, but the kind of person we will be" (pp. 7–8). Willard (1988, p. 118) suggests that "Habitual reliance upon God as we dedicate our bodies to righteous behavior and to all reasonable preparation for righteous behavior makes sin dispensable, even uninteresting and revolting—just as righteousness was revolting to us when our behavior was locked into the sin system. Our desires and delights are changed because our actions and attitudes are based upon the reality of God's Kingdom." See Willard (1988) and Foster (1988) for explanations of the spiritual disciplines. A brief discussion of Willard's list of spiritual disciplines appears as the application section in chapter 9. See Tables 4.4 and 4.5 for specific guidance on developing new habits (chap. 4).

15. Two key concepts in measurement theory are "reliability" and "validity." Reliability signifies that we would get a similar result no matter how many times we measured an item. A synonym for validity is accuracy. Does the measurement tool actually measure what it claims to measure? Let's illustrate the concepts by using a yard stick, a common measuring tool. Imagine that the yard stick is made of plastic, and somehow—after being heated—it stretches, but the inch markers do not appear distorted. Now the yard stick is longer than a yard and each inch marker no longer is exactly an inch. In using this longer yard stick, we would get reliable results—we could mark off a number of pieces of wood with the same effect. But these markings would not be accurate. When we move from the physical world to measure characteristics of learning, such as achievement or personality tests, measurement theory becomes a little more complex.

Testing theory for classrooms incorporates two quite distinct emphases: norm-referenced tests and criterion-referenced tests. Standardized tests are based on a norm-referenced orientation. Their main purpose is to compare students' results in order to develop a ranking from top to bottom. Grades using this orientation would be based on the normal bell curve and, theoretically, would yield a few A's, B's, D's, and F's—but mostly C's. Criterion-referenced tests help individual students assess how well they scored against the standards of mastery set up by the teacher. Thus, in a class using this "mastery learning" model, all students could theoretically earn A's if they reached a certain level of achievement.

16. In fact, some outcomes never surface; they may be quite private for good reasons (Matt. 6:1–6), or it may be that the student's learning was all "talk" and no "show" (Matt. 23:3).

17. For example, the "guess and go" technique used by one first-grade teacher has significant implications for learning. While writing in their journals, students would ask the teacher, "How do I spell —?" To which the teacher replied, "Guess and go." Translated, that meant don't worry about your spelling right now; concentrate on your thoughts and what you are writing, and the spelling will take care of itself. By the second or third grade, it did. This technique allowed first-graders to focus on the skill and enjoyment of writing, because they weren't required to have perfect spelling at this point in their writing careers.

# Chapter 3: Learning by Processing Information

1. See Habermas (1993c) concerning extrabiblical sources of truth which affect our instruction.

2. Some educational psychology texts discuss another theory: humanistic principles of education. This theory arose primarily in reaction to the more mechanistic behavioral psychology that dominated the first half of this century in American educational research. In contrast to an emphasis on the similarities among people, humanistic theory attempts to highlight the uniqueness of each person—and to provide a more humane learning environment. Much of this concept fits more into the Affective Level of learning than any other. Two humanistic pioneers have been Carl Rogers (1983) and Abraham Maslow (1987). Maslow's famous hierarchy of needs is treated in chapter 9. A current popular method in schools, cooperative learning, fits in well with many of the personal values promoted by humanistic theory. Major proponents of this approach have been Johnson and Johnson (1991).

3. For ease of memory, the learning *family* and its matched set of *Avenues* begin with the same letter of the alphabet.

4. The term "Information-Processing" is used by Joyce et al. (1992) with reference to our "drive to make sense of the world by acquiring and organizing data, sensing problems, and generating solutions to them, and developing concepts and language for conveying them" (p. 71).

5. Since the miraculous feeding of the five thousand demonstrates effective use of all six learning Avenues, this special learning event will also be included in chapters 4 and 5.

6. The concept of identification or "meaningful" learning is developed by Ausubel (1963, 1968).

7. Since such metaphors are culturally and historically-specific, we must transform these biblical illustrations into contemporary ones. "Shepherds," "sheep," and "vineyards" are no longer relevant to many present-day Christians.

8. The advance organizer was developed by Ausubel (1968). Some confuse this technique with a brief overview at the beginning of class when the teacher outlines the material to be covered in that session. This particular activity is helpful—it explains the lesson agenda—but it is not an advance organizer. The advance organizer attempts to fit new information within a *conceptual* outline of a broader knowledge base. For example, the acrostic, "LEARN," with its related five part framework is an advance organizer for the concept of learning.

Levels of learning—What can we learn?

Extent of learning—How well can we learn?

Avenues of learning—In what ways can we learn?

Readiness for learning—Are we prepared to learn?

Nature of learning—What is the essence of learning?

9. The theoretical background for the Inquiry Avenue stems from Festinger's (1957) cognitive dissonance theory and Piaget's (1977) concept of equilibration. An introductory treatment of Piaget's cognitive development theory will be provided in chapter 8. Related to Inquiry is the term "discovery learning," which emphasizes students' participation in the learning process through guided experiences, so they develop solutions and principles themselves.

10. Appreciation is expressed to Rev. Larry Gadbaugh for this illustration.

11. Since using questions in the classroom has been so highly touted as an effective teaching method, some teachers have assumed that *any* use of questions is appropriate. The worst use of classroom questions is the "fishing game." Teachers ask questions and "fish for" answers with the exact phrasing that they have in mind. When a student gives an answer in this situation, teachers usually respond with, "That's not exactly what I had in mind," and continue receiving answers until the expected response surfaces. Rather than wasting class time and frustrating students, it's better to present the concept directly, and then use participatory teaching methods to guide students' deeper thought about the issue.

# Chapter 4: Learning by Association

1. "Conditioning Learning family" is our term for Behavioral Learning theories. One must make a distinction between "behavioral learning theory" and "behaviorism." The first is a label used to include explanations about how we tend to act—looking at efficient causes. "Behaviorism" is a mechanistic, deterministic, metaphysical view about the final causes of all human behaviors. As Christians, we can use principles from the former, but we must reject the latter.

2. Andi Kalugin, Ed.D. student, School of Intercultural Studies, Biola University. See Luccock and Hutchinson (1949, pp. 168–71) for an example of how the class leader might encourage and admonish members during a typical Wesleyan class meeting during the nineteenth century.

3. In addition, our conscience is designed as an internal monitor to provide feedback regarding our thoughts and actions (Rom. 2:15). For helpful studies of conscience, see Toon (1984) and Issler (1993).

4. The Consequence Avenue is based on "operant" or "respondent" behavioral conditioning, as initially developed by Skinner (1953). A treatment of these concepts from a Christian perspective is provided by Bufford (1981). Although experiencing pleasure and pain are important components of operant conditioning, we would not deify these as the only values of worth, as did Jeremy Bentham (1748–1832) when he developed hedonistic utilitarian ethics: "Nature has placed mankind under the governance of two sovereign masters, pain and pleasure. It is for them alone to point out what we ought to do, as well as what we shall do" (Bentham 1789).

5. Even though certain disciples were initially introduced to Jesus by John the Baptist as the Lamb of God (John 1:29), it took about two years for the disciples to fully recognize Jesus as the Messiah. Besides the resurrection, the feeding of the five thousand is the only miracle that is recorded by all four Gospel writers, signifying its importance.

6. Such diverse skills as learning a foreign language and playing the piano depend on the Cue Avenue. For example, in playing the piano, we make a linkage between the different dots on a page and the appropriate keys to play.

7. John Johnson, Ed.D. student, School of Intercultural Studies, Biola University.

8. The Cue Avenue (or "classical" conditioning) with its basic concept of "conditioned reflex" was developed in America by Watson (1930). A brief, readable discussion of principles undergirding both Consequence and Cue Avenues can be found in chapters 5–7 of Mager (1984), Gagne (1985), and, from a Christian perspective, in Meier et al. (1991, chap. 6). Gagne discusses the concept of "chaining." He explains how habits are developed through the combination of the Consequence (operant conditioning) and Cue (classical conditioning) Avenues.

9. The distinctive features of the three modes of education (formal, nonformal,

and informal) are discussed in our book (Habermas and Issler 1992, pp. 145–46). See Habermas (1994a) for more information on educating children within the family context.

10. See Hoekema (1986) for a helpful theological discussion of the concept of self-image. See Dobson (1974) for ways to help children develop a positive self-image.

11. "What keeps Rocco from the road? Just a detail," Mark Hulig, New York Times News Service, as reported in *The [Portland] Oregonian* (Dec. 5, 1987).

12. Bolton et al. (1987) explain how to effectively employ such Bible learning activities.

13. Sprinthall and Sprinthall (1990, chap. 20) outline a developmentally appropriate classroom management strategy based on Kohlberg's moral reasoning theory. For additional information on rearing and teaching children, see Meier et al. (1993) and Ratcliff (1988b, 1992).

# Chapter 5: Learning by Example

1. Reported in *The Orange County Register*, (Santa Ana, Calif.) "Sideshow/A Lighter Side" May 25, 1992, p. A2.

2. Reported in *The Orange County Register*, (Santa Ana, Calif.) Dec. 27, 1991, p. A10.

3. Charles Colson encourages parents to introduce their children to biographies of great Christians. His recent book, *The Body* (Word 1992), includes a number of dramatic stories about heroes of the faith.

4. Routines and habits can be placed in this category. That is, a particular routine was either planned prior to the first instance, or thought to be worth repeating after the first instance.

5. Some professional models have refused to advertise certain products because they believe they have "a responsibility not to encourage people to use such products" (Chapelle 1988, L5). Jeffrey Calenberg, who founded Models for Christ with his wife, also a model, does not appear in ads for cigarettes or alcohol. "I choose not to do them because I know there are hundreds of thousands of people who die from cigarette-re-

lated causes and millions who die from alcohol-related causes each year."

6. It is difficult to call anything our Lord did "spontaneous," since he always knew what he was doing. From the disciples' perspective, new events, such as this miracle, were spontaneous to them, as participants, and they are spontaneous to us as readers. Technically, such happenstance events are the essence of this Avenue of modeling.

7. The "classroom meeting," an informal discussion in which teacher and students evaluate the class, is another means of bringing Spontaneous Modeling into the classroom. The idea is to have a "town hall" meeting to talk about how the class is progressing (Joyce and Weil 1986). An understanding of Spontaneous Modeling should also encourage teachers to increase out-of-class contacts with students.

8. In our pairing of Social Learning theory and teaching youth, we reject a "mindless mentoring" in which adults only passively associate with teens. We think leaders should be more intentional about being a role model. For example, adults should model critical thinking skills in facing the problems of today. Teens can then learn how we as adults integrate our faith as we confront our world.

9. See Dockery (1989) for twelve practical lessons on teen relationships.

10. See Burns (1988, pp. 114–17) for how a peer ministry can be developed. Additional resources are Reynolds (1983) and Varenhorst (1983).

11. In a typical worship time, other learning Avenues are evident, such as in the reading of Scripture (Cue Avenue and Structured Modeling) and in congregational singing (Cue Avenue).

12. Issler (1990) outlines alternate strategies for nurturing healthy marriages and families in the church based on some of the Avenues of learning: Inquiry Avenue ("seizing the teachable moment"), Consequence Avenue ("providing meaningful feedback"), and Spontaneous Modeling ("modeling biblical norms").

13. Suggested responses for this second "Try It Out" exercise can be found in Appendix A.

# Chapter 6: Sensitivity to Student Motivation

1. What happens when a teacher falsely assumes that each student has "normal" mental and physical functioning? For instance learning-disabled students or physically handicapped learners require alternative teaching strategies. The field of "special education" attempts to be sensitive to these developmental concerns in guiding instruction and learning. Some guidelines are suggested in the application section in chapter 7.

2. We can make some generalizations applicable to all students since they share similar developmental phases from childhood through adulthood, though some differences may emerge due to varying cultural contexts and expectations of what it is to be mature.

3. "Willing" is a factor of the will. Students choose to participate or not to participate. We need to build on our students' natural desire to learn and cultivate a disposition for higher-order learning, despite the effort it may take. Adult educator Patricia Cross says it well: "Ideally, the task of educators is to develop the taste for good learning—to develop gourmet learners who are able to tailor and utilize the resources in the learning society to their own needs" (cited in Wlodkowski 1985, p. 281).

4. Wlodkowski and Jaynes (1990, pp. 7–11) discuss these kinds of learning barriers in more detail.

5. Keller (1987) offers another helpful and integrative model of motivation in which he summarizes four basic motivational factors summarized as "ARCS": Attention, Relevance, Confidence, and Satisfaction. The substance of these four parallels the substance of Wlodkowski's six-factor model as Wlodkowski himself suggests (1985, pp. 276–77). Another commonly used analytical tool for motivation is Maslow's hierarchy of needs. This model is discussed under personality development in chapter 9.

6. Information about how attitudes are developed, largely through the Cue Avenue, is available in chapter 4 and in Mager (1984).

7. Appreciation is expressed to Rev. Tom Mosley for pointing out this fourfold comparison.

8. Lewis (1987) suggests a provocative psychological ordering approach in teaching basic reading skills:

Students' motivation to read can be stifled by the kinds of reading assignments commonly found on reading lists. Often material is of little interest and does not encourage reading as a life-long pastime. Students are usually required to read the "classics," which are someone else's idea of what is interesting. . . . It may be possible to help students read more and at the same time to pique their interest in the classics by suggesting that they read the works of Louis L'Amour [the famous Western novelist]. . . . L'Amour mentions authors, scholars, and books that the best educated in our society would find impressive. . . . The gains from introducing L'Amour works to preadolescents and adolescents may be threefold. First, students might be stimulated to read action-packed adventure tales told by a master storyteller. Second, the novels expose students to a strong advocate of the value of education in the classic sense. Third, the books might stimulate interest in the classical literature referenced in L'Amour's works (pp. 261–62).

9. As Richards (1970) suggests, not every lesson has a "Took" segment. A series of lessons (e.g., with six lessons) may build toward one significant "Took" during the final session. Thus, the first couple of lessons may just include "Hook" and "Book" emphases. Later lessons may include a "Hook," a brief review of the previous "Book" material, and more emphasis on "Look" implications. The sixth lesson may be totally taken up with "Look" and "Took" segments. The Hook, Book, Look, Took theoretical framework is primarily useful for teaching teens and adults. Although the principles are applicable to children, the segments are not as discrete. Children's sessions use a variety of

combinations of "Hook-Book" activities and "Look-Took" methods.

10. A lesson design format widely used in public education was developed by Hunter (1982). This model includes seven basic elements (notice certain similarities with Richards' four-part model):

- anticipatory set (gaining student attention)
- objective and purpose of lesson (what students will learn and why)
- input (new information needed)
- modeling (teacher activities to illustrate content or skill)
- guided practice (student activities to practice in class)
- checking for understanding (gauging level of student learning)
- independent practice (homework)

For additional information on designing lessons, see Ford (1978) and Posner and Rudnitsky (1989).

11. Helping students set their own learning goals can also address issues of relevance and student readiness. Setting their own goals may also encourage their ownership and responsibility in the learning process.

12. To make group activities and projects more successful, we need to eliminate as much as possible destructive competitive elements among group members. For example, our evaluation and grading practices can significantly affect our students' willingness to work together. If course grades are based on a normal curve (a certain percentage will earn A's, B's, C's, etc.) then a student may wish to withhold giving help to others so that he or she will earn the highest grade. If a "mastery model" of learning is used wherein students earn grades based on their own mastery (and not primarily in comparison to the achievement of other students), then students may be more willing to cooperate on assignments.

13. For example, one of us used this handicapping technique to teach his son, Daniel, the game of chess. I wanted to encourage his progress, yet let him face the reality of losing fairly. In this vein, I removed three playing pieces from my side of the board: a rook, a bishop, and a knight (we tried taking off pawns, but that didn't work well). If Daniel beat me five games in a row, I would add one piece at the next game. If I won a series of five games, one piece would come off from my side. (In addition, I did warn him whenever his queen was in danger.) Over a two-year period we went back and forth, adding and taking off pieces—and both of us enjoyed the game. Eventually, Daniel was able to beat me ten games in a row, even though I had all of my pieces!

14. We are used to giving awards for meritorious achievement. Awards can help students focus on the kinds of standards we wish to highlight, whether they be academic, attitudinal, or behavioral. The "warm fuzzy jar" is one interesting reinforcement technique. The teacher places a marble in a glass bowl when she catches her students being good (the marble represents a "warm fuzzy" award). She takes a marble out when any student misbehaves. If the jar is full at the end of the week, the whole class enjoys a special treat (e.g., extra snack, game time, or play time out at the park). This particular approach encourages group effort as well as peer pressure to develop self-discipline in students.

Incentives can also be used to encourage students to try a new activity—to take a risk. Here a reward is given regardless of how well a student performs the action—just for the sake of an attempt. We know one grandfather who used monetary prizes if a grandchild would try a new food item ("It's worth a quarter if you taste this"). Speaking of food, it's always appropriate to celebrate the end of a class with an "R & R"—refreshments and reflection on what students have learned in the class.

15. The "Learning Style Inventory" (a twelve-item questionnaire), based on Kolb's cognitive model, is available from McBer and Company, 137 Newbury St., Boston, MA 02116. Learning Style Inventories based on Dunn's multidimensional model (a one hundred-item task) are available for those in grades 3–12 and for adults ("Productivity Environmental Preference Survey") from Price Systems, Box 1818, Lawrence, KS 66044.

16. A helpful overview of learning styles, especially as it relates to multicultural education, can be found in Bennett (1990). Though no research has attempted yet to address this issue, many of the particular learning modes may largely stem from a student's personality temperament. Chapter 9 presents one four-factor temperament theory that could easily be paired with Kolb's four learning styles:

| Temperament | Kolb's Styles |
|---|---|
| Expressive | Innovative |
| Analytical | Analytical |
| Amiable | Common sense |
| Driver | Dynamic |

# Chapter 7: Human Nature: Birthday Gifts for Growth and Learning

1. Even the angelic host are placed in a position of subservience to humankind (Ps. 8:5; 1 Cor. 6:3; Heb. 1:14). Undoubtedly we are in a class by ourselves—a privileged class of all of God's creatures, despite the current accusation of "speciesism" (an unjustified preference for one species over another; thus humans and animals are equally valuable, an implication of evolutionary theory). See Habermas (1993b) concerning insights and implications of the image of God in all people.

2. "We know from the Bible, however, that God chose to become incarnate in a creature very much like himself. It is quite possible that God's purpose in making man in his own image was to facilitate the incarnation which would someday take place" (Erickson 1985, p. 737).

3. "In Jesus, for the first time a human being was developing under ideal conditions, unimpeded by heredity or acquired defects" (Thomas and Gundry 1988, p. 40). Erickson (1985) comments on the deity and humanity of our Lord:

"The union of the two natures meant that they did not function independently. . . . His [Jesus'] actions were always those of divinity-humanity. This is the key to understanding the functional limitations which the humanity imposed upon the divinity. For example, he still had the power to be ev-

erywhere (omnipresence). However, as an incarnate being, he was limited in the exercise of that power by possession of a human body. Similarly, he was still omniscient, but he possessed and exercised knowledge in connection with a human organism which grew gradually in terms of consciousness, whether of physical environment or eternal truths. Thus, only gradually did his limited human psyche become aware of who he was and what he had come to accomplish. Yet this should not be considered a reduction of the power and capacities of the Second Person of the Trinity, but rather a circumstance-induced limitation on the exercise of his power and capacities" (p. 735).

4. "The question is not whether Jesus was fully human, but whether we are. He was not merely as human as we are; he was more human than we are. He was, spiritually, the type of humanity that we will possess when we are glorified. . . . We should define humanity, not by integrating our present empirical observations, but by examining the human nature of Jesus, for he most fully reveals the true nature of humanity" (Erickson 1985, p. 736).

5. For further comments on points 1 and 2, see Appendix B.

6. These differences between Condition B and Condition C bring greater complexity for Christians regarding the study of human growth and learning. We must be careful to identify which aspects of humankind remain the *same* between Condition B and Condition C and which aspects have been *changed*. Secular psychology primarily studies persons in Condition B. Moreover, non-Christian psychologists approach their task with Condition B "perspectives" (i.e., a fallen mind). They measure, collect, and interpret data within a "Condition B" mindset. When these psychologists study features of humanity that have a significant continuity between Condition B and Condition C, Christians can readily use their research (e.g., intelligence testing). *Yet when these psychologists study features that have been significantly changed between Condition B and Condition C* (e.g., a renewed conscience that has greater sensitivity to sin), *their interpretations should be held with some suspicion.* In such cases, greater credibility must be given

to researchers with a biblical frame of reference, all other issues being equal (e.g., research skills and competence).

Thus, in understanding matters of human and spiritual growth, we must keep in mind that, currently, no person is fully human (in the same sense as we will be in our glorified condition) since both Condition B and Condition C characteristics still prevail. For a survey of a theology of human nature, see Saucy (1993).

7. In the New Testament, the primary word translated as "growth" is *auxanō* ("to grow"). This word takes its point of reference from the botanical sphere. "Behind the use of the simple form there plainly stands the thought of growth in creation, especially in the plant kingdom. . . . The combination with *karpopherō* (Col. 1:16 and 10) again shows that we have here an image from the plant kingdom" (Delling 1972, p. 518). The *auxanō* word group, appearing twenty-five times in the New Testament, is used of lilies (Matt. 6:28), mustard trees (Matt. 13:32), and the body (Luke 1:80). Metaphorically, it points to the spiritual growth of the body of Christ (Col. 2:19). With reference to such figurative growth in believers, Scripture records use of *auxanō* in relation to the ministry of God's word (Acts 12:24; Col. 1:16); believers (Eph. 4:15; 1 Pet. 2:2); and specific factors such as faith (2 Cor. 10:15), the knowledge of God (Col. 1:10), and the grace of the Lord (2 Pet. 3:18)."

Of significance in this botanical metaphor is that there must be a correspondence between the nature of the *seed* and the nature of the *mature plant* (cf. James 3:12). The analogy of the seed conveys the appropriate imagery of our spiritual-human nature. We are complete, based on both *natural* birth and *spiritual* rebirth. As we obey and trust God, our human nature unfolds and matures (Phil. 2:12–13).

8. God placed within our bodies an internal developmental clock that regulates both the timing and sequence of the physical maturation process. For example, we have baby teeth before we have adult teeth. In addition, this clock regulates the outside boundaries of our bodies, such as height (cf. Luke 12:25). A different "clock setting" is

given to God's other creatures. For example, it takes approximately one to two years for horses to reach adult form.

9. Rev. J. Singh, who directed an orphanage in India, kept a journal of the progress of two young girls who had been reared by wolves (Singh and Zingg 1939). Both girls died before they reached adolescence. The second half of this book recounts other bizarre cases in which children lived under extremely repressive conditions. More recently, the Associated Press reported a case in which a four-year-old had been kept in a dirt-floored pen with sixty dogs (Tacoma *News Tribune,* March 17, 1990). The newly assigned foster parents were astounded that "he ran wildly through the house, crashing into walls, and most of the time he ran on all fours. If he wanted attention, he would run up to us and paw at our bodies, rub his head on us and whimper" (p. 1).

10. The list only includes those disorders based on physical impairments. Disorders not physically based include "Behavior Disorders" and "Learning Disability". These are catch-all categories used when no specific cause can be identified. The first category is associated with aggressive and disruptive behavior. The second category primarily is used when there is a significant discrepancy between student academic performance and overall ability (e.g., one has poor reading skills yet is fairly capable in other areas of life). For sake of completeness, the category of "gifted and talented" students should also be included here since it typically occurs in discussions of special education.

11. For further reading on physical disabilities and special education see Hallahan and Kauffman (1991), Hardman et al. (1990), Haring and McCormick (1990), and Slavin et al. (1989); from a Christian perspective see Ratcliff (1980), and Newman and Tada (1987), Sutton et al. (1993)—primarily on mental impairment, see Ratcliff (1985b, 1990) and Anthony (1992).

12. In the early years before the flood, people lived much longer than today. For example, Adam and Methuselah lived over 900 years (Gen. 5:5, 27)! Current limits appear to be around 120 years, as recorded by the Guinness records (cf. Ps. 90:10).

# Chapter 8: Developmental Changes in Our Thinking

1. Responses are taken from interviews conducted by students of the EMS 503 Learning Process class at Western Seminary, 1990.

2. The purpose of 1 Corinthians 13:11 in Paul's argument in verses 8–12 is to provide a human example of two different perspectives: one that is limited (our current *earthly* viewpoint—"now I know in part") and one that is full (our future heavenly viewpoint—"then I shall know fully"). See Habermas (1993a) for serious implications that emerge when "childlikeness" is not differentiated from "childishness." For another example from Scripture regarding differences in reasoning ability, consider the concept of the "age of moral accountability." The idea assumes some kind of a demarcation in cognitive capacity, that moral accountability cannot be reckoned to those who are incapable of full cognizance of their actions, such as very small children and those who are severely mentally retarded. Deuteronomy 1:39 gives some support for such a concept: "And the little ones that you said would be taken captive, your children who do not yet know good from bad—they will enter the land. I will give it to them and they will take possession of it" (see also Isa. 7:15–16).

3. Piaget (1896–1981) offered a theory of cognitive-structural development that has significantly influenced psychology and education ever since. In testing the IQ of children in France, Piaget was puzzled about the wrong answers children supplied. Further assessment led him to postulate that children's reasoning ability moves through *qualitatively* different forms before achieving full adult capabilities (Piaget and Inhelder 1969).

The concept of intelligence is a complex one, but typically incorporates three broad abilities: to deal with abstractions, to solve problems, and to learn (Gage and Berliner 1991, p. 52). Yet cultures vary as to which ability is more important and what particular abstractions or problems are necessary to solve. See Habermas (1989) for insights as to how doubts (dissonance) affect both quantitative and qualitative changes in knowledge and faith.

4. The age ranges listed for each stage are suggestive and not prescriptive.

5. Modified from Dworetzky 1981, p. 316.

6. Reported by Larry Wood.

7. The use of geometric shapes to portray the qualitative changes in cognitive development was suggested by J. T. Dillon, associate professor of education, University of California, Riverside.

8. Current discussions of Piaget's theory are incorporating revisions in light of continuing research (see Fischer and Knight 1990, and Case 1991 for recent Neo-Piagetian perspectives). For example, some researchers claim that Piaget underestimated the complexity of younger children's cognitive abilities and overestimated the formal operational skills of adolescents. For a critical review of Piagetian theory for religious education, see Ratcliff (1988a) and Hyde (1990, appendix G). Alternate or additional explanations of cognitive development are offered by Gagne, Vygotsky, and "Information Processing Theory." Gagne's (1985) "cumulative learning" theory attempts to explain the effects predicted by Piagetian theory without reference to any qualitative or structural stage changes. "Learning is cumulative then, because particular intellectual skills are transferable to a number of higher-order skills and to a variety of problems to be solved. . . . These cumulative effects of learning are the basis for observed increases of intellectual 'power' in developing human beings" (p. 130). Vygotsky suggested that the social context—particularly children's private speech—plays an important role in children's cognitive development (see Tharp and Gallimore, 1988; Wertsch, 1991). Information Processing theory is modeled after the computer and approaches learning primarily from a study of short- and long-term memory (see Gagne 1985; Anderson 1990).

9. In an unpublished handout, Ward draws a parallel between Piaget's four stages and God's progressive dealings with his people throughout history.

• Sensorimotor     Adam → Noah

Leadership and communication are personal, active, experiential.

· Preoperational    Babel → Exodus

Communication is through signs, events, and people used as examples and signs.

· Concrete          Sinai → Christ
  Operations

Abstractions are made specific in "stone" tables and codes of law with special emphasis on ritual and concrete symbols. God's word is put into Scripture for the first time.

· Formal            Christ → Now
  Operations

Emphasis is transferred to the underlying and unifying principles; for example, sacrifices are transferred to "living sacrifice."

"There is a parallel between the stages of cognitive development of a human being (as understood through the research of the Swiss psychologist Jean Piaget) and development of God's progressive revelations. It is not clear *why* the parallel exists." These are general parallels for the whole period as God's mode of communication. It does not signify that individual persons within that period operated only at that cognitive stage.

10. For example, in addition to reciting a verse, students should also explain what it means.

Psalm 119:11 is often misinterpreted to indicate that simple memorization of Bible verses prevents a believer from sinning. Yet the true meaning of the passage underscores a more complex process. When the principles of God's word become a part of the deep convictions of the heart or conscience, then one will tend to avoid sinful ways. Such a believer will choose to live righteously (see also Heb. 5:14). Therefore, Christians should not only be able to recite God's word, but also to entrust their lives fully to its principles.

11. Answers for the reading level and Bible version quiz:

A.  11th grade    New American Standard
                  Version (1960/1971)

B.  3rd grade     International Children's
                  Version (1986)

C.  12th grade    King James Version (1611)

D.  9th grade     New King James Version
                  (1980/1983)

E.  7th grade     New International Version
                  (1973/1978)

Reading levels are from Kohlenberger (1987, p. 6) based on an analysis of thirty-six passages using the Fog Reading Index. Kohlenberger discusses two main criteria to consider in selecting a Bible translation: accuracy and readability. Numbers in parentheses represent the year when the version was published. When two numbers appear, the first one indicates the publication date of the New Testament; the second, publication of the whole Bible.

12. The Greek of the New Testament was not the literary or classical Greek, but the common (koine) Greek that was spoken in the marketplace. Up until the time of the Reformation, the most common Bible version in the Western church was Jerome's fourth-century Latin translation, the Vulgate (also meaning "common").

13. Fowler (1981, 1986) has offered a (fairly cognitive) theory of "faith" stages. This stage theory is significantly influenced by his former Harvard colleague, Kohlberg, and by Piaget. The thought of H. Richard Niebuhr provided the theological foundations of Fowler's understanding of faith (Fowler's doctoral dissertation is an investigation of Niebuhr's theology). We would agree with Fowler's purpose for developing his theory: "Our restlessness for divine companionship, if denied, ignored, or distorted, dehumanizes us and we destroy each other. Recognized and nurtured, it brings us into that companionship with God which frees us for genuine partnership with our sisters and brothers, and for friendship with creation" (1986, p. 40). Yet two foundational difficulties with Fowler's understanding stand out for evangelical believers: (1) Fowler's understanding of "faith" is so broad and ecumenical that *all* persons have faith (i.e., there is no such thing as "unbelief" or "unfaithfulness"); and (2) the most mature form of faith is defined not by some content or particular belief about God, but rather by one's *capacities for perspective-taking and reflection*, whether or not one is a Christian, a

Jew, or a Muslim. See Dykstra and Parks (1986) for a summary and critique of Fowler's theory. See Lee (1990) for a helpful study of the concept of faith, primarily within the Christian tradition. For a review of research on faith and religion, see Steele (1989) and Maloney (1990).

In attempting to measure the progress of faith in believers we are caught in a double-bind situation. One means of assessing faith development is to collect self-reports about one's relationship with God from a variety of individuals in different seasons of life. Similarly, we could study the reports of how one's awareness of and conception of God changes. (For summaries of this line of research see Godin 1965; Ratcliff 1985; and Meier et al. 1991, pp. 249–50). Yet James 2:14–26 indicates that such verbal expressions of faith are not very reliable indicators. Genuine faith must express itself in observable ways, since "faith without deeds is dead" (v. 26). Another means to study faith development would be to study the actions and personal habits of those who give evidence of great faith (cf. Willard 1988). Yet, in focusing on good deeds we encounter another problem. Jesus claimed that good deeds alone will not guarantee that living faith exists (cf. Matt. 7:22–23). Thus, the more holistic a picture we are able to glean, the more accurate will be our understanding of faith development. And, we should be cautious and tentative about investigations into faith development.

14. One important interpersonal skill for believers to master is that of conflict resolution. In our litigious society, Americans use immature and destructive means to get their way. In response to the challenge of 1 Corinthians 5, the Christian Conciliation Service was formed as a means to help believers resolve large and small conflicts within the church (see Buzzard and Eck 1982).

15. See Issler (1993) for a recent study of conscience.

16. Predominantly cognitively oriented social science researchers tend to publish findings under the term "moral development" and "moral education" (see Sapp 1986). Behaviorial-oriented researchers tend to use the term "prosocial behavior" to describe their work (see Staub et al. 1984;

Bridgeman 1983). Kurtines and Gewirtz (1987) include various research traditions in their edited work. A few studies have investigated moral development issues at Christian colleges and Bible colleges (Shaver 1985, 1987; Rahn 1991) and at seminaries (Issler and Ward 1989).

In an attempt to draw upon the findings of all schools of research about the subject, Rest (1983, 1986) suggests that there are at least four components involved in taking a moral action: (1) moral sensitivity (being aware of and correctly interpreting a situation as involving a moral issue); (2) moral reasoning (making a decision as to the ideal course of action); (3) moral motives and values (considering extenuating factors that will affect the final course of action to be taken); and (4) moral character or courage (executing the plan of action, despite any countervailing forces). Rest then organizes various past research efforts under these four major headings. See Holmes (1991) for an eleven-task outline for Christian moral education.

17. The following discussion is also based on Kohlberg's theory of stages of moral reasoning. Rather than focusing on six stages or three levels of hierarchical reasoning, we focus on the three lenses of concern identified in Kohlberg's three levels. This adaptation, though related to Kohlberg's theory, issues from a scriptural basis.

Though aspects of Kohlberg's stage theory of moral reasoning are useful in Christian education, evangelicals should be aware of his problematic assumptions: (1) the highest stage of moral reasoning is one of moral autonomy (literally "self-law") in which one is free from all outside influences, including divine authority; (2) justice is understood as the essence of morality—for believers, God's nature is the essence of morality in which the twin themes of love and justice are foundational; (3) individual rights and decision-making are highlighted to the neglect of individual responsibility, the patterns of decision-making that shape one's character, and corporate accountability (i.e., the church). In his movement toward a "just community" approach to moral education, Kohlberg began to modify some of these initial assumptions. See Kuhmerker (1991) for a recent summary of Kohlberg's theory.

18. Kohlberg's theory suggests, and we would agree, that becoming an adult does not guarantee that one would regularly incorporate God's principles in decision-making. Reaching adulthood only suggests that we are now *capable* of such thinking, not that we actually *use* it. Thus, we see the need to challenge teens and adults to more comprehensive patterns of thinking.

19. In 1974 Kohlberg began to study growth in both moral reasoning *and* moral behavior in what was labeled the "just community." Working with a few groups of high school students (in an on-campus alternative setting in which both students and staff participated by choice), students were challenged to deal with their own "real-life" moral situations. Staff and students would agree on corporate solutions and actions regarding matters of school governance (related to both academic and student conduct issues). The central feature of the program involved a "town hall"-like meeting in which policy was debated and enacted and punishment was meted out to those who violated these policies. Based on this kind of research (especially studies completed within the last decade of his life), Kohlberg concluded that the most effective way for individuals to become people of justice and morality is to experience this within a democratically oriented "just community" (Power, Higgins, and Kohlberg 1989). Since the church aspires to be a community of holiness, this particular line of research offers potential implications for church leaders to consider.

20. In the words of Bushnell, "that the child is to grow up a Christian, and never know himself as being otherwise" (1916, p. 4). Although Bushnell's comments are harshly (and often unfairly) judged, in fact, much of what he suggests parallels contemporary Christian strategies.

21. Further reading on the evangelism and salvation of children is available from Jeschke (1983), Hayes (1986, chap. 23), Richards (1983, chap. 20), Downs (1983), Ingle (1970), Yoder (1959), and Cragoe (1987).

22. Church leaders should adapt these practices to fit their own ecclesiastical tradition. See Sparkman (1983, Appendix 5) for a detailed outline of words and music that could accompany such ceremonies.

23. Yoder (1955) identifies a crucial blind spot in church ministry—one that can ruin the health of the church today.

Throughout Mennonite history, a major cause of spiritual decline in times of tolerance, apart from the possession of wealth, has been the *too-easy integration of the children of Christians into the church.* As long as persecution continued, it was clear to everyone what was involved in confessing one's faith, and the request for baptism retained its character of a dangerous and conscious commitment to break with the world. With persecution gone it became easier for a young person to stay in the church community, which was also his family, than to leave it. Baptism became an act of conformity rather than a break with the world, and young people, ever so serious and well-meaning, could not really know what commitment was involved. Two generations of such practice, coupled with a lack of discipline, suffice to render any church *lukewarm*" (p. 29, emphasis added).

Periodic intensive instructional classes and public ceremonies for children and teens may help address this blind spot.

24. For a scholarly treatment of baptismal practices in the early church, see Jewett (1978).

25. One church presented parents with a candle, which was to be lit every year on the anniversary date of this occasion. Thus, with the lighting of the candle, parents were to rehearse with the child the story of the dedication, including any visual reminders of the ceremony, such as a written covenant, pictures, and videos.

26. Hayes (1986, p. 409) suggests these general guidelines for inviting children to respond to a gospel presentation:

1. Ask children to respond "inside" before asking for outward response.
2. Make the invitation clear.
3. Use natural situations to talk to children about receiving Christ.
4. Avoid making the invitation so easy that acceptance is not genuine.
5. Avoid group decisions with the young.

For additional suggestions for teaching children about God, see Haystead (1974).

27. "Tertullian in an early work (*circa* 198–200) advocates delaying baptism until adolescence, so that the candidate may be old enough fully to understand the grave step that he is taking. . . . The truth is that much of the greater portion of new Christians were converts; furthermore, baptism was a very solemn act which called for a long period of preparation, and putting off this sacrament [baptism] until manhood or even until late in life was customary even when both parents of a candidate were Christians" (Laister 1951, pp. 33–34).

28. The word "convert" is used purposefully in light of the previous comments about evangelism as both *product* (a point in time) and *process* (a sensitive reappraisal and renewal of faith commitments, partially based on developmental needs). Because of their new thinking skills teens may be imminently ready to make significant reaffirmations to Christ.

29. Topics for study and reflection include such themes as spiritual gifts, stewardship, and the biblical view of vocation. For further reading on vocation, see Fowler (1987), particularly pp. 27–51. Westerhoff argues that the current practice of confirmation in mainline denominations should become an adult rite. It should be understood as "calling forth the Holy Spirit to 'ordain' adults for their ministry in church and society" (1982, pp 114–15).

30. A potential problem with such church ceremonies would arise if children or teens were made to pass through these experiences at a *required* age, regardless of their *personal* response to God. As suggested here, movement through the phases is dependent on the *initiative and qualifications of the individual*—no age is designated as a maximum; *minimal* age ranges may be appropriate. Although children or teens attend group classes, readiness for the public commitment of the ceremony is based on *individual* assessment. These general phases could be used, in a modified way, for new adult converts, as was the practice in the early church's form of Christian education, the catechumenal schools (see Gangel and Benson 1983, pp. 88–90).

# Chapter 9: Mapping Our Personality Growth

1. In contemporary educational psychology, human nature is primarily viewed as a machine—a material object, with no corresponding immaterial component. This is an interesting reversal since the term "psychology" itself was originally coined to describe a scholarly discussion of the soul (Greek, *psuchē* or *psychē*). For a book-length discussion of the existence of the soul, see Swinburne (1986); from a distinctly evangelical perspective, see the chapter by Moreland (1993).

In an interesting departure from standard social science textbooks, the opening chapter of Weiner's (1992) summary text of motivational theories includes a philosophical discussion of the mind-body problem. Without acknowledging that souls exist, Weiner attempts to provide a meaningful synthesis of current motivational theories by grouping theories under two main metaphors: "machine-like" (e.g., drive theories, relating to subhuman or animal actions) and "God-like" (e.g., attribution theory, relating to human actions). "It is these two visions—the person as machine and the person as Godlike—that shaped motivational thought and supply the overriding framework for the organization of the motivational theories that are presented in this book" (p. 14). An additional unique feature is that he notes the positive contribution of Christian theology to the study of human nature: "What has been evident in the prior discussion is that Christian theology had a considerable impact and influence on the development of Western science" (p. 9).

"Hence, just as Christian theology was in part responsible for Cartesian dualism, the separation of humans from infrahumans, and the metaphors of the person as Godlike and the person as machine, it also is in the background for the disparate Godlike metaphors and the dominance of judgements and behaviors guided by the perceived worth of others" (p. 342).

2. The technical term for this process and tension is "object relations," or more properly, "subject-object relations" (see Kegan 1982, chap. 3). Object-relations theory suggests that healthy growth of the self takes place within good relationships. Steele (1990, pp. 107–8) briefly discusses this concept as one of five essential components of Christian maturity. One central factor that we must integrate into a healthy sense of self is gender (see Van Leeuwen 1990). Further comments about gender are offered in Appendix B.

3. See Thomas (1991) for a brief survey of this "death-life paradox" concept in the New Testament.

4. See Dobson (1974) for helpful information about guiding a child's self-esteem.

5. The crucial criterion for distinguishing temperament from other personality traits is inheritance (Buss and Plomin 1984, p. 84). For additional comprehensive discussion of temperament, see Buss and Plomin (1975) and Thomas and Chess (1977). Ratcliff (1993) has proposed a three-temperament matrix to synthesize the current discussion of temperament theory [unpublished manuscript, available from the author at Toccoa Falls College, Tocca Falls, GA 30598).

6. Each of the following inventories is based on a similar four-factor view of style: the *Personal Profile System* (DiSC), a twenty-page, self-scored interpretive booklet from Carlson Learning Company, is distributed through the Charles E. Fuller Institute of Evangelism and Church Growth, P.O. Box 91990, Pasadena, CA 91109, (800) C-FULL-ER. *Social Styles*, a PC-scored inventory, can be purchased through University Associates, 8517 Production Avenue, San Diego, CA 92121 (619) 578-5900. The *Social Style Profile*, a computer-scored inventory, is available from Tracom Corp., 3773 Cherry Creek North Drive, West Tower, Suite 950, Denver, CO 80209 (800) 221-2321.

7. Answers: Beaver (3); Golden Retriever (4); Lion (2); Otter (1). Smalley and Trent (1990) use the four animal names. For additional information about these four behavioral patterns, see Merrill and Reid (1981) and Bolton and Bolton (1984); for a Christian perspective, see Phillips (1989), Voges and Braund (1989), and Perkins and Cooper (1989). To identify which style best matches your own perspective complete a simple test found in chapter 2 of Phillips' (1989) book or select one of the fuller assessment inventories listed in note 6 above. The treatment of these social style instruments is included in the text to indicate some of the practical implications of a study of temperaments. The instruments identified above, although offering insights into how we act, are not comprehensive in nature and do not incorporate the precision outlined in Buss and Plomin's (1984) theory of temperament.

8. Research on identical twins may provide some answers. For example, one University of Minnesota study of 348 pairs, including some reared in different homes, indicates that heredity has a stronger influence than environment on many central personality traits (Goleman 1986).

Attempts have been made to study innate factors specifically related to the kinds of tasks required at work. Through years of testing, Bradley (Bradley and Carty 1991) has uncovered fifty-four possible natural talents—our "aptitudes for excellence." Bradley suggests that aligning our talents with our job responsibilities is the key to enjoying one's work. An extensive career assessment package, based on these natural talents, is available from IDAK, 7931 N.E. Halsey, Portland, OR 97213 (503) 252-3495. The Kolbe Conative Index is another career-related inventory to be used to isolate inherent drives related to our actions (Kolbe 1990). "Conation [or 'striving'] is our knack for getting things done" (p. 9)—our striving toward a goal—"how we use our creativity and channel our mental energy to act and do" (p. xiv). The four action modes are: fact finder, follow thru, quick start, and implementor. A simple test is included in the book and can be scored when sent to Kolbe Concepts, Inc. 3421 N. 44th St., Phoenix, AZ 85018.

9. The particular theories cited here were all developed with the predominant

cultural context in mind. Those from other geographical areas may wish to identify similarities and differences with the particular patterns resident there. Ultimately, it would be worthwhile to outline the distinctive patterns of your own culture.

10. For a more extensive discussion of the theory and practice of Erikson's psychosocial stages from a Christian perspective, see Steele (1990, chaps. 10–12), Aleshire (1988), and Sparkman (1983). Steele's (p. 132) adaptation of the stages is listed below:

| | |
|---|---|
| Infancy: | Nurturing versus Neglecting |
| Childhood: | Enculturating and Training versus Ignoring |
| Early Adolescence: | Belonging versus Alienating |
| Adolescence: | Searching versus Entrenching |
| Young Adulthood: | Consolidating versus Fragmenting |
| Middle Adulthood: | Re-appraising versus Re-entrenching |
| Later Adulthood: | Anticipating versus Dreading |

11. Despite the practical utility of the theory, the major criticism is that it has been difficult to substantiate empirically. Recent research suggests that some of Erikson's polarities may not actually be true polarities existing on eight separate continua, but rather, contributing features of two major dimensions: positive factors and negative factors.

Ledbetter (1991) analyzed various proposals for understanding Erikson's theory as: a two-factor theory (positive and negative factors); a three-factor theory, (positive, negative, and a third factor), an eight-factor-theory (traditional view of Erikson's theory) and an eleven-factor theory (a combination of bipolar and unipolar factors). Ledbetter's study is based on the national sample data of the "Measures of Psychosocial Development" developed by Hawley (1988).

In our own understanding of Erikson's theory, we prefer to coordinate the various crises with the four lifespan themes of our model of Christian maturity (see chap. 10).

Thus, we believe the issues highlighted by Erikson are equally important throughout life as suggested below.

| Four Themes | Erikson's Psychosocial Crises |
|---|---|
| Communion | Trust versus Mistrust |
| Community | Intimacy versus Isolation |
| Character | Autonomy versus Shame and Doubt |
| | Integrity versus Despair |
| Commission | Initiative versus Guilt |
| | Industry versus Inferiority |
| | Generativity versus Stagnation |

12. Other theories of personality development offer additional insight for this essential aspect of our human growth (e.g., Kegan 1982; Loevinger 1976). Kegan, building on a Piagetian cognitive-structural base, outlines six stages. The first three are linked to the sensorimotor, preoperational, and concrete operational periods, respectively. The final three stages fit within the formal operations stage.

# Chapter 10: The Goal: Christian Maturity

1. Another recent model of maturity is presented by Pazmiño (1992, pp. 45–55). He identifies five principal tasks of the church. Listed below is a rough comparison between Pazmiño's concepts and ours. His model tends to give more emphasis to what we have designated as "Commission."

| Issler-Habermas Model: | Pazmiño's Model: |
|---|---|
| Communion | • Worship—celebration and creativity (leitourgia) |
| Community | • Community—community and covenant (koinonia) |
| Character | [Aspects of his "Community" fit here also] |
| Commission | • Proclamation—call and commitment (kerygma) |
| | • Service—care and concern (diakonia) |
| | • Advocacy—conscience and challenge (propheteia) |

2. "Community is so easily taken for granted. Like the soil, we hardly even notice it is there. At the beginning of this century, forty per cent of the land in the country of Ethiopia was covered by trees. But over the years, the trees were cut down, leaving only three per cent of the land under forest. The country's rich soil, which had been held together by the trees, was simply washed away into the rivers. This damage, which helped to cause the devastating droughts in the mid-1980's, will take many years to put right.

"It takes centuries to build up a heritage of community, which can enrich the lives of so many people. But like the soil, once it is lost, the damage is very hard to put right. Our culture has shed its community values almost overnight, casually exchanging these hard-won values for the modern cult of self-fulfillment. The church, which rightly lives in the world, but wrongly is so deeply affected by it, has also suffered in the stripping away of community" (Houston 1989, pp. 286–87). In rebuilding community norms and expectations, leaders will face four critical issues:

(a) *Establishing* norms—what particular norms will be identified as essential for all members of the community and how will these norms be identified.

(b) *Endorsing* norms—how will the norms be voluntarily owned and adopted by members.

(c) *Encouraging* norm adherence—how will members be regularly reminded (and occasionally honored) for living by the norms.

(d) *Enforcing* norm adherence—what level of accountability will be used when a particular norm violation occurs (i.e., if no consequence follows a norm violation, then, in practice there is no norm).

3. Holmes (1991) presents a similar outline in a recent work on moral education. The book provides a brief explanation of each of the eleven steps.

Phase 1: Forming the Conscience: (1) consciousness-raising; (2) consciousness-sensitizing; (3) values analysis; (4) values clarification; (5) values criticism.

Phase 2: Learning to Make Wise Decisions: (6) moral imagination; (7) ethical analysis; (8) moral decision-making.

Phase 3: Developing Character: (9) responsible agents; (10) virtue development; (11) moral identity.

4. This "test" is adapted from one suggested by Rev. Tom Mosley.

5. In his discussion of the concept of "vocation," Fowler (1984) first outlines what vocation is not (a job, a profession, or a career) before he proposes that "vocation is the response a person makes with his or her total self to the address of God and to the calling of partnership. The shaping of vocation as total response of the self to the address of God involves the orchestration of our leisure, our relationships, our work, our private life, our public life, and of the resources we steward, so as to put it all at the disposal of God's purposes in the services of God" (pp. 94–95).

6. Foster (1988) has a slightly different list of disciplines within three broad categories: (a) inward disciplines (meditation, prayer, fasting, study), (b) outward disciplines (simplicity, solitude, submission, service), and (c) corporate disciplines (confession, worship, guidance, celebration). In the acknowledgment of the first edition of the book (1978), Foster states his indebtedness to Dallas Willard: "It was through the friendship and teaching of Dallas Willard that I first saw the meaning and necessity of the Spiritual Disciplines. For four years and more he was my mentor in the Disciplines. His life is the embodiment of the principles of this book" (p. vi).

# Chapter 11: A Lifelong Call to Change

1. If learning sometimes involves discomfort and pain, why do we have to go through the learning process? Why didn't God just create us all as mature adults? Or, at least, when we become Christians, why doesn't he just take us home to be with him in heaven? Why do we have to go through the learning process? It's because learning is part and parcel of how God made us. Just as our bodies go through physical changes from birth to adulthood, our souls go through a maturing process. To be human is to be a learner. It is an essential function of our nature as finite human beings. Knowing

everything is reserved for the only infinite being that exists: God. God's nature precludes learning. No one was his teacher or counselor (Isa. 40:13–14). In taking on human nature, in that respect, Jesus was placed in the role of a learner. "Although he was a son, he learned obedience from what he suffered" (Heb. 5:8).

2. Answer to the first "Try It Out": "Learning for Christians is change [Nature] facilitated through deliberate or incidental experience [Avenues], under the supervision of the Holy Spirit [Nature], and in which one acquires and regularly integrates [Extent] age-appropriate [Readiness] knowledge, attitudes, values, emotions, skills, dispositions, and habits [Levels] into an increasingly Christ-like life [Nature]."

3. On this point, see Sapp's (1994) chapter "Compassion in Religious Education."

4. Tharp and Gallimore (1988) catalog six specific "means of assisting performance" that are evident in either nontechnological or industrialized societies in order to articulate a comprehensive theory of teaching. Although there isn't an exact one-to-one correspondence, both models incorporate concepts that overlap fairly well:

| *Our 5 - E Model:* | *Tharp and Gallimore:* |
| --- | --- |
| Emphasis | Instruction and Cognitive Structuring |
| Examples | Modeling (Instruction) |
| Exercise | Questioning and Cognitive Structuring (Instruction) |
| Encouragement | Contingency Management |
| Evaluation | Feeding-back (Contingency Management) |

(1) *Instructing:* "In typical educational settings, instructions are used primarily in two contexts: on matters of deportment and in assigning tasks" (p. 56). (2) *Cognitive Structuring:* "'Cognitive structuring' refers to the provision of a structure for thinking and acting. It may be a structure for beliefs, for mental operations, or for understanding. It is an organizing structure that evaluates,

groups, and sequences perception, memory, and action" (p. 63). (3) *Modeling:* "Modeling is the process of offering behavior for imitation" (p. 47). (4) *Questioning:* "Assessment questions compose the major interaction of the recitation script. The *assessment question* inquires to discover the level of the pupil's ability without assistance. . . . The *assistance question,* on the other hand, inquires in order to produce a mental operation that the pupil cannot or will not produce alone" (pp. 59–60). (5) *Contingency management:* "Contingency management is the means of assisting performance by which rewards and punishments are arranged to follow on behavior, depending on whether or not the behavior is desired" (p. 51). (6) *Feeding-back:* "Feedback . . . implies the existence of a closed loop; that is, for information to be considered feedback, it must be fed to a system that has a standard, as well as a mechanism for comparing a performance to the standard. . . . In the self-regulation literature, therefore, much is made of the necessity for setting standards (as goals and sub-goals) and for setting up specific procedures for regular comparison of feedback information to that standard" (pp. 54–55).

# Appendix B: Unity in Diversity: Body, Soul, and Gendeer

1. Regarding the physical body, the most common term used in the New Testament is *soma* ("body"). On occasion *sarx* ("flesh") is translated in a neutral sense as "body" (2 Cor. 4:11), although this term is usually employed to convey a mode of existence apart from Christ in opposition to a life indwelt by the Spirit (Rom. 8:9 NASB; see Russell 1993). Once Paul refers to the body as the "outer man" (2 Cor. 4:16), once as a "house" (2 Cor. 5:1), and twice as an "earthly tent" (2 Cor. 5:1,4). Gundry (1987) argues that "*soma* denotes the physical body" (p. 50) and only the physical body. He claims that the term never refers to the whole person.

2. We will be using the philosophical term "soul" to refer to the immaterial aspect of our being. Saucy (1993) presents an al-

ternate view: "The spirit is thus immaterial in essence, whereas the soul encompasses the total person, material and immaterial" (p. 33).

The dichotomous (two substances: body and soul/spirit) and trichotomous (three substances: body, soul, and spirit) views will be grouped together since their agreements (both hold to anthropological dualism) are greater than their differences. The trichotomous view makes a further distinction in the immaterial aspects of humanity—between soul and spirit.

3. The "extinction-recreation" view of the afterlife is the only logically defensible conclusion of ontological monism and is represented in MacKay (1980) and Reichenbach (1983—although he does not hold to an intermediate state). The other posited view, "immediate resurrection," involves an instantaneous "body switch" at death. This particular view is held by Anderson (1982) and Harris (1985) and may be inferred in Carey (1977). Yet, if continuity of existence is posited, then some form of dualism must be affirmed (Cooper 1989, pp. 180–85).

4. The monism-dualism debate has surfaced again largely due to the results of brain research. It has been found that states of consciousness are significantly dependent on brain functioning. Electrical stimulation of the brain and the use of certain chemicals can influence a person's thoughts and emotions. In response to these and other findings, MacKay (1980) and Myers (1978) have opted for a monistic view of personhood. For further treatment of the issue within a Christian understanding, from a social science perspective, see Van Leeuwen (1985, chap. 6); from a philosophical perspective, see Evans (1981) and Moreland (1993).

5. The following summaries are quoted from a forty-five-page report prepared for the Conservative Baptist Association by a committee of seminary faculty. It reviews the major terms, issues, and passages that concern the debate. The study packet is available for purchase from the Western Seminary Bookstore, 5511 S.E. Hawthorne Boulevard, Portland, OR 97215.

6. For a representative of the egalitarian position, see Van Leeuwen (1990) and Bilezikian (1985). Hurley (1981) represents a moderate position (yet hierarchical applications tend to be offered). For a more hierarchical presentation, see Clark (1980). Ordination of women is a related but separate issue. See Van Leeuwen (1993) and Cook and Lee (1993) for more recent treatment of these issues.

# References

Aleshire, Daniel. 1988. *Faithcare: Ministering to all God's people through the ages of life.* Philadelphia: Westminster.

Anderson, J. R. 1990. *Cognitive psychology and its implications.* 3d ed. New York: Freeman.

Anderson, Ray. 1982. *On being human: Essays in theological anthropology.* Grand Rapids: Eerdmans.

Anthony, Michael. 1992. Special education ministries. In *Foundations of ministry: An introduction to Christian education for a new generation,* ed. Michael Anthony, Wheaton, Ill.: Bridgepoint, pp. 360–78.

Arnold, Clinton E. 1992. *Powers of darkness: Principalities and powers in Paul's letters.* Downers Grove, Ill.: InterVarsity.

Ausubel, David. 1963. *The psychology of meaningful verbal learning: An introduction to school learning.* New York: Grune and Stratton.

———. 1968. *Educational psychology: A cognitive approach.* New York: Holt, Rinehart and Winston.

Backus, William and Marie Chapin. 1980. *Telling yourself the truth.* Minneapolis: Bethany House.

Bandura, Albert. 1977. *Social learning theory.* Englewood Cliffs, N.J.: Prentice-Hall.

———. 1986. *Social foundations of thought and action: A social cognitive theory.* Englewood Cliffs, N.J.: Prentice-Hall.

Barlow, Daniel L. 1985. *Educational psychology: The teaching-learning process.* Chicago: Moody.

Bartlett, Josiah. 1848. *An inquiry into the degree of certainty in medicine, and into the nature and extent of its power over disease.* Philadelphia: Lea and Blanchard. (Cited in King 1991, p. 200.)

Bayly, Joseph. 1982, Nov. Out of My Mind. *Eternity,* p. 59.

Beechick, Ruth. 1982. *A Biblical psychology of learning: How your mind works.* Denver, Colo.: Accent.

Bellezza, Francis. 1981. Mnemonic devices: Classification, characteristics and criteria. *Review of Educational Research* 51 (2): 247–75.

Bennett, Christine L. 1990. Learning styles: Interactions between culture and the individual. In *Comprehensive multicultural education: Theory and practice.* 2d ed. Boston: Allyn and Bacon.

Bentham, Jeremy. 1789. *An introduction to the principles of morals and legislation.* reprinted in Louis Pojman, ed., *Ethical theory* (Belmont, Ca.: Wadsworth, 1989), pp. 111–14.

Biehler, Robert F. and Jack Snowman. 1993. *Psychology applied to teaching.* 7th ed. Boston: Houghton Mifflin.

Bilezikian, Gilbert. 1985. *Beyond sex roles.* Grand Rapids: Baker.

Bloom, Benjamin, et al. 1956. *Taxonomy of educational objectives. Handbook 1: Cognitive domain.* New York: David McKay.

Boehlke, Robert R. 1962. *Theories of learning in Christian education.* Philadelphia: Westminster.

Bolton, Barbara, Charles T. Smith, and Wes Haystead. 1987. *Everything you wanted to know about teaching children: Grades 1–6.* Ventura, Calif.: Regal.

Bolton, Robert and Dorothy Grover Bolton. 1984. *Social styles/Management styles: Developing productive work relationships.* New York: American Management Association.

Bonham, L. Adrienne. 1988. Learning style use: In need of perspective. *Lifelong Learning: An Omnibus of Practice and Research* 11 (5): 14–17, 19.

Bradley, John and Jay Carty. 1991. *Unlocking your sixth suitcase: How to do what you love and love what you do.* Colorado Springs, Colo.: NavPress.

Bridgeman, Diane L. 1983. *The nature of prosocial development.* New York: Academic.

Bufford, Rodger. 1981. *The human reflex: Behavioral psychology in biblical perspective.* San Francisco: Harper and Row.

Burns, Jim. 1988. *The youth builder.* Eugene, Oreg.: Harvest House.

Bushnell, Horace. 1916. *Christian nurture.* New Haven, Conn.: Yale University.

Buss, Arnold H. and Robert Plomin. 1975. *A temperament theory of personality development.* New York: Wiley-Interscience.

———. 1984. *Temperament: Early developing personality traits.* Hillsdale, N.J.: Erlbaum.

Buzzard, Lynn R., and Laurence Eck. 1982. *Tell it to the church: Reconciling out of court.* Elgin, Ill.: David C. Cook.

Carey, George. 1977. *I Believe in man.* Grand Rapids: Eerdmans.

Case, R. ed. 1991. *The mind's staircase: Stages in the development of human intelligence.* Hillsdale, N.J.: Erlbaum.

Chapelle, Tony. 1988. August 14. Scrupulous models just saying no. *The Sunday [Portland] Oregonian* [New York Times News Service].

Christie, Les. 1987. *Unsung heroes: How to recruit and train volunteer youth workers.* Grand Rapids: Zondervan.

Clark, Stephen B. 1980. *Man and woman in Christ.* Ann Arbor, Mich.: Servant.

Conservative Baptist Seminaries. 1989. *Women's ministry roles and ordination study packet.* Portland, Oreg.: Western Seminary.

Cook, Kaye and Lance Lee. 1993. *Man and woman: Alone and together.* Wheaton, Ill.: Victor/Bridgepoint.

Cook, Stuart. 1988. Measurement and evaluation. In *The Christian educator's handbook on teaching: A comprehensive resource on the distinctiveness of true Christian teaching,* ed. Kenneth O. Gangel and Howard G. Hendricks. Wheaton, Ill.: Victor.

Cooper, John W. 1989. *Body, soul, and life everlasting: Biblical anthropology and the monism-dualism debate.* Grand Rapids: Eerdmans.

Copeman, W. S. C. 1960. *Doctors and diseases in Tudor times.* London: Dawsons of Pall Mall.

Cornett, Claudia. 1983. *What you should know about teaching and learning styles.* Bloomington, Ind.: Phi Delta Kappa Foundation.

Cosgrove, Mark. 1987. *The amazing body human: God's design for personhood.* Grand Rapids: Baker.

Cragoe, Thomas. 1987. An examination of the issue of infant salvation. Ann Arbor: University Microfilms (#8729700). Doctoral diss., Dallas Theological Seminary, 1987.

Davis, Robert H., Lawrence T. Alexander, and Stephen L. Yelon. 1974. *Learning system design: An approach to the improvement of instruction.* New York: MacGraw-Hill.

Delling, G. 1972. Huperauxano. In *Theological dictionary of the New Testament,* ed. G. Friederich. Vol. 5. Grand Rapids: Eerdmans.

Dembo, Myron H. 1991. *Applying educational psychology in the classroom.* 4th ed. N.Y.: Longman.

Dillon, J. T. 1988. *Questioning and teaching: A manual of practice.* New York: Teacher's College.

Dobson, James. 1974. *Hide or seek.* Old Tappan, N.J.: Revell.

Dockery, Karen. 1989. *Combined efforts: A youth worker's guide to ministry to and through parents.* Wheaton, Ill.: Victor.

Downs, Perry. 1983. Child evangelization. *Christian Education Journal* 3 (2): 5–13.

Dunn, Rita, Jeffrey Beaudry, and Angela Klavas. 1989. Survey of research on learning styles. *Educational Leadership* 46 (6): 50–58.

Dunn, Rita, and Kenneth Dunn. 1978. *Teaching students through their individual learning styles: A practical approach.* Reston, Va.: Reston Publishing.

Dunn, Rita, and S. A. Griggs. 1988. *Learning style: Quiet revolution in American secondary schools.* Reston, Va.: National Association of Secondary School Principals.

Dworetzky, John. 1981. *Introduction to child development.* St. Paul, Minn.: West Publishing.

Dykstra, Craig. 1990. Learning theory. In *Harper's encyclopedia of religious education,* ed. Iris V. Cully and Kendig B. Cully. San Francisco: Harper and Row.

Dykstra, Craig, and Sharon Parks, eds. 1986. *Faith development and Fowler.* Birmingham, Ala.: Religious Education Press.

Elkind, David, and Irving B. Weiner. 1978. *Development of the child.* New York: Wiley.

Erickson, Millard. 1985. *Christian theology.* Grand Rapids: Baker.

Erikson, Erik. 1963. *Childhood and society.* 2d ed. New York: W. W. Norton.

———. 1968. *Identity: Youth and crisis.* New York: W. W. Norton.

———. 1982. *The life cycle completed: A review.* New York: W. W. Norton.

Evans, Stephen. 1981. Separable souls: A defense of minimal dualism. *Southern Journal of Philosophy* 19: 313–31.

Festinger, Leon. 1957. *A theory of cognitive dissonance.* Stanford, Calif.: Stanford University Press.

Fischer, Kurt W. and C. C. Knight. 1990. Cognitive development in real children: Levels and variations. In *Learning and thinking styles: Classroom interactions,* R. McClure ed. Washington, D.C.: National Education Association.

Flavell, John H., and E. Markham, eds. 1983. Cognitive development. Vol. 3. In *Handbook of child psychology,* ed. Paul Mussen. New York: John Wiley and Sons.

Ford, LeRoy. 1978. *Design for teaching and training.* Nashville, Tenn.: Broadman.

Foster, Richard. [1978] 1988. *Celebration of discipline.* San Francisco: Harper and Row.

Fowler, James. 1981. *Stages of faith: The psychology of human development and the quest for meaning.* San Francisco: Harper and Row.

———. 1984. *Becoming adult, becoming Christian: Adult development and Christian faith.* San Francisco: Harper and Row.

———. 1986. Faith and the structure of meaning. In *Faith development and Fowler,* ed. Craig Dykstra and Sharon Parks. Birmingham, Ala.: Religious Education Press.

———. 1987. *Faith development and pastoral care.* Philadelphia, Pa.: Fortress.

Fuller, Daniel. 1978. The Holy Spirit in biblical interpretation. In *Scripture, tradition, and interpretation,* ed. W. Ward Gasque and William Sanford LaSor. Grand Rapids: Eerdmans.

Gaebelein, Frank. 1954. *Patterns of God's truth.* Chicago: Moody.

Gage, Nathan L., and David C. Berliner. 1992. *Educational psychology.* 5th ed. Boston: Houghton Mifflin.

Gagne, Robert. 1985. *The conditions of learning and theory of instruction.* 4th ed. New York: Holt, Rinehart and Winston.

Gangel, Kenneth. 1974. *24 ways to improve your teaching.* Wheaton, Ill.: Victor.

———. 1989. *Feeding and leading: A practical handbook on administration in churches and Christian organizations.* Wheaton, Ill.: Victor.

Gangel, Kenneth, and Warren Benson. 1983. *Christian education: Its history and philosophy.* Chicago: Moody.

Glare, P. W. G., et al. 1968. *Oxford Latin dictionary.* London: Clarendon Press.

Godin, A. J., ed. 1965. *From religious experience to a religious attitude.* Chicago: Loyola University Press.

Goldsmith, H. H. 1983. Genetic influences on personality from infancy to adulthood. *Child Development* 54: 331–55.

Goldsmith, H. H., et al. 1987. Roundtable: What is temperament? Four approaches. *Child Development* 58: 505–29.

Goleman, D. 1986. Major personality study finds that traits are mostly inherited. *New York Times,* Dec. 2, 17–18.

Gonzales, Arturo F., Jr. 1987. Giving a sucker an even break. *MD:* Feb. 65–69.

Good, Thomas L. and Jere E. Brophy. 1990. *Educational psychology: A realistic approach.* N.Y.: Longman.

Griffin, Em. 1982. *Getting together: A guide for good groups.* Downers Grove, Ill.: InterVarsity.

———. 1984. (Fall) How to gauge the closeness of a group. *Leadership* 84–90.

Gundry, Robert. 1987. *Soma in biblical theology, with an emphasis on Pauline anthropology.* Grand Rapids: Zondervan.

Guralnik, David B., ed. 1984. *Webster's new world dictionary of the American language.* 2d college ed. New York: Simon and Schuster.

Habermas, Ronald. 1985. Social development as a curriculum component of Protestant theological education. (Ph.D. diss., Michigan State University).

———. 1989. Summer. Doubt is not a four-letter word. *Religious Education* 84 (3), 402–10.

———. 1993a, March 8. Does Peter Pan corrupt our children? *Christianity Today,* 30–33.

———. 1993b, Winter. Practical dimensions of *Imago Dei. Christian Education Journal* 8 (2), 83–92.

———. 1993c, Winter. using extrabiblical truth in your teaching. *Youthworker 9* (3), 82–87.

———. 1994a. The family as a context for spiritual formation. In *Christian educator's handbook,* Vol. III, eds., Kenneth Gangel and Jim Wilhoit. Wheaton, Ill.: Victor.

———. 1994b. The purpose of Christian education. In *Leadership handbooks of practical theology, Vol. 2: Outreach and care.* Grand Rapids: CTI/Baker.

———. in press. The developmental use of lecturing. In *Developmental Christian education,* eds. John Dettoni and Jim Wilhoit. Wheaton, Ill.: Victor.

Habermas, Ronald and Klaus Issler. 1992. *Teaching for reconciliation: Foundations and practice of Christian educational ministry.* Grand Rapids: Baker.

Hallahan, D. P., and J. M. Kauffman. 1991. *Exceptional children: Introduction to special education.* 5th ed. Boston: Allyn and Bacon.

Hamacheck, Don. 1990. *Psychology in teaching, learning, and growth.* 4th ed. Boston: Allyn and Bacon.

Hardman, M. L., C. J. Drew, M. W. Egan and B. Wolf. *Human exceptionality.* 3d ed. Boston: Allyn and Bacon.

Haring, Norris G., and Linda McCormick, eds. 1990. *Exceptional children and youth.* 5th ed. Columbus, Ohio: Merrill.

Harner, Nevin C. 1939. *The educational work of the church.* New York: Abingdon-Cokesbury.

Harris, Murray J. 1985. *Raised immortal: Resurrection and immortality in the New Testament.* Grand Rapids: Eerdmans.

Harrow, A. 1969. *A Taxonomy of the psychomotor domain: A guide for developing behavioral objectives.* New York: David McKay.

Hauerwas, Stanley. 1975. *Character and the Christian Life.* San Antonio, Texas: Trinity University Press.

Havighurst, Robert. [1952]1972. *Developmental tasks and education.* 3d ed. New York: Longman.

Hawley, Gwen. 1988. *Measures of psychosocial development.* A professional manual. Odessa, Fla.: Psychological Assessment Resources, Inc.

Hayes, Edward. 1986. Evangelism of children. In *Childhood education in the church,* ed. Robert E. Clark, Joanne Brubaker, and Roy B. Zuck. Chicago: Moody.

Haystead, Wes. 1974. *Teaching your child about God: You can't begin too soon.* Ventura, Calif.: Regal.

———. 1989. *Everything you wanted to know about teaching young children: Birth-6 years.* Ventura, Calif.: Gospel Light.

Hendricks, Howard G. 1987. *Teaching to change lives.* Portland, Oreg.: Multnomah Press.

Hersey, Paul, and Ken Blanchard. 1982. *Management or organizational behavior: Utilizing human resources.* 4th ed. Englewood Cliffs, N.J.: Prentice-Hall.

Hoekema, Anthony. 1986. *Created in God's image.* Grand Rapids: Eerdmans.

Hoffman, Martin. 1977. Personality and social development. *Annual Review of Psychology* 28:259–331.

Holmes, Arthur. 1977. *All truth is God's truth.* Grand Rapids: Eerdmans.

———. 1991. *Shaping character: Moral education in the Christian college.* Grand Rapids: Eerdmans.

House, H. Wayne. 1988. *Schooling choices: An examination of private, public and home education.* Portland, Oreg.: Multnomah.

Houston, James. 1989. *The transforming friendship: A guide to prayer.* Oxford: Lion.

Hunter, Madeline. 1982. *Mastery teaching.* El Segundo, Calif.: TIP Publishers.

Hurley, James. 1981. *Man and woman in biblical perspective.* Grand Rapids: Zondervan.

Hyde, Kenneth E. 1990. *Religion in childhood and adolescence.* Birmingham, Ala.: Religious Education Press.

Ingle, Clifford, ed. 1970. *Children and conversion.* Nashville, Tenn.: Broadman.

Issler, Klaus. 1984. Moral development as a component of the education of Protestant ministers. (Ph.D. diss., Michigan State University).

———. 1990. Nurturing marriage and family life. *Christian Educational Journal* 10 (2): 75–85.

———. 1993. Conscience: moral sensitivity and moral reasoning. In *Christian perspectives on being human: A multidisciplinary approach,* ed. J. P. Moreland and David Ciocchi. Grand Rapids: Baker.

Issler, Klaus, and Ted W. Ward. 1989. Moral development as a curriculum emphasis in American Protestant theological education. *Journal of Moral Education* 18 (2):131–43.

Jackson, Philip. 1986. *The practice of teaching.* New York: Teacher's College Columbia.

Jeschke, Marlin. 1983. *Believers baptism for children of the church.* Scottdale, Pa.: Herald.

Jewett, A., and M. Mullan. 1977. Movement process categories in physical education in teaching-learning. In *Curriculum Design: Purposes and Procedures in Physical Education Teaching-Learning.* Washington, D.C.: American Alliance for Health, Physical Education and Recreation.

Jewett, Paul K. 1978. *Infant baptism and the Covenant of Grace.* Grand Rapids: Eerdmans.

Joy, Donald. 1985. *Bonding: Relationships in the Image of God.* Waco, Tex.: Word.

———. 1986. Why reach and teach children? In *Childhood education in the church,* ed. Robert E. Clark, Joanne Brubaker, and Roy B. Zuck. Chicago: Moody.

Joyce, Bruce, and Marsha Weil. 1989. *Models of Teaching.* 3d ed. Englewood Cliffs, N.J.: Prentice Hall.

Joyce, Bruce, Marsha Weil, with Beverly Showers. 1992. *Models of Teaching.* 4th ed. Englewood Cliffs, N.J.: Prentice Hall.

Kagan, Jerome. 1972. A conception of early adolescence. In *Twelve to Sixteen: Early adolescence,* ed. Robert Coles, et al. New York: Norton.

Keefe, J. W. 1983. Assessing student learning styles: An overview. In *Student learning styles and brain behavior.* Reston, Va.: National Association of Secondary School Principals.

Kegan, Robert. 1982. *The evolving self: Problem and process in human development.* Cambridge, Mass.: Harvard University.

Keillor, Garrison. 1987. Leaving home. New York: Viking.

Keller, John. 1987. Development and use for the ARCS model of instructional design. *Journal of Instructional Development* 10 (3): 2–10.

Keyes, Ralph. 1976. *Is there life after high school?* New York: Warner.

Kibler, R., L. Barker, and D. Miles. 1970. *Behavior objectives and instruction.* Boston: Allyn and Bacon.

King, Lester, M.D. 1991. *Transformations in American medicine: From Benjamin Rush to William Osler.* Baltimore: Johns Hopkins University.

Kohlberg, Lawrence. 1981. *The philosophy of moral development.* San Francisco: Harper and Row.

———. 1984. *Essays on moral development: Volume 2. The psychology of moral development.* San Francisco: Harper and Row.

Kohlberg, Lawrence, Charles Levine, and Alexandra Hewer. 1983. *Moral stages: A current formulation and a response to critics.* Basel, Switzerland: Karger.

Kohlenberger, John. 1987. *Words about the Word.* Grand Rapids: Zondervan.

Kolb, David. 1984. *Experiential learning: Experience as the source of learning and development.* Englewood Cliffs, N.J.: Prentice-Hall.

Kolbe, Kathy. 1990. *The conative connection: Uncovering the link between who you are and how you perform.* Reading, Mass.: Addison-Wesley.

Krathwohl, David, Benjamin Bloom, and Bertram Masia. 1964. *Taxonomy of educational objectives—The classification of educational goals. Handbook II: Affective Domain.* New York: David McKay.

Kuhmerker, Lisa. 1991. *The Kohlberg legacy for the helping professions.* Birmingham, Ala.: R.E.P.

Kurtines, William M., and Jacob L. Gewirtz, eds. 1987. *Moral development through social interaction.* New York: John Wiley and Sons.

Laister, Max L. W. 1951. *Christianity and pagan culture in the later Roman empire.* Ithaca: Cornell University Press.

LeBar, Lois E. [1958] 1981. *Education that is Christian.* Old Tappen, N.J.: Fleming H. Revell. (See also the newly-revised edition, under the same title, organized by James E. Plueddemann, Victor Books, 1989.)

Ledbetter, Mark. 1991. An evaluation of the construct validity of the Measures of Psychosocial Development using the normative sample: A confirmatory factor approach. Psy.D. doctoral diss., George Fox College.

Lee, James M. 1985. *The content of religious instruction.* Birmingham, Ala.: Religious Education.

Lee, James M., ed. 1990. *Handbook of faith.* Birmingham, Ala.: Religious Education.

LeFever, Marlene. 1985. *Creative teaching methods.* Elgin, Ill.: David C. Cook.

Lefrancois, Guy. 1993. *Psychology for Teaching.* Belmont, Ca.: Wadsworth.

Levin, Michael. 1990. Can ethics be taught. *Reader's Digest:* March 113–14.

Lewis, Gordon, and Bruce Demarest. 1987. *Integrative theology: Vol. I: Knowing ultimate reality, the living God.* Grand Rapids: Zondervan.

———. 1990. *Integrative theology: Vol. II: Our primary need, Christ's atoning provisions.* Grand Rapids: Zondervan.

Lewis, Harold E. 1987, Feb. L'Amour on education. *The Clearing House* 60 (6): 261–62.

Leypoldt, Martha. 1971. *Learning is change: Adult education in the church.* Valley Forge, Pa.: Judson.

Lickona, Thomas. 1983. *Raising good children: Helping your child through the stages of moral development.* New York: Bantam.

Loevinger, Jane. 1976. *Ego development: Conceptions and theories.* San Francisco: Jossey-Bass.

Lorayne, Harry, and Jerry Lucas. 1974. *The memory book.* New York: Ballantine.

Luccock, Harford E., and Paul Hutchinson. 1949. *The Story of Methodism.* Nashville: Abingdon.

McCarthy, Bernice. 1987. *The 4MAT system: Teaching to learning styles with right/left mode techniques.* Rev. ed. Barrington, Ill.: Excel, Inc.

McDonald, H. D. 1984. Man, Doctrine of. In *Evangelical dictionary of theology,* ed. W. A. Elwell. Grand Rapids: Baker.

MacKay, Donald. 1980. *Brains, machines, and persons.* Grand Rapids: Eerdmans.

McNabb, Bill, and Steven Mabry. 1990. *Teaching the Bible creatively: How to awaken your kids to scripture.* Grand Rapids: Zondervan

Mager, Robert. 1984. *Developing attitude toward learning.* Belmont, Calif.: David S. Lake Publishers.

Maloney, H. Newton. 1990. The concept of faith in psychology. In *Handbook of faith,* ed. James Michael Lee. Birmingham, Ala.: Religious Education.

Maslow, Abraham. 1968. Self-actualization and beyond. In *Human dynamics in psychology and education: Selected readings,* ed. Don E. Hamachek. Boston: Allyn and Bacon.

———. 1987. *Motivation and personality,* ed. R. Frager, J. Fadiman, C. McReynolds, and R. Cox. 3d ed. New York: Harper and Row.

Meier, Paul D., Frank B. Minirth, Frank B. Wichern, and Donald E. Ratcliff. 1991. *Introduction to psychology and counseling: Christian perspectives and applications.* 2d ed. Grand Rapids: Baker.

Meier, Paul, Donald E. Ratcliff and Fred Rowe. 1993. *Child-rearing and personality development.* 2d ed. Grand Rapids: Baker.

Merrill, David W., and Roger H. Reid. 1981. *Personal styles and effective performance.* Radnor, Pa.: Chilton.

Mininnger, Joan, and Eleanor Dugan. 1988. *Make your mind work for you.* Emmaus, Pa.: Rodde Press.

Moreland, J. P. 1987. *Scaling the secular city: A defense of Christianity.* Grand Rapids: Baker.

———. 1989. *Christianity and the nature of science: A philosophical investigation.* Grand Rapids: Baker.

———. 1993. A defense of substance dualist view of the soul. In *Christian perspectives on being human: A multidisciplinary approach to integration,* ed. J. P. Moreland and David Ciocchi. Grand Rapids: Baker.

Morgan, Elisa. 1991. *Chronicles of childhood: Recording your child's spiritual journey.* Colorado Springs, Colo.: NavPress.

Myers, David. 1978. *The human puzzle: Psychological research and Christian belief.* San Francisco: Harper and Row.

Newman, Gene, and Joni Eareckson Tada. 1987. *All God's Children: Ministry to the disabled.* Grand Rapids: Zondervan.

*Oxford English Dictionary.* 1971. Compact ed. Oxford: Oxford University Press.

Packer, J. I. 1973. *Knowing God.* Downers Grove, Ill.: IVP.

Pazmiño, Robert. 1988. *Foundational issues in Christian education: An introduction in evangelical perspective.* Grand Rapids: Baker.

———. 1992. *Principles and practices of Christian education: An evangelical perspective.* Grand Rapids: Baker.

Perkins, Bill, and Rod Cooper. 1989. *Kids in sports: Shaping a child's character from the sidelines.* Portland, Oreg.: Multnomah.

Phillips, Bob. 1989. *The delicate art of dancing with porcupines: Learning to appreciate the finer points of others.* Ventura, Calif.: Regal.

Piaget, Jean. 1977. *The development of thought: Equilibration of cognitive structures.* New York: Viking.

Piaget, Jean, and Barbel Inhelder. 1969. *The psychology of the child.* New York: Basic Books.

Posner, George, and Alan Rudnitsky. 1989. *Course design: A guide to curriculum development for teachers.* 4th ed. New York: Longman.

Postman, Neil. 1985. *Amusing ourselves to death.* New York: Viking.

Postman, Neil, and Charles Weingartner. 1969. *Teaching as a subversive activity.* New York, New York: Delacorte.

Potter, David, and Martin P. Anderson. 1976. *Discussion in small groups: A guide to effective practice.* 3d ed. Belmont, Ca.: Wadsworth.

Power, F. Clark, Ann Higgins, and Lawrence Kohlberg. 1989. *Lawrence Kohlberg's approach to moral education.* New York: Columbia University.

Premack, David. 1965. Reinforcement Theory. In *Nebraska Symposium on Motivation,* ed. D. Levine. Lincoln: University of Nebraska Press.

Pulaski, Mary Ann. 1980. *Understanding Piaget: An introduction to children's cognitive development.* Rev ed. New York: Harper and Row.

Rahn, David. 1991. Faith domain distinctions in the conceptualization of morality and social convention for evangelical Christians. Ph.D. diss., Purdue University.

Ratcliff, Donald E. 1980. Toward a Christian perspective of developmental disability. *Journal of Psychology and Theology* 8, 328–335.

———. 1985a. The development of children's religious concepts: Research review. *Journal of Psychology and Christianity* 4 (1): 35–43.

———. 1985b. Ministering to the mentally retarded. *Christian Education Journal* 6 (1), 24–30.

———. 1988a. The cognitive development of preschoolers. In *Handbook of preschool religious education,* ed. Donald Ratcliff. Birmingham, Ala.: Religious Education Press.

———, ed. 1988b. *Handbook of preschool religious education.* Birmingham, Ala.: Religious Education Press.

———. 1990. Counseling parents of the mentally retarded: A Christian perspective. *Journal of Psychology and Theology* 18 (4), 318–325.

———, ed. 1992. *Handbook of children's religious education.* Birmingham, Ala.: Religious Education Press.

———. 1993. Temperament in childhood: Three key dimensions—activity, emotionality, and sociability. [unpublished paper]

Reichenbach, Bruce. 1983. *Is man the phoenix? A study of immortality.* Grand Rapids: Eerdmans.

Rest, James. 1983. Morality. In *Cognitive development, Vol. III*, ed. J. H. Flavell and E. Markman. In *Handbook of child psychology*, ed. Paul Mussen. New York: John Wiley and Sons.

——. 1986. *Moral development: Advances in research and theory.* New York: Praeger.

Reynolds, Brian. 1983. *A Chance to serve.* Winona, Minn.: St. Mary's Press.

Richards, Lawrence. 1970. *Creative Bible teaching.* Grand Rapids: Zondervan.

——. 1975. *A theology of Christian education.* Grand Rapids: Zondervan.

——. 1983. *A theology of children's ministry.* Grand Rapids: Zondervan.

Rogers, Everett M. 1983. *Diffusion of innovations.* 3d ed. New York: Free Press.

Roberts, Randal. 1984. The relationship between the perspicuity of Scripture and the nature of spiritual illumination. Unpublished master's thesis, Western Conservative Baptist Seminary (Portland, Oreg.).

Rogers, Carl. 1983. *Freedom to learn.* Columbus, Oh.: Merril.

Russell, Walt. 1993. The apostle Paul's view of the "sin nature"/"new nature" struggle. In *Christian perspectives on being human: A multidisciplinary approach*, eds. J. P. Moreland and David Ciocchi. Grand Rapids: Baker.

Sapp, Gary L. 1994. Compassion in religious instruction. In *Compassionate ministry*, ed. Gary L. Sapp. Birmingham, Ala.: Religious Education Dress.

——, ed. 1986. *Handbook of moral development.* Birmingham, Ala.: Religious Education Press.

Saucy, Robert L. Theology of human nature. In *Christian perspectives on being human: A multidisciplinary approach to integration*, eds. J. P. Moreland and David M. Ciocchi. Grand Rapids: Baker.

Schimmels, Cliff. 1989. *Parents' most-asked questions about kids and schools.* Wheaton, Ill.: Victor.

Schneidau, Herbert N. 1976. *Sacred discontent: The Bible and western tradition.* Baton Rouge, La.: Louisiana State University.

Schultz, Thom and Joani Schultz. 1993. *Why nobody learns much of anything at church: And how to fix it.* Loveland, Colo.: Group.

Seifert, Kelvin L. 1991. *Educational psychology.* 2d ed. Boston: Houghton Mifflin.

Sell, Charles M. 1985. *Transition.* Chicago, Ill.: Moody.

Shaver, D. G. 1985. A longitudinal study of moral development as a conservative religious liberal arts college. *Journal of College Student Personnel*, 26: 400–4.

——. 1987. Moral development of students attending a Christian liberal arts college and a Bible college. *Journal of College Student Personnel* 28 (3): 211–18.

Simpson, Elizabeth. 1966. Taxonomy of objectives: Psychomotor domain. Unpublished manuscript. University of Illinois, Urbana.

Singh, J., and R. Zingg. 1939. *Wolf-children and feral man.* New York: Harper and Row.

Skinner, B. F. 1953. *Science and human behavior.* New York: Macmillan.

Slavin, Robert E., N. L. Karweit, and N. A. Madden. 1989. *Effective programs for students at risk.* Boston: Allyn and Bacon.

Smalley, Gary, and John Trent. 1990. *The two sides of love.* Pomona, Calif.: Focus on the Family.

Smedes, Lewis. 1986. *Choices: Making right decisions in a complex world.* San Francisco: Harper and Row.

Sparkman, G. Temp. 1983. *The salvation and nurture of the child of God: The story of Emma.* Valley Forge, Pa.: Judson.

Sprinthall, Norman, and Richard Sprinthall. 1990. *Educational psychology: A developmental approach*. 5th ed. New York: Random House.

Staub, Ervin, et al., eds. 1984. *Development and maintenance of prosocial behavior*. New York: Plenum.

Steele, Les. 1989, Winter. Research on faith development. *Christian Education Journal 9* (2): 21–30.

———. 1990. *On the way: A practical theology of Christian formation*. Grand Rapids: Baker.

Steinaker, Norman, and M. Robert Bell. 1979. *The experiential taxonomy: A new approach to teaching and learning*. New York: Academic.

Stevens, Doug. 1985. *Called to care: Youth ministry and the church*. Grand Rapids: Zondervan.

Sutton, Joe, Connie Sutton, and E. Gail Everett. 1993, Spring. Special education in Christian schools: A commitment to *all* the children? *Journal of Research on Christian Education 2* (1): 65–79.

Swinburne, Richard. 1986. *The evolution of the soul*. Oxford: Clarendon Press.

Tharp, Roland, and Ronald Gallimore. 1988. *Rousing minds to life: Teaching, learning, and schooling in social context*. Cambridge: Cambridge University Press.

Thomas, A. and S. Chess. 1977. *Temperament and development*. New York: Bruner/Mazel.

Thomas, Robert L. 1991, March. Improving evangelical ethics: An analysis of the problem and a proposed solution. *Journal of the Evangelical Theological Society 34* (1): 3–19.

Thomas, Robert L., and Stanley Gundry. 1988. *The NIV harmony of the Gospels*. San Francisco: Harper and Row.

Toon, Peter. 1984. *Your conscience as your guide*. Wilton, Conn.: Morehouse-Barlow.

Van Leeuwen, Mary Stewart. 1985. *The person in psychology: A contemporary Christian appraisal*. Grand Rapids: Eerdmans.

———. 1990. *Gender and grace: Love, work and parenting in a changing world*. Downers Grove, Ill.: InterVarsity.

———, ed. 1993. *After Eden: Facing the challenge of gender reconciliation*. Grand Rapids: Eerdmans.

Varenhorst, Barbara B. 1983. *Real friends*. San Francisco: Harper and Row.

Voges, Ken, and Ron Braund. 1989. *Understanding how others misunderstand you: A unique and proven plan for strengthening personal relationships*. Chicago: Moody.

Vygotsky, Lev. S. 1978. *Mind in society: The development of higher psychological processes* (M. Cole, V. John-Steiner, S. Scribner, and E. Souberman, eds. and trans.). Cambridge, Mass.: Harvard University Press.

———. 1986. *Thought and language*. Cambridge, Mass.: MIT Press.

Ward, Ted. 1989. *Values begin at home*. 2d ed. Wheaton, Ill.: Victor.

———. (n.d.) Non-formal education. Unpublished manuscript.

Watson, David, and R. Tharp. 1989. *Self-directed behavior*. 5th ed. Monterery, Calif.: Brooks/Cole.

Watson, John B. 1930. *Behaviorism*. Rev. ed. New York: Norton.

Weiner, Bernard. 1992. *Human motivation: Metaphors, theories, and research*. Newbury Park, Calif.: Sage.

Wertsch, J. V. 1991. *Voices of the mind: A sociocultural approach to mediated action*. Cambridge, Mass.: Harvard University Press.

Westerhoff, John. 1982. Aspects of adult confirmation. In *Confirmation examined*, ed. Kendig Brubaker Cully. Wilton, Conn.: Morehouse-Barlow.

Wilhoit, Jim. 1991. *Christian education and the search for meaning.* Rev. ed. Grand Rapids: Baker.

Wilkins, Michael. 1992. *Following the master: Discipleship in the steps of Jesus.* Grand Rapids: Zondervan.

Willard, Dallas. 1988. *The Spirit of the disciplines.* San Francisco: Harper and Row.

Williams, Reed G., and Thomas M. Haladyna. 1982. Logical operation for generating intended questions (LOGIQ): A typology for higher level test items. In *A technology for test-item writing,* ed. Gale H. Roid and Thomas M. Haladyna. New York: Academic.

Williamson, William. 1970. *Language and concepts in Christian education.* Philadelphia: Temple University.

Wlodkowski, Raymond J. 1985. *Enhancing adult motivation to learn.* San Francisco, Calif.: Jossey-Bass.

Wlodkowski, Raymond J., and Judith H. Jaynes. 1990. *Eager to learn: Helping children become motivated and love learning.* San Francisco: Jossey-Bass.

Wolterstorff, Nicholas. 1980. *Educating for responsible action.* Grand Rapids: Eerdmans.

Woolfolk, Anita E. 1993. *Educational psychology.* 5th ed. Boston: Allyn and Bacon.

Worthen, Blaine, and James Sanders. 1987. Educational evaluation: Alternative approaches and practical guidelines. New York: Longman.

Yaconelli, Mike, and Jim Burns. 1986. *High school ministry.* Grand Rapids: Zondervan.

Yoder, Gideon. 1959. The nurture and evangelism of children. Scottdale, PA: Herald.

Yoder, John Howard. 1955, Jan-Mar. Discipleship as missionary strategy. The Christian Ministry 8.

# Index of Scripture

# Index of Authors

# Index of Subjects